About this book

Here is a cookery book full of imaginative ideas for well-balanced meals without meat!

Super Meals Without Meat will introduce you to unusual and interesting new dishes, and will also provide excitingly different ways to cook old favourites. There are many recipes to delight the budget-conscious cook and plenty of superbly elegant dishes for impressive dinner parties. This book aims to show you that non-meat cookery is both creative and fun, and even the most dedicated meat eaters will enjoy meatless meals.

There is so much to choose from and experiment with – home-baked breads, soups, pies, casseroles, mouth-watering cakes and desserts.

Just to give you an idea of how delicious meatless meals can be, here are two sample menus:

Family meal: Spring or Winter Vegetable Soup
Frittata con Ricotta (Italian Cheese Omelet)
  with Tomato Salad and Wholewheat Bread
Fresh Peaches with Raspberry Syrup

Dinner party: Avocado Pâté
Greek Pilaff with Caesar Salad
A selection of French or Italian cheeses
Bombe Coppelia or Soufflé Grand Marnier
Suggested wines: An Alsatian Sylvaner followed
  by Tavel Rosé or a good Beaujolais

Each section has a general introduction giving analyses of the ingredients used. As you will see, wholemeal flours and pasta, unpolished rice, compost-grown vegetables and other natural foods are suggested in the recipes. This is because most people generally agree that wholefoods are not only healthier but tastier.

The nutrition chart on the next page will guide you in the preparation of well-balanced meals. Providing your family with a healthy diet is *so* easy as long as you remember when planning your daily menus to ensure that they are getting plenty of all the essential proteins, vitamins and minerals.

Each recipe has a short introduction containing helpful hints about how and when the dish should be served, the preparation and cooking times and number of servings. The recipes are written so clearly that the most inexperienced cook will find it easy to create super meals and the experienced cook will enjoy enlarging her repertoire.

So, why spend the earth buying even the cheapest cuts of meat when, for much less cost, you can create the most superb, health-giving meals with fruit, vegetables, eggs and cheeses?

Nutrition Guide

Foods	Protein	Vitamins	Minerals	What they do
Milk, yogurts, cheeses, butter, eggs	very high	A, B complex, C and D	Calcium Phosphorus Potassium	**Proteins** provide energy and play a vital role in the growth, maintenance and repair of body tissue.
Wholegrain flours, unpolished rice, wholemeal pastas, millet and other grain products	medium to high	B complex	Calcium, Iron Magnesium Phosphorus Potassium	**Vitamin A** aids good eyesight and skin. **Vitamin B Complex** important for nervous and digestive system and heart.
Vegetable oils, margarine		A, D and E		**Vitamin B$_2$** maintains healthy growth of skin, nails and hair.
Nuts (walnuts, hazelnuts, peanuts, almonds, cashews)	very high	B complex, E	Calcium, Iron Potassium Magnesium Phosphorus	**Vitamin B$_6$** essential for growth in children and in maintaining healthy skin.
Pulses (peas, lentils, dried beans)	high	A, B complex, C	Calcium, Iron Potassium Phosphorus	**Vitamin B$_{12}$** essential for all cell functions, especially for growth in nerve cells.
Soya beans, T.V.P. (Textured Vegetable Protein)	very high	B complex	Calcium, Iron Potassium Phosphorus	**Vitamin D** very important for babies and children, promotes healthy teeth and bones.
Green vegetables	low	A, B, C, E and K	Calcium Potassium Phosphorus	**Vitamin E** once known as the fertility vitamin – vitamin E maintains normal metabolism. **Vitamin K** absolutely essential for normal clotting of the blood.
Root vegetables (potatoes, carrots, onions, leeks)	low	A, B complex, C	Potassium Phosphorus	**Calcium** for the proper development and maintenance of bones and teeth. **Phosphorus** works with Calcium to form the hard structure of bones and teeth.
All salad vegetables (lettuce, cress, tomatoes, radishes, etc.)	low	A, B complex, C	Potassium Phosphorus	**Iron** is present in the red colouring pigment of blood. It is most important that women have a sufficient amount of iron per day.
Fresh fruit (citrus, peaches, strawberries, raspberries, apples, pears, etc.)	low	C, B and A	Calcium Potassium Phosphorus	**Magnesium** an important constituent of all soft tissue and bone.
Dried fruit (sultanas, raisins, figs, dates, etc.)	low		Calcium Magnesium Potassium	**Potassium** together with Sodium and Chloride, Potassium maintains an inner balance of body fluids.

Dry Measures: Equivalents

British and American	Metric
1 oz.	28.3 grams (approx. 30 grams)
3 oz.	85 grams
1 lb. (16 oz.)	454 grams (approx. 500 grams or ½ kg.)
35 oz. (2 lb. 3 oz.)	1000 grams or 1 kg.

Liquid Measures: Equivalents

British	American	Metric
⅙ fl. oz.	1 teaspoon	5 ml. approx.
½ fl. oz.	1 tablespoon	15 ml. approx.
1 fl. oz.	2 tablespoons	30 ml. approx.
8 fl. oz.	1 cup	2.27 dl.
10 fl. oz. (½ pint)	1¼ cups	2.83 dl.
16 fl. oz.	1 pint (2 cups)	4.5 dl. or .45 litre approx. ½ litre
20 fl. oz. (1 pint)	2½ cups	5.68 dl.
35 fl. oz. (2 lb. 3 oz.)	4⅓ cups	10 dl. or 1 litre

Oven Temperatures

	Fahrenheit	Centigrade	Gas
Very cool	250°F	130°C	Gas Mark ½
	275°F	140°C	Gas Mark 1
Cool	300°F	150°C	Gas Mark 2
Warm	325°F	170°C	Gas Mark 3
Moderate	350°F	180°C	Gas Mark 4
Fairly hot	375°F	190°C	Gas Mark 5
	400°F	200°C	Gas Mark 6
Hot	425°F	220°C	Gas Mark 7
Very hot	450°F	230°C	Gas Mark 8
	475°F	240°C	Gas Mark 9
	500°F	250°C	Gas Mark 10

To convert Fahrenheit into Centigrade:
   subtract 32, multiply by 5, divide by 9
To convert Centigrade into Fahrenheit:
   multiply by 9, divide by 5, add 32

Readers Please Note: Equivalents for American ingredients are given in the text in square brackets.

If you have any difficulty in obtaining self-raising flour, use plain [all-purpose] flour or wholemeal [wholewheat] flour with baking powder in the proportion of 4 level teaspoons of baking powder to 1 pound [4 cups] of flour.

CONTENTS

Breads

Most of you would agree that it is more convenient to buy a packet of plastic-wrapped, sliced bread, but it will not give you the sense of achievement you will have when you share your first loaves of crusty home-made bread – still warm from the oven – with your family and friends. Bread-making is very simple, and if you plan your baking day, you will wonder why so much fuss is made about yeast cookery.

More and more people are experimenting with bread-making and as a result many stores and even some supermarkets are stocking fresh and dried yeast, and many different types of flours.

Fresh yeast is now readily available in most health food stores, and as long as you remember that it is a living cell and treat it kindly, you will find it very easy to work with. Only temperatures over 110°F or 'old age' will kill yeast. (Never use yeast which is dry and streaky.) Fresh yeast can be stored for at least a week in the refrigerator. Dried yeast will keep much longer, because the yeast plants are inert and must be reactivated in warm water or milk before using.

Among the variety of flours available, the best for bread-making are the 100 per cent and 81 per cent wholewheat, wholemeal and rye flours. These flours contain more protein, calcium, iron and roughage than white flours (as well as a high proportion of Vitamins E and the B complex).

All the recipes in this section are very comprehensive. If they are followed exactly, with the understanding that yeast doughs cannot be hurried by leaving them to prove in too warm a place, you will find that your very first attempt will produce a successful loaf of bread.

Wholewheat Bread

Home-made wholewheat bread is far superior to any commercial brown bread. Although it is most delicious when freshly baked and spread with butter, honey or cheese, stored correctly the bread keeps extremely well and can be served up to a week after baking. For variation, the loaves may be baked in well-greased flower pots, or shaped into cottage loaves on a baking sheet.
Preparation and cooking time: 4 hours

FOUR 1-POUND LOAVES

1½ teaspoons butter or margarine
1 oz. fresh yeast
1 teaspoon brown sugar
1½ pints [3¾ cups] plus 4 teaspoons lukewarm water
3 lb. [12 cups] stone-ground wholewheat flour
1¼ tablespoons rock salt or 1 tablespoon table salt
2 tablespoons honey
1 tablespoon vegetable oil
4 tablespoons cracked wheat (optional)

Grease four 1-pound loaf tins with the butter or margarine. Set aside.

Crumble the yeast into a small mixing bowl and mash in the brown sugar with a kitchen fork. Add 4 teaspoons of the water and cream the water, sugar and yeast together to form a smooth paste. Set the bowl aside in a warm, draught-free place for 15 to 20 minutes, or until the yeast mixture has risen and is puffed up and frothy.

Put the flour and salt into a warmed, large mixing bowl. Make a well in the centre of the flour mixture and pour in the yeast mixture, the honey, the remaining lukewarm water and the oil. Using your fingers or a spatula, gradually draw the flour into the liquid. Continue mixing until all the flour is incorporated and the dough comes away from the sides of the bowl.

Turn the dough out on to a floured board or marble slab and knead it for about 10 minutes, reflouring the surface if the dough becomes sticky. The dough should then be elastic and smooth.

Rinse, thoroughly dry and lightly grease the large mixing bowl. Shape the dough into a ball and return it to the bowl. Dust the top of the dough with a little flour and cover the bowl with a clean, damp cloth. Set the bowl in a warm, draught-free place and leave it for 1 to 1½ hours, or until the dough has risen and has almost doubled in bulk.

Turn the risen dough out of the bowl on to a floured surface and knead it vigorously for about 10 minutes. Using a sharp knife, cut the dough into four pieces. Roll and shape each piece into a loaf. Place the loaves in the tins.

If you prefer a country-style loaf, use a heated, sharp knife or kitchen scissors to make a deep gash on the top of each loaf and then dust them with a little wholewheat flour. Otherwise, if you are using the cracked wheat, sprinkle 1 tablespoon on to the top of each loaf. Cover the tins with a damp cloth and return to a warm place for 30 to 45 minutes, or until the dough has risen to the top of the tins.

Preheat the oven to very hot 475°F (Gas Mark 9, 240°C).

Place the tins in the centre of the oven and bake for 15 minutes. Then lower the oven temperature to hot 425°F (Gas Mark 7, 220°C), put the bread on a lower shelf in the oven and bake for another 25 to 30 minutes.

After removing the bread from the oven, tip the loaves out of the tins and rap the undersides with your knuckles. If the bread sounds hollow, like a drum, it is cooked. If the bread does not sound hollow, lower the oven temperature to fairly hot 375°F (Gas Mark 5, 190°C), return the loaves, upside-down, to the oven and bake for a further 10 minutes.

Cool the loaves on a wire rack.

Egg Bread

This beautifully light Egg Bread, or Challah, is plaited [braided] and sprinkled with poppy seeds. It is traditionally baked for Jewish Sabbaths and festivals. For Rosh Hashana the same bread is shaped into round loaves.

Preparation and cooking time: 5 hours
ONE 2-POUND LOAF

½ oz. fresh yeast
1½ tablespoons sugar
6 fl. oz. [¾ cup] lukewarm milk
1 lb. [4 cups] flour
1½ teaspoons salt
2 eggs, lightly beaten
1 tablespoon vegetable oil
½ teaspoon butter or margarine
1 egg yolk, beaten with 1 tablespoon cold water
2 tablespoons poppy seeds

Crumble the yeast into a small mixing bowl and mash in ½ teaspoon of the sugar with a kitchen fork. Add 2 teaspoons of the warm milk and cream the milk and yeast together to form a smooth paste. Set the bowl aside in a warm, draught-free place for 15 to 20 minutes, or until the yeast mixture has risen and is puffed up and frothy.

Sift the flour, remaining sugar and the salt into a large, warmed mixing bowl. Make a well in the centre of the flour mixture and pour in the yeast mixture. Add the remaining milk, the eggs and oil. Using your fingers or a spatula, gradually draw the flour into the liquid. Continue mixing until all the flour is incorporated and the dough comes away from the sides of the bowl.

Cover the bowl with a clean damp cloth. Set the bowl in a warm, draught-free place and leave it for 1½ to 2 hours, or until the dough has risen and has doubled in bulk.

Grease a large baking sheet with the butter or margarine. Set aside.

Turn the risen dough out of the bowl on to a lightly floured surface and knead it for about 5 to 8 minutes. Divide the dough into three ropes, each about 12-inches long. Fasten the ropes together at one end and loosely plait [braid] the three pieces together, fastening again at the end.

Place the loaf on the greased baking sheet and cover it again with a clean cloth. Set it aside in a warm place for 2 to 2½ hours, or until the loaf has risen and expanded across the baking sheet.

Preheat the oven to hot 425°F (Gas Mark 7, 220°C).

With a pastry brush, paint the top of the loaf with the egg yolk glaze and sprinkle the poppy seeds over the top. Place the baking sheet in the centre of the oven and bake for 10 minutes. Then reduce the oven temperature to fairly hot 375°F (Gas Mark 5, 190°C) and bake for a further 25 to 30 minutes or until the loaf is deep golden brown.

After removing the bread from the oven, tip the loaf off the baking sheet and rap the underside with your knuckles. If the bread sounds hollow, like a drum, it is cooked. If it does not sound hollow, return it to the oven for a further 5 to 10 minutes. Cool the loaf on a wire rack.

Corn Bread

In the United States, Corn Bread is served hot with butter and honey as an accompaniment to blackeye beans. It is also delicious for tea, spread with butter and jam.

Preparation and cooking time: 50 minutes
8-INCH SQUARE BREAD

1 teaspoon butter or margarine
5½ oz. [1 cup] yellow corn meal
4 oz. [1 cup] flour
2 teaspoons baking powder
1 teaspoon salt
2½ oz. [¼ cup plus 1 tablespoon] vegetable fat
8 fl. oz. [1 cup] milk
1 egg

Preheat the oven to fairly hot 400°F (Gas Mark 6, 200°C).

Using the teaspoon of butter or margarine, lightly grease an 8-inch baking tin. Sift the corn meal, flour, baking powder and salt into a medium-sized mixing bowl. Add the vegetable fat and, with a table knife, cut the fat into the flour until it is in small pieces. With your fingertips, rub the fat into the flour until the mixture resembles fine breadcrumbs.

In a small mixing bowl, beat the milk and egg together with a fork.

Using a wooden spoon, stir the egg-and-milk mixture into the flour mixture until the ingredients are well blended.

Turn the mixture into the greased baking tin. Place the tin in the oven and bake for 25 minutes, or until a skewer inserted into the centre of the bread comes out clean.

Remove the tin from the oven. Cut the corn bread into 2-inch squares and lift them out of the tin on to a serving plate. Serve at once.

Bran Bread

A nutritious bread that is ideal for slimmers, Bran Bread is both inexpensive and easy to make. Unlike other breads, it requires only one rising of only 30 minutes, so it can be made in the morning and will be ready at lunchtime.

Preparation and cooking time: 2¼ hours
ONE 2-POUND LOAF

1 teaspoon vegetable oil
1 oz. fresh yeast
½ teaspoon sugar
1 pint [2½ cups] lukewarm water
1½ lb. stone-ground wholemeal flour [6 cups wholewheat flour]
1 oz. [¼ cup] soya flour
1½ teaspoons salt
3 oz. [1 cup] plus 2 tablespoons bran

Lightly grease a baking sheet with the oil. Set aside.

Crumble the yeast into a small mixing bowl and mash in the sugar with a kitchen fork. Add 2 tablespoons of the water and cream the water and yeast together to form a smooth paste. Set the bowl aside in a warm, draught-free place for 15 to 20 minutes or until the yeast mixture has risen and is puffed up and frothy.

Put the flours and salt into a large mixing bowl. Add 3 ounces [1 cup] of the bran. Make a well in the centre and pour in the yeast mixture and remaining water. Using your hands or a spatula, gradually draw the flour mixture into the liquids. Continue mixing until all the flour is incorporated and the dough comes away from the sides of the bowl.

Turn the dough out on to a lightly floured board or marble slab and knead it for 10 minutes, reflouring the surface if the dough becomes sticky. The dough should then be elastic and smooth.

Shape the dough into a ball and place it on the baking sheet. Sprinkle the remaining bran on top. Cover the sheet with a clean, damp cloth and set it in a warm, draught-free place. Leave it for 30 minutes or until the dough has risen and expanded across the baking sheet.

Preheat the oven to hot 450°F (Gas Mark 8, 230°C).

Place the baking sheet in the oven and bake the bread for 1½ hours. Then lower the temperature to moderate 350°F (Gas Mark 4, 180°C) and continue baking for 10 minutes.

After removing the bread from the oven, tip the loaf off the baking sheet and rap the underside with your knuckles. If the bread sounds hollow, like a drum, it is cooked. If it does not sound hollow, return the loaf, upside-down, to the oven and bake for a further 5 to 10 minutes.

Cool the loaf on a wire rack.

Christmas Bread

A large, dark loaf with an unusual flavour Christmas Bread is an old traditional Swedish recipe. The bread is served at lunch on the day before Christmas, and is usually decorated with softened unsalted butter piped on top in a decorative pattern. Christmas Bread is particularly delicious with butter and cheese or honey.

Preparation and cooking time: 4 hours

THREE 1-POUND LOAVES

¾ oz. fresh yeast
½ teaspoon brown sugar
2 tablespoons lukewarm water
1 pint [2½ cups] stout or dark brown ale
2 oz. [¼ cup] plus 1 tablespoon butter or margarine
1½ lb. [6 cups] rye flour
12 oz. [3 cups] flour
1 teaspoon salt
8 fl. oz. [1 cup] molasses
grated rind of 4 oranges
2 tablespoons aniseed, crushed

GLAZE
1 tablespoon molasses mixed with 3 tablespoons hot water

Crumble the yeast into a small mixing bowl and mash in the sugar with a kitchen fork. Add the water and cream the yeast and water together. Set the bowl aside in a warm, draught-free place for 15 to 20 minutes, or until the yeast mixture has risen and is puffed up and frothy.

Meanwhile, in a medium-sized saucepan, warm the stout or ale over low heat. Add 2 ounces [¼ cup] of the butter or margarine and heat the mixture for 2 to 3 minutes or until it is just lukewarm and the butter or margarine has melted. Remove the pan from the heat.

Sift the flours and salt into a large mixing bowl. Make a well in the centre and pour in the yeast and stout mixtures, the molasses, the orange rind and the aniseed. Using your fingers or a spatula, gradually draw the flour into the liquid. Continue mixing until all the flour is incorporated and the dough comes away from the sides of the bowl.

Turn the dough out on to a lightly floured board and knead it for 5 minutes, reflouring the surface if the dough is sticky. It should be elastic and smooth.

Rinse, thoroughly dry and lightly grease the large mixing bowl. Form the dough into a ball and return it to the bowl. Cover the bowl with a clean cloth and set it aside in a warm, draught-free place for 1½ to 2 hours, or until the dough has risen and almost doubled in bulk.

Lightly grease three baking sheets with the remaining tablespoon of butter or margarine. Set aside.

Turn the risen dough out on to a lightly floured surface and knead it for 10 minutes. Divide the dough into three equal pieces and shape each piece into a long loaf, slightly shorter than the baking sheets. Transfer the loaves to the baking sheets and cover them with clean cloths. Return them to a warm place for 45 minutes to 1 hour, or until the loaves have risen and expanded across the sheets.

Preheat the oven to very cool 250°F (Gas Mark ½, 130°C).

Uncover the loaves and prick them all over with a fork. Place the baking sheets in the oven and bake for 20 minutes.

Remove the loaves from the oven and brush them with the molasses and water glaze. Return the loaves to the oven and bake for a further 20 minutes.

After removing the bread from the oven, tip the loaves off the baking sheets and rap the undersides with your knuckles. If the bread sounds hollow, like a drum, it is cooked. If it does not sound hollow, return the loaves to the oven and bake for a further 10 to 15 minutes.

Cool the loaves on a wire rack.

Spicy Cheese Bread

Spicy Cheese Bread is both nourishing and satisfying. Serve it with vegetable soup for an economical and filling meal.

Preparation and cooking time: 3 hours

TWO 2-POUND LOAVES

¾ oz. fresh yeast
1 teaspoon sugar
2 tablespoons lukewarm water
12 fl. oz. [1½ cups] milk
1 oz. [2 tablespoons] butter or margarine
8 oz. wholemeal flour [2 cups wholewheat flour]
14 oz. [3½ cups] rye flour
1 teaspoon salt
1 teaspoon white pepper
⅛ teaspoon cayenne pepper
¼ teaspoon dried thyme
1 egg
4 oz. [1 cup] Lancashire or other hard cheese, grated
2 teaspoons vegetable oil

Crumble the yeast into a small mixing bowl and mash in the sugar with a kitchen fork. Add the water and cream the yeast and water together to form a smooth paste. Set the bowl aside in a warm, draught-free place for 15 to 20 minutes or until the yeast mixture has risen and is puffed up and frothy.

Meanwhile, in a small saucepan, scald the milk over moderate heat (bring to just under boiling point). Remove the pan from the heat. Add the butter or margarine and set the pan aside to allow the milk to cool to lukewarm.

Put the flours, salt, pepper and cayenne into a warmed large mixing bowl and sprinkle over the thyme. Make a well in the centre of the flour mixture and pour in the yeast mixture, cooled milk mixture and the egg.

Using your fingers or a spatula, gradually draw the flour mixture into the liquids. Continue mixing until all the flour is incorporated and the dough comes away from the sides of the bowl. Add more flour if the dough is too sticky.

Add the cheese and lightly work it into the dough. Turn the dough out on to a lightly floured board or marble slab. Knead it for 10 minutes to distribute the cheese evenly. Reflour the surface if the dough is sticky. It should be elastic, stiff and smooth.

Rinse, thoroughly dry and lightly grease the large mixing bowl. Form the dough into a ball and return it to the bowl. Cover the bowl with a clean, damp cloth and set it aside in a warm, draught-free place for 1 to 1½ hours, or until the dough has risen and almost doubled in bulk.

Lightly grease two 2-pound loaf tins with the oil. Set aside.

Turn the risen dough out of the bowl on to a floured surface and knead it for 8 to 10 minutes. Form the dough into a roll and with a sharp knife divide it into two equal pieces. Shape each piece into a loaf and place them in the tins. Cover the tins with a clean cloth and return them to a warm place for about 30 to 45 minutes, or until the dough has almost doubled in bulk again.

Preheat the oven to hot 425°F (Gas Mark 7, 220°C).

Place the tins in the centre of the oven and bake the loaves for 15 minutes. Then lower the temperature to fairly hot 375°F (Gas Mark 5, 190°C), put the tins on a lower shelf in the oven and continue baking for 30 to 35 minutes.

After removing the bread from the oven, tip the loaves out of the tins and rap the undersides with your knuckles. If the bread sounds hollow, like a drum, it is cooked. If it does not sound hollow, lower the oven temperature to moderate 350°F (Gas Mark 4, 180°C), return the loaves, upside-down, to the oven and bake for a further 5 to 10 minutes.

Cool the loaves on a wire rack.

Onion and Herb Loaf

Fragrant Onion and Herb Loaf is best made with fresh herbs. Dried herbs may be used in smaller quantities, but the aroma will not be as pungent.

Preparation and cooking time: 3¼ hours

ONE 1-POUND LOAF

- ½ oz. fresh yeast
- ½ teaspoon sugar
- 4 fl. oz. [½ cup] lukewarm water
- 2 fl. oz. [¼ cup] milk
- 1 tablespoon butter or margarine
- 10 oz. wholemeal flour [2½ cups wholewheat flour]
- 1 teaspoon salt
- 1 teaspoon finely chopped fresh sage
- 2 teaspoons finely chopped fresh tansy, wormwood or savory
- 1 small onion, minced
- 1 teaspoon vegetable oil

Crumble the yeast into a small mixing bowl and mash in the sugar with a kitchen fork. Add 2 tablespoons of the water and cream the yeast and water together to form a smooth paste. Set the bowl aside in a warm, draught-free place for 15 to 20 minutes or until the yeast mixture has risen and is puffed up and frothy.

Meanwhile, in a small saucepan scald the milk over moderate heat (bring to just under boiling point). Remove the pan from the heat and add the butter or margarine and the remaining water. Set the pan aside to allow the milk mixture to cool to lukewarm.

Put the flour and salt into a warmed large mixing bowl. Sprinkle over the herbs and onion. Make a well in the centre of the flour mixture and pour in the yeast and milk mixtures. Using your fingers or a spatula, gradually draw the flour mixture into the liquids. Continue mixing until all the flour is incorporated and the dough comes away from the sides of the bowl.

Turn the dough out on to a lightly floured board or marble slab. Knead the dough for 10 minutes, reflouring the surface if the dough becomes sticky. The dough should then be elastic and smooth.

Rinse, thoroughly dry and lightly grease the large mixing bowl. Form the dough into a ball and return it to the bowl. Cover the bowl with a clean, damp cloth and set it aside in a warm, draught-free place for 1 to 1½ hours or until the dough has risen and doubled in bulk.

Lightly grease a 1-pound loaf tin with the oil. Set aside.

Turn the dough out on to a floured surface and knead it for 8 to 10 minutes. Form the dough into a loaf and place it in the tin. Cover the tin with a cloth and return it to a warm place for 30 to 45 minutes or until the dough has doubled in bulk again.

Preheat the oven to moderate 350°F (Gas Mark 4, 180°C).

Place the tin in the centre of the oven and bake the bread for 1 hour.

After removing the bread from the oven, tip the loaf out of the tin and rap the underside with your knuckles. If the bread sounds hollow, like a drum, it is cooked. If it does not sound hollow, return the loaf, upside-down, to the oven and bake for a further 5 to 10 minutes.

Cool the loaf on a wire rack.

Stollen

A rich, spicy bread, Stollen is a traditional German and Austrian Christmas bread, filled with candied fruit and nuts and covered with a vanilla-flavoured icing.

Preparation and cooking time: 5¼ hours

1 STOLLEN

- 6 oz. [¾ cup] plus 1 teaspoon butter or margarine
- ½ oz. fresh yeast
- 5 oz. [⅝ cup] plus 1 teaspoon sugar
- 1 tablespoon lukewarm water
- 6 fl. oz. [¾ cup] milk
- 1 lb. [4 cups] flour
- ½ teaspoon salt
- ½ teaspoon ground cinnamon
- ¼ teaspoon ground cardamom
- 2 eggs, lightly beaten
- 4 oz. [⅔ cup] raisins
- 4 oz. [⅔ cup] currants
- 2 oz. [⅓ cup] chopped mixed candied peel
- 2 oz. [⅓ cup] glacé cherries, chopped
- 4 oz. [¾ cup] walnuts or pecans, chopped
- 2 tablespoons melted butter or margarine

ICING

- 6 oz. icing sugar [1 cup confectioners' sugar]
- ¼ teaspoon vanilla essence
- 3 tablespoons hot water
- 12 walnut or pecan halves

Lightly grease a large baking sheet with the teaspoon of butter or margarine. Set aside.

Crumble the yeast into a small mixing bowl and mash in the teaspoon of sugar with a kitchen fork. Add the lukewarm water and cream the yeast and water together. Set the bowl aside in a warm, draught-free place for 15 to 20 minutes, or until the yeast mixture has risen and is puffed up and frothy.

Meanwhile, in a small saucepan, scald the milk over moderate heat (bring to just below boiling point). Remove the pan from the heat and add half of the remaining butter or margarine. Set the pan aside to allow the butter or margarine to melt and the milk to cool to lukewarm.

Place the remaining butter or margarine in a small mixing bowl and cream it with a wooden spoon until it is soft and fluffy. Set aside.

Sift the flour, salt, cinnamon, cardamom and remaining sugar into a large, warmed mixing bowl. Make a well in the centre and pour in the yeast and milk mixtures and the eggs. Using your fingers or a spatula, gradually draw the flour into the liquid. Continue mixing until all the flour is incorporated and the dough comes away from the sides of the bowl.

Turn the dough out on to a lightly floured surface. Knead the dough for 8 minutes, reflouring the surface if the dough is sticky. It should then be elastic and smooth.

Spread or roll the dough out into a large circle. Sprinkle the raisins, currants and candied peel over the surface and bring the dough up over them. Knead the dough for another 2 to 3 minutes to distribute the fruits and peel evenly.

Rinse, thoroughly dry and lightly grease the large mixing bowl. Form the dough into a ball and return it to the bowl. Cover the bowl with a clean cloth and set it aside in a warm, draught-free place for 1 to 1½ hours, or until the dough has risen and has almost doubled in bulk.

Turn the dough out on to a lightly floured surface. Knead it for 5 minutes.

Spread or roll the dough out into an oval about 12 x 8 inches. Cover the surface with the softened butter or margarine. Sprinkle the cherries and walnuts or pecans over the butter or margarine. Fold the dough lengthways over the cherries and nuts and press the edges lightly together.

Carefully transfer the folded dough to the greased baking sheet and shape it into a crescent. Cover with a clean cloth and set aside in a warm, draught-free place for 45 minutes to 1 hour, or until the dough has risen and expanded across the baking sheet.

Preheat the oven to fairly hot 400°F (Gas Mark 6, 200°C).

Uncover the dough and place the baking sheet in the oven. Bake the stollen for 10 minutes. Then reduce the oven temperature to moderate 350°F (Gas Mark 4,

9

180°C) and continue baking for 25 minutes.

After removing the stollen from the oven, tip it off the baking sheet and rap the underside with your knuckles. If it sounds hollow, like a drum, the stollen is cooked. If it does not sound hollow, return it to the oven, upside-down, and continue baking for 5 to 10 minutes.

Transfer the stollen to a wire rack and brush it with the melted butter or margarine. Leave it to cool to room temperature.

To make the icing, sift the sugar into a small mixing bowl. Add the vanilla essence and enough of the hot water to make an icing that is not runny.

When the stollen is cool, spread the icing over it. Decorate with the walnut or pecan halves.

Birnbrot

Birnbrot, a luscious Swiss bread that is rolled around a filling of pears, prunes, raisins and walnuts, is usually served with steaming cups of hot chocolate, but it will go equally well with tea or coffee.
Preparation and cooking time: 5½ hours

ONE 2-POUND LOAF

½ oz. fresh yeast
2 oz. [¼ cup] plus 1 teaspoon sugar
5 fl. oz. [⅝ cup] lukewarm water
2 oz. [¼ cup] plus 1 tablespoon butter or margarine
10 oz. [2½ cups] flour
⅛ teaspoon salt
1 egg, lightly beaten
½ egg beaten with 1 tablespoon milk (for glaze)
FILLING
8 fl. oz. [1 cup] water
8 oz. [1⅓ cups] dried pears, coarsely chopped
4 oz. [⅔ cup] stoned, dried prunes, coarsely chopped
2 oz. [⅓ cup] raisins
juice of ½ lemon
2 oz. [½ cup] walnuts, chopped
2 tablespoons sugar
2 tablespoons kirsch
grated rind of 1 lemon
¼ teaspoon ground cinnamon
¼ teaspoon grated nutmeg
1½ tablespoons dry red wine

Crumble the yeast into a small mixing bowl and mash in 1 teaspoon of the sugar with a kitchen fork. Add 2 tablespoons of the water and cream the yeast and water together. Set the bowl aside in a warm, draught-free place for 15 to 20 minutes or until the yeast mixture has risen and is puffed up and frothy.

Meanwhile, pour the remaining water

into a small saucepan and add 2 ounces [¼ cup] of the butter or margarine. Place the pan over moderate heat and stir to melt the butter or margarine. Remove the pan from the heat and set it aside to cool slightly.

Sift the flour, salt and remaining sugar into a large, warmed mixing bowl. Make a well in the centre and pour in the yeast and water mixtures and the egg. Using your fingers or a spatula, gradually draw the flour into the liquid. Continue mixing until all the flour is incorporated and the dough comes away from the sides of the bowl.

Turn the dough out on to a lightly floured surface and knead it for 10 minutes, reflouring the surface if the dough becomes sticky. It should be smooth and elastic.

Rinse, thoroughly dry and lightly grease the large mixing bowl. Shape the dough into a ball and return it to the bowl. Cover the bowl with a cloth and place it in a warm, draught-free place for 1 to 1½ hours or until the dough has doubled in bulk.

While the dough is rising, prepare the filling. In a small saucepan, bring the water to the boil over low heat. Add the pears, prunes, raisins and lemon juice to the water and reduce the heat to low. Stirring frequently, simmer for 10 minutes, or until the fruit is tender and can be mashed easily with the back of a spoon.

Drain the fruit thoroughly. Purée it in a blender or rub it through a strainer with the back of a wooden spoon. Stir the walnuts, sugar, kirsch, grated lemon rind, cinnamon and nutmeg into the fruit purée.

When the ingredients are well mixed, stir in the wine a little at a time. The purée should be very thick, so add the wine with caution.

Grease a large baking sheet with the remaining tablespoon of butter or margarine. Set aside.

Lightly dust a piece of greaseproof or waxed paper, which is about 18-inches square, with flour. Punch the dough to get rid of air pockets. Transfer it to the paper. Knead the dough lightly and roll it out into a square about ¼-inch thick.

With a palette knife, spread the filling over the dough, covering it smoothly to within 1 inch of its edges. Fold the edges over the filling and roll up the dough like a Swiss [jelly] roll, using the paper to lift the dough.

Transfer the roll to the greased baking sheet and lightly prick the surface all over with a fork. Put the roll in a warm place to rise for about 1 hour.

Preheat the oven to fairly hot 400°F (Gas Mark 6, 200°C).

Brush the top, sides and ends of the roll with the egg-and-milk mixture. Place the baking sheet in the middle of the oven and bake for 10 minutes. Then reduce the oven temperature to moderate 350°F (Gas Mark 4, 180°C) and continue baking for a further 50 minutes, or until the crust of the bread is golden and crisp.

Transfer the bread to a wire rack to cool.

Date and Walnut Loaf

A moist tea bread, Date and Walnut Loaf is best eaten 2 or 3 days after baking. If stored in an airtight tin, it will keep for 2 weeks.
Preparation and cooking time: 1¼ hours

ONE 2-POUND LOAF

4 oz. [½ cup] plus 2 teaspoons butter or margarine
1 lb. wholemeal flour [4 cups wholewheat flour]
1 teaspoon salt
2 teaspoons baking powder
4 oz. [⅔ cup] dark brown sugar
6 oz. [1 cup] dates, stoned and finely chopped
2 oz. [⅓ cup] walnuts, coarsely chopped
1 egg
6 fl. oz. [¾ cup] milk

Preheat the oven to fairly hot 375°F (Gas Mark 5, 190°C).

Generously grease a 2-pound loaf tin with 2 teaspoons of the butter or margarine. Set aside.

Put the flour, salt and baking powder into a large mixing bowl. Add the remaining butter or margarine and cut it into small pieces with a table knife. With your fingertips, rub the fat into the flour until the mixture resembles coarse breadcrumbs. Stir in the sugar, dates and walnuts.

In a small bowl, lightly beat the egg and 4 fluid ounces [½ cup] of the milk together with a fork. Add the egg and milk mixture to the flour mixture and thoroughly blend the ingredients. If necessary, add some of the remaining milk to form a soft dough.

Form the dough into a loaf-shape and place it in the tin. Brush the top of the dough with a little milk. Place the tin in the centre of the oven and bake for 50 minutes. Cool the loaf on a wire rack.

Banana Walnut Loaf

A moist bread, Banana Walnut Loaf is very easy to make and good to serve at tea-time or with coffee.

Preparation and cooking time: 1 hour 20 minutes

ONE 1-POUND LOAF

1½ oz. [3 tablespoons] plus 1 teaspoon vegetable fat
5 oz. [⅝ cup] sugar
3 eggs
4 bananas, mashed
8 oz. [2 cups] flour
1 teaspoon baking powder
½ teaspoon salt
¼ teaspoon bicarbonate of soda [baking soda]
6 oz. [1 cup] walnuts, chopped

Preheat the oven to moderate 350°F (Gas Mark 4, 180°C). Grease a 1-pound loaf tin with 1 teaspoon of the vegetable fat. Set aside.

In a medium-sized mixing bowl, beat the sugar, remaining vegetable fat and eggs together with a wooden spoon. Beat until the mixture is light and fluffy. Beat in the bananas.

Sift the flour, baking powder, salt and soda into the banana mixture and beat well.

Stir in the walnuts.

Pour the mixture into the loaf tin and place it in the oven. Bake for 1 hour, or until a skewer inserted into the centre of the loaf comes out clean.

Turn the loaf out of the tin on to a wire rack and allow it to cool before slicing.

Gingerbread

Moist, slightly sticky Gingerbread is a favourite treat for children. But don't let them be impatient and open the oven door too soon, or the top of the gingerbread will be uneven.

Preparation and cooking time: 1 hour 20 minutes

ONE 12-INCH GINGERBREAD

8 oz. [1 cup] plus 2 teaspoons butter or margarine
5 fl. oz. black treacle [⅝ cup molasses]
3 fl. oz. golden syrup [⅜ cup light corn syrup]
8 oz. [1⅓ cups] dark brown sugar
2 eggs
12 oz. [3 cups] flour
½ teaspoon salt
2½ teaspoons baking powder
1 tablespoon ground ginger
1 teaspoon ground cinnamon
1 teaspoon ground allspice
1 teaspoon ground coriander
10 fl. oz. [1¼ cups] milk

Preheat the oven to warm 325°F (Gas Mark 3, 170°C).

Grease a shallow 10- x 12-inch baking tin with 1 teaspoon of the butter or margarine. Cut out a piece of greaseproof or waxed paper the same size as the bottom of the tin and grease it with 1 teaspoon of the butter or margarine. Line the tin with the greased paper and set it aside.

In a medium-sized saucepan, heat the treacle [molasses], syrup, sugar and remaining butter or margarine over low heat, stirring to dissolve the sugar. As soon as the butter has melted and the sugar has dissolved, remove the pan from the heat.

Add the eggs, one at a time, stirring constantly. Set the pan aside.

Sift the flour, salt, baking powder, ginger, cinnamon, allspice and coriander into a large mixing bowl. Make a well in the centre and pour in the syrup mixture. Using a wooden spoon, gradually draw the flour into the liquid. When all the flour has been incorporated, slowly beat in the milk, adding just enough to make a soft batter with a dropping consistency.

Pour the batter into the baking tin and place it in the oven. Bake the gingerbread for 50 minutes, or until it has pulled away from the sides of the tin and a skewer inserted into the centre comes out clean.

Allow the gingerbread to cool slightly in the tin. Then cut it into squares and serve warm.

Oatcakes

A Scottish speciality, Oatcakes are best served while still warm with lots of butter, and will be welcome at any time.

Preparation and cooking time: 45 minutes

12 OATCAKES

1 teaspoon butter or margarine
8 oz. [2⅔ cups] oatmeal
3 oz. wholemeal flour [¾ cup wholewheat flour]
1 teaspoon baking powder
2½ oz. [¼ cup plus 1 tablespoon] vegetable fat
2 oz. [⅓ cup] dark brown sugar
3 to 4 tablespoons milk

Preheat the oven to warm 325°F (Gas Mark 3, 170°C).

Lightly grease a large baking sheet with the butter or margarine. Set aside.

In a medium-sized mixing bowl, combine the oatmeal, flour and baking powder. Add the vegetable fat and cut it into small pieces with a table knife. With your fingertips, rub the fat into the oatmeal mixture until it resembles coarse breadcrumbs.

Stir in the sugar. Gradually add enough of the milk to make a firm dough.

Turn the dough out on to a lightly floured surface and knead it for 2 minutes. Roll it out to a circle about ¼-inch thick. With a 2½-inch diameter pastry cutter, cut out circles of dough. Gather up the trimmings and roll them out again to make more circles until all the dough is used.

Transfer the circles to the baking sheet and place it in the centre of the oven. Bake the oatcakes for 20 to 25 minutes, or until they are golden brown.

Cool the oatcakes on a wire rack.

Raisin Drops

Nourishing and chewy little Raisin Drops are lovely served straight from the oven for Sunday afternoon tea.

Preparation and cooking time: 40 minutes

10-12 BISCUITS

2 oz. [¼ cup] plus 1 teaspoon butter or margarine
7 oz. [1¾ cups] flour
1 teaspoon baking powder
2 tablespoons wheatgerm
2 oz. [⅓ cup] dark brown sugar
1 egg
8 oz. [1¼ cups] raisins
5 to 6 tablespoons milk

Preheat the oven to fairly hot 375°F (Gas Mark 5, 190°C).

Lightly grease a large baking sheet with the teaspoon of butter or margarine. Set aside.

Sift the flour and baking powder into a medium-sized mixing bowl. Stir in the wheatgerm. Add the remaining butter or margarine and cut it into small pieces with a table knife. With your fingertips, rub the fat into the flour until the mixture resembles coarse breadcrumbs.

In a small bowl, mix together the sugar and egg with a fork. Add to the flour and wheatgerm mixture with the raisins and blend the ingredients thoroughly. Gradually stir in enough milk to make a stiff dough.

Turn the dough out on to a lightly floured surface and knead it for 2 to 3 minutes to be sure the raisins are evenly distributed. Roll out the dough to a circle about ½-inch thick. With a 2½-inch diameter pastry cutter, cut out circles of dough. Gather up the trimmings of dough and roll them out again and make more circles until all the dough is used.

Transfer the circles to the baking sheet. With a pastry brush, coat the circles with the remaining milk. Place the baking sheet near the top of the oven and bake the drops for 10 to 15 minutes, or until they are golden brown.

Stocks, Soups, Accompaniments and Sauces

Soup stimulates the appetite, which makes it an excellent first course to serve at any time of the year. A hearty vegetable or bean soup, such as Winter Vegetable Soup, should be followed by a light omelet, a cheese flan or salad, and Cream of Tomato Soup – a puréed soup – by a savoury bake or casserole.

The basis for all good soups – hot or cold, creamed or clear – and some sauces is a home-made stock. The two basic stock recipes included in this section may also be used to make rice pilaffs, pulaos and risottos.

In Britain and Europe sauces have been justifiably popular since medieval times. In fact an English city census taken during the fourteenth century has an individual listing for 'Sauce-makers'.

Sauces balance the flavour, texture and appearance of almost any vegetable, cheese or egg dish. They are extremely versatile – for instance, Béchamel Sauce can be changed, just with the addition of cheese, spices, herbs or mushrooms, to suit any savoury dish – and, in general, they are very easy to make.

Dark Vegetable Stock

Stocks are the basis of so many sauces and soups, with a myriad of other uses, that a home-made dark vegetable stock is invaluable. Leeks, cauliflower, swedes [rutabaga] or any other vegetables you have on hand may be used. Remember that vegetable peelings and cooking liquid are good additions.

Preparation and cooking time: 1 hour

2 PINTS [5 CUPS]

4 carrots
4 oz. turnips
4 oz. mushrooms, wiped clean
2 medium-sized onions, peeled
4 celery stalks
4 oz. tomatoes
2 tablespoons corn or other
 vegetable oil
2½ pints [6¼ cups] water
2 teaspoons salt
 bouquet garni, consisting of 2
 parsley sprigs, 1 thyme spray and 1
 bay leaf tied together
3 black peppercorns

Wash the carrots and turnips but do not peel them. With a sharp knife, chop all the vegetables into walnut-sized pieces.

In a large saucepan, heat the oil over moderate heat. Add the chopped vegetables to the pan and fry them, stirring occasionally, for 8 to 10 minutes or until the turnips and onions are lightly browned and all the oil has been absorbed.

Pour the water into the pan and add the salt, bouquet garni and peppercorns. Increase the heat to high and bring the liquid to the boil, stirring occasionally. Reduce the heat to low and simmer the stock for 30 minutes.

Strain the stock into a medium-sized bowl, pressing down on the vegetables with the back of a wooden spoon to extract as much of their juices as possible. Discard the vegetables and seasonings left in the strainer.

Set the stock aside to cool to room temperature, then cover the bowl with plastic wrap and keep it in the refrigerator until you are ready to use it.

Light Vegetable Stock

Another basic and useful stock, Light Vegetable Stock may also be made with leeks and cauliflower, or any light vegetable peelings.

Preparation and cooking time: 1 hour

2 PINTS [5 CUPS]

6 oz. parsnips
6 oz. turnips
2 medium-sized onions, peeled
4 whole celery stalks
2 tablespoons corn or other
 vegetable oil
4 tablespoons chopped mushroom
 stalks

2½ pints [6¼ cups] water
2 teaspoons salt
 bouquet garni, consisting of 2
 parsley sprigs, 1 thyme spray and 1
 bay leaf tied together
3 black peppercorns

Wash the parsnips and turnips but do not peel them. With a sharp knife, chop the parsnips, turnips, onions and celery into walnut-sized pieces.

In a large saucepan, heat the oil over moderate heat. Add the chopped vegetables to the pan (including the mushrooms) and fry them, stirring occasionally, for 5 to 7 minutes or until the onion is soft and translucent.

Do not allow the vegetables to become brown.

Pour the water into the pan and add the salt, bouquet garni and peppercorns. Increase the heat to high and bring the liquid to the boil, stirring occasionally. Reduce the heat to low and simmer the stock for 30 minutes.

Strain the stock into a medium-sized bowl, pressing down on the vegetables with the back of a wooden spoon to extract as much of their juices as possible. Discard the vegetables and seasonings left in the strainer.

Set the stock aside to cool to room temperature. Then cover the bowl with plastic wrap and keep it in the refrigerator until you are ready to use it.

Spring Vegetable Soup

Make this colourful soup when young and tender vegetables are plentiful. If the carrots are very young, they need not be scraped before cooking.

Preparation and cooking time: 40 minutes

6-8 SERVINGS

1 oz. [2 tablespoons] butter or margarine
6 carrots, scraped and sliced
4 spring onions [scallions], finely chopped
4 pints [5 pints] Light Vegetable Stock
6 oz. fresh shelled peas
4 oz. fresh or canned and drained corn
$\frac{1}{4}$ teaspoon salt
$\frac{1}{8}$ teaspoon black pepper
$\frac{1}{2}$ teaspoon dried marjoram

In a large saucepan, melt the butter or margarine over moderate heat. When the foam subsides, add the carrots and spring onions [scallions]. Fry them for 5 to 7 minutes or until the onions [scallions] are soft but not brown.

Add the stock, peas, fresh corn, salt, pepper and marjoram and bring the soup to the boil. Reduce the heat to low and simmer for 20 minutes, or until all the vegetables are cooked but still firm. If using canned corn, add it 5 minutes before the cooking time is completed.

Turn the soup into a warmed tureen or individual soup bowls and serve.

Winter Vegetable Soup

Winter Vegetable Soup is a meal-in-itself with bread and butter to accompany it. Any seasonal vegetables may be used in addition to, or instead of, those suggested.

Preparation and cooking time: 40 minutes

4 SERVINGS

4 tablespoons vegetable oil
1 medium-sized onion, finely chopped
1 garlic clove, crushed
2 oz. wholemeal flour [$\frac{1}{2}$ cup wholewheat flour]
1$\frac{1}{4}$ pints [3 cups] water
6 oz. Brussels sprouts, roughly chopped
4 oz. carrots, scraped and sliced
2 tomatoes, blanched, peeled and roughly chopped
$\frac{1}{2}$ teaspoon salt
$\frac{1}{4}$ teaspoon black pepper
6 oz. canned soya or red kidney beans, drained (optional)
10 fl. oz. [1$\frac{1}{4}$ cups] milk or single [light] cream
1 tablespoon chopped fresh parsley

In a large saucepan, heat the oil over moderate heat. Add the onion and garlic and fry them, stirring occasionally, for 5 to 7 minutes or until the onion is soft and translucent but not brown. With a wooden spoon, stir in the flour to make a smooth paste. Continue cooking and stirring for 1 to 2 minutes.

Remove the pan from the heat and gradually add the water, stirring constantly. Return the pan to the heat and bring the liquid to the boil, stirring occasionally. Add the Brussels sprouts, carrots, tomatoes, salt and pepper and stir to mix. Reduce the heat to low and simmer the soup for 15 to 20 minutes or until the vegetables are tender but still firm.

Stir in the beans, if you are using them, and milk or cream and continue simmering for 5 minutes to heat the beans thoroughly.

Pour the soup into a warmed tureen or individual bowls. Sprinkle over the parsley and serve.

Corn Chowder

This is a delicious American soup of sweetcorn, onion, green pepper and mushrooms that is ideal to serve for a cold winter night's supper.

Preparation and cooking time: 45 minutes

4-6 SERVINGS

1 oz. [2 tablespoons] butter or margarine
1 medium-sized onion, finely chopped
1 green pepper, white pith removed, seeded and chopped
1 tablespoon flour
2 medium-sized potatoes, parboiled for 10 minutes in boiling salted water, drained and finely chopped
1 lb. canned sweetcorn, drained
8 fl. oz. [1 cup] Light Vegetable Stock
10 fl. oz. [1$\frac{1}{4}$ cups] milk
4 oz. mushrooms, wiped clean and sliced
1 teaspoon salt
$\frac{1}{4}$ teaspoon white pepper
8 fl. oz. double cream [1 cup heavy cream]

In a small frying-pan, melt the butter or margarine over moderate heat. When the foam subsides, add the onion and green pepper. Cook, stirring occasionally, for 5 to 7 minutes, or until the onion is soft and translucent but not brown. Remove the frying-pan from the heat. With a wooden spoon, stir in the flour to make a smooth paste. Set the pan aside.

Put the potatoes, sweetcorn, stock and

milk in a large saucepan and, over moderate heat, bring the mixture to the boil, stirring occasionally. Pour a little of the liquid on to the onion, green pepper and flour mixture. Stir to form a smooth, thick liquid and stir this into the potato mixture. Add the mushrooms. Cover the saucepan, reduce the heat to very low and simmer the chowder for 15 to 20 minutes.

Season with the salt and pepper and add the cream, stirring to blend it thoroughly into the mixture. Heat for a further 2 minutes over very low heat. Serve immediately.

Cream of Tomato Soup

Cream of Tomato Soup is perhaps the most popular of all soups, and this version is especially delicious. Serve it for a special dinner party with Diablotins.

Preparation and cooking time: 50 minutes

4 SERVINGS

1$\frac{1}{2}$ oz. [3 tablespoons] butter or margarine
1 shallot, finely chopped
1$\frac{1}{2}$ lb. ripe tomatoes, blanched, peeled, seeded and coarsely chopped
$\frac{1}{2}$ teaspoon sugar
bouquet garni, consisting of 4 parsley sprigs, 1 thyme spray and 1 bay leaf tied together
1 teaspoon salt
$\frac{1}{2}$ teaspoon black pepper
$\frac{1}{4}$ teaspoon dried basil
$\frac{1}{4}$ teaspoon dried sage
1 pint [2$\frac{1}{2}$ cups] hot Light Vegetable Stock
2 tablespoons flour
4 fl. oz. single cream [$\frac{1}{2}$ cup light cream]
5 tablespoons Cognac

In a large, heavy saucepan melt 1 tablespoon of the butter or margarine over low heat. When the foam subsides, add the shallot and cook it for 5 minutes, stirring occasionally. Add the tomatoes, sugar, bouquet garni, salt, pepper, basil and sage and cook for a further 2 to 3 minutes. Stir in the stock. Cover the pan and simmer for 15 minutes.

Strain the mixture into a large mixing bowl, pressing down on the vegetables in the strainer to extract as much of their juices as possible. Set aside.

In a medium-sized saucepan, melt the remaining butter or margarine over moderate heat. Remove the pan from the heat and, with a wooden spoon, stir in the flour to make a smooth paste. Return the pan to the heat and gradually add the strained tomato mixture, stirring constantly. Bring the mixture to the boil, still stirring.

Remove the pan from the heat and stir in the cream and Cognac, mixing briskly until all the ingredients have blended. Reduce the heat to low and return the pan to the heat. Heat the soup very gently until it is hot but not boiling.

Turn the soup into a warmed tureen or individual soup bowls and serve.

Cucumber and Beer Soup

This refreshing cold summer soup, made from cucumber and light ale, has a delicate and unusual flavour.
Preparation and cooking time: 1¼ hours
6 SERVINGS

4 fl. oz. [½ cup] sour cream
12 fl. oz. [1½ cups] light ale
1 medium-sized cucumber, peeled and finely chopped
1½ teaspoons salt
1 garlic clove, crushed
½ teaspoon sugar
1 teaspoon paprika

In a large mixing bowl, combine the sour cream and ale together, beating with a wire whisk until they are thoroughly mixed. Add the chopped cucumber, salt, garlic and sugar to the mixture and stir until all the ingredients have blended.

Transfer the soup to a deep serving bowl and place it in the refrigerator to chill for at least 1 hour. Just before serving, sprinkle it with the paprika.

French Onion Soup

An adaptation of a traditional French recipe, this Onion Soup is a very warming main dish soup. For an authentic French touch, reminiscent of the cafés around Les Halles in Paris, use lots of coarsely ground black pepper.
Preparation and cooking time: 45 minutes
4 SERVINGS

3 tablespoons olive oil
2 lb. onions, thinly sliced
1 teaspoon salt
½ teaspoon black pepper
2½ pints [6¼ cups] Dark Vegetable Stock
4 thick slices of bread
2 garlic cloves, halved
4 oz. [1 cup] hard cheese, grated

In a large saucepan, heat the oil over moderate heat. Add the onions and reduce the heat to low. Cook the onions slowly, stirring occasionally, for about 15 minutes, or until they are lightly browned.

Preheat the grill [broiler] to high.

Sprinkle the salt and pepper over the onions and stir in the stock. Increase the heat to moderately high and bring the soup to the boil. Reduce the heat to low again and simmer for 15 minutes.

Meanwhile, toast the slices of bread on both sides. Rub the cut side of the garlic cloves over the slices of toast. Discard the garlic. Place a slice of toast in each of 4 individual flameproof soup bowls. Spoon the onion soup over the toast and liberally sprinkle the top of each bowl with grated cheese.

Place the bowls under the grill [broiler] and cook for 5 to 6 minutes or until the cheese is melted and bubbling. Serve at once.

Asparagus Cream Soup

This delicious soup is made with fresh asparagus, cream and eggs. It looks as beautiful as it tastes.
Preparation and cooking time: 1¼ hours
4 SERVINGS

2 lb. asparagus
1 small onion, thinly sliced
5 pints [6¼ pints] Light Vegetable Stock
10 fl. oz. [1¼ cups] water
1 teaspoon salt
½ teaspoon white pepper
1 oz. [2 tablespoons] butter or margarine
2 tablespoons flour
2 egg yolks
5 fl. oz. single cream [⅝ cup light cream]

Wash and trim the asparagus. Cut off 2 inches from the tips and set them aside. Peel the stalks and cut them into 1-inch pieces.

Put the pieces of asparagus stalks and the onion in a medium-sized saucepan. Pour over the stock and place the pan over moderately high heat. Bring the stock to the boil. Reduce the heat to low and simmer for 30 minutes.

Meanwhile, in another medium-sized saucepan, bring the water and ½ teaspoon of the salt to the boil over high heat. Drop the asparagus tips into the water and boil them for 5 minutes, or until they are tender. Drain the asparagus tips and set them aside.

Strain the asparagus and stock mixture into a medium-sized mixing bowl, rubbing the vegetables through the strainer with a wooden spoon. Alternatively, purée the mixture in a blender.

Return the purée to the saucepan and return the pan to the heat. Add the pepper and the remaining salt. Cook, stirring occasionally, for 5 minutes.

In a small bowl, mash together the butter or margarine and flour to form a smooth paste (beurre manié). Roll the beurre manié into small pieces.

Remove the saucepan from the heat. Add the beurre manié to the hot asparagus mixture, one piece at a time, stirring constantly. When all the beurre manié has been incorporated, return the pan to moderate heat. Bring the mixture to the boil, stirring constantly. Remove the pan from the heat.

In a small bowl, lightly beat the egg yolks and cream together with a fork. Stir in 4 tablespoons of the hot asparagus mixture. Stir this into the remaining asparagus mixture in the saucepan.

Place the pan over low heat and gently cook and stir the soup for 2 minutes. Do not allow it to boil.

Turn the soup into a warmed tureen or individual bowls. Garnish with the asparagus tips and serve.

Carrot and Lemon Soup

A subtle blend of flavours and textures makes Carrot and Lemon Soup a cheerful offering.
Preparation and cooking time: 1¼ hours
4 SERVINGS

2 tablespoons vegetable oil
1 medium-sized onion, finely chopped
2 lb. carrots, scraped and chopped
1½ pints [3¾ cups] Light Vegetable Stock
grated rind and juice of ½ lemon
¼ teaspoon salt
⅛ teaspoon white pepper
2 tablespoons chopped fresh parsley

In a large saucepan, heat the oil over moderate heat. Add the onion and carrots and fry them, stirring occasionally, for 5 to 7 minutes or until the onion is soft and translucent but not brown. Stir in the stock, lemon juice, half the lemon rind, the salt and the pepper. Bring the liquid to the boil.

Reduce the heat to low and simmer, stirring occasionally, for about 40 minutes, or until the carrots are very tender.

Strain the carrot mixture into a large mixing bowl, rubbing the vegetables through the strainer with a wooden spoon. Alternatively, purée the mixture in a blender. Return the purée to the saucepan and stir in the remaining lemon rind. Replace the pan on the heat and cook the soup, stirring constantly, for 5 minutes.

Turn the soup into a warmed tureen or individual soup bowls, sprinkle over the parsley and serve.

Borscht

BEETROOT [BEET] SOUP

This is a classic summer Borscht, a light clear soup that may be served hot or cold. It is traditionally served hot with boiled potatoes as well as with sour cream. This recipe can be varied by whisking two beaten eggs into the hot soup just before serving.

Preparation and cooking time: 1¾ hours

6 SERVINGS

- 5 large, raw beetroots [beets], peeled and coarsely grated
- 3 pints [7½ cups] water
- 1 onion, chopped
- 3 oz. tomato purée
- 1 tablespoon lemon juice
- 1 teaspoon salt
- ½ teaspoon black pepper
- 1 teaspoon sugar
- 10 fl. oz. [1¼ cups] sour cream

Place the beetroots [beets], water and onion in a large saucepan over high heat. Bring the liquid to the boil. Reduce the heat to low, cover the pan, and simmer for 45 minutes.

Stir in the tomato purée, lemon juice, salt, pepper and sugar. Cover the pan again and continue cooking for 45 minutes.

Remove the pan from the heat. Strain the soup into a tureen or individual bowls. Discard the vegetables. Top the borscht with the sour cream and serve.

Celery Soup

An economical soup based on a stock made with the leaves of the celery, this soup has a very pleasant taste and an interesting texture.

Preparation and cooking time: 1½ hours

4-5 SERVINGS

- 2 heads of celery, with the leaves
- 1¼ pints [3 cups] water
- 3 tablespoons vegetable oil
- 1 large leek, white part only, cut into ½-inch pieces
- 1 garlic clove, finely chopped
- ¼ teaspoon salt
- ⅛ teaspoon white pepper
- 10 fl. oz. [1¼ cups] milk or single [light] cream

With a sharp knife, cut the leaves from the heads of celery and put them in a large saucepan. Pour over the water and place the pan over moderately high heat. Bring the water to the boil. Reduce the heat to low and simmer for 20 minutes.

Strain the celery leaf liquid into a medium-sized bowl or jug and set aside. Discard the celery leaves.

With a sharp knife, cut the celery stalks into ½-inch pieces.

Wash and dry the saucepan and in it heat the oil over moderate heat. Add the celery and leek pieces and fry them, stirring continuously, for 5 to 7 minutes, or until they are slightly soft but not brown. Stir in the celery leaf liquid and garlic and bring the liquid to the boil. Reduce the heat to low and simmer for 40 minutes.

Add the salt and pepper and stir in the milk or cream. Continue simmering for 5 minutes, stirring occasionally.

Turn the soup into a warmed tureen or individual soup bowls and serve it immediately.

Creamed Spinach Soup

Beautifully green, with a swirling pattern of white on the surface, Creamed Spinach Soup is as pleasing to the eye as it is to the palate.

Preparation and cooking time: 55 minutes

4 SERVINGS

- 1½ oz. [3 tablespoons] butter or margarine
- 1 large potato, peeled and chopped
- 1 medium-sized onion, finely chopped
- 1 lb. spinach, washed, drained and coarsely chopped
- 1½ pints [3¾ cups] Dark Vegetable Stock
- ¼ teaspoon salt
- ⅛ teaspoon white pepper
- ⅛ teaspoon ground mace
- ½ teaspoon lemon juice
- 4 fl. oz. single cream [½ cup light cream]

In a large saucepan, melt the butter or margarine over moderate heat. When the foam subsides, add the potato and onion. Fry them, stirring occasionally, for 5 to 7 minutes or until the onion is soft and translucent but not brown.

Add the spinach, stock, salt, pepper, mace and lemon juice and bring the soup to the boil. Reduce the heat to low and simmer the soup, stirring occasionally, for 15 to 20 minutes, or until the potatoes are thoroughly cooked.

Strain the soup into a large mixing bowl, rubbing the vegetables through the strainer with a wooden spoon. Alternatively, purée the soup in a blender. Return the soup to the saucepan and place the pan back on the heat. Cook the soup gently, stirring occasionally, for 5 minutes.

Turn the soup into a warmed tureen or individual soup bowls and swirl in the cream. Serve immediately.

Jerusalem Artichoke Soup

Suitable for people who have to watch their sugar intake, Jerusalem Artichoke Soup is both easily digestible and very tasty.

Preparation and cooking time: 45 minutes

4-6 SERVINGS

- 2 fl. oz. [¼ cup] vegetable oil
- 1 large onion, finely chopped
- 2 pints [5 cups] water
- 2 garlic cloves, crushed
- 2 lb. Jerusalem artichokes, finely chopped
- ¼ teaspoon salt
- ⅛ teaspoon white pepper
- 2 tablespoons snipped fresh chives

In a large saucepan, heat the oil over moderate heat. Add the onion and fry it, stirring occasionally, for 8 to 10 minutes or until it is just turning golden brown. Stir in the water and garlic and bring the liquid to the boil. Add the artichokes. Reduce the heat to low and simmer for 20 minutes or until the artichokes are soft and mushy.

Remove the pan from the heat and, with a wire whisk or rotary beater, beat the soup until it is smooth and creamy. Alternatively, purée the soup in a blender. Stir in the salt and pepper.

Return the pan to the heat and reheat the soup for 2 to 3 minutes. Turn the soup into a warmed tureen or individual bowls. Sprinkle over the chives and serve.

Mushroom Soup

This creamy Mushroom Soup has an attractive garnish of thinly sliced mushrooms floating on the top.

Preparation and cooking time: 1½ hours

4-6 SERVINGS

- 2 tablespoons vegetable oil
- 1 small onion, finely chopped
- 8 oz. button mushrooms, wiped clean and finely chopped
- 1½ pints [3¾ cups] Light Vegetable Stock
- ¼ teaspoon salt
- ⅛ teaspoon black pepper
- 2 tablespoons flour dissolved in 2 tablespoons water
- 10 fl. oz. [1¼ cups] milk or single [light] cream
- 4 button mushrooms, wiped clean and thinly sliced
- 1 teaspoon lemon juice
- 2 tablespoons water

In a large saucepan, heat the oil over moderate heat. Add the onion and fry it, stirring occasionally, for 8 to 10 minutes, or until it is just turning golden brown. Add the chopped mushrooms and stir to blend them with the oil and onion mixture. Continue cooking, stirring occasionally, for 3 minutes.

Stir in the stock, salt and pepper and bring the liquid to the boil. Reduce the heat to low and simmer for 50 minutes.

Strain the mushroom mixture into a large mixing bowl, rubbing the vegetables through the strainer with a wooden spoon. Alternatively, purée the mixture in a blender. Return the purée to the saucepan and stir in the flour and water mixture.

Replace the pan over the heat and cook, stirring constantly, for 5 minutes, or until the soup is slightly thickened and smooth. Stir in the milk or cream and continue cooking and stirring for 5 minutes.

Meanwhile, in a small saucepan bring the sliced mushrooms, lemon juice and water to the boil over moderate heat. Simmer the mushrooms for 4 minutes. Remove the pan from the heat and drain the mushrooms thoroughly.

Turn the soup into a warmed tureen or individual bowls. Float the mushroom slices on top and serve.

Fennel Soup

A warming soup with an unusual flavour, Fennel Soup may be served with Sesame Seed and Honey Fingers.

Preparation and cooking time: 45 minutes
4 SERVINGS

1 oz. [2 tablespoons] butter or
   margarine
1 large onion, chopped
1 garlic clove, crushed
1 large potato, peeled and chopped
1 large head of fennel, chopped, and
   feathery leaves roughly chopped
   and reserved
1½ pints [3¾ cups] hot Light Vegetable
   Stock
¼ teaspoon sea salt
⅛ teaspoon freshly ground black
   pepper
4 tablespoons single [light] cream
   (optional)

In a large saucepan, melt the butter or margarine over moderate heat. When the foam subsides, add the onion and garlic and fry them for 5 to 7 minutes, or until the onion is soft and translucent but not brown.

Add the potato and fennel to the pan and stir gently to coat them with the butter and onion mixture. Cover the pan and cook the vegetables for 10 to 15 minutes, or until the potato and fennel are tender, shaking the pan occasionally

to prevent the vegetables from sticking to the bottom.

Stir in the stock, salt and pepper and bring the soup to the boil. Reduce the heat to low and simmer the soup gently for 5 minutes. Taste the soup and add more salt and pepper if necessary.

Remove the pan from the heat. Pour the soup through a strainer into a large mixing bowl, pushing the vegetables through the strainer with a wooden spoon. Alternatively, purée the soup in a blender. If you prefer, purée only two-thirds of the soup vegetables, leaving the remainder in small pieces.

Return the puréed soup to the saucepan and return the pan to the heat. Cook the soup for a further 5 minutes.

Turn the soup into a warmed tureen or individual soup bowls. If you are using the cream, spoon a tablespoonful on to the top of each bowl and swirl it in. Sprinkle over the reserved fennel leaves and serve.

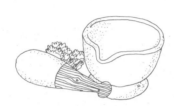

Cold Pear and Cherry Soup

Cold fruit soups are relatively unknown in English-speaking countries, which is a shame as they make a refreshing and unusual start to a meal. In the summer especially, they are much lighter and easier to digest than cooked hors d'oeuvre or hot soup.

Preparation and cooking time: 1¾ hours
6 SERVINGS

2 lb. firm dessert pears, peeled,
   cored and diced
10 fl. oz. [1¼ cups] water
1 cinnamon stick
1 lb. canned, stoned Morello
   cherries
6 fl. oz. [¾ cup] red wine
3 oz. [⅜ cup] sugar
   grated rind and juice of ½ lemon

Put the pears into a large saucepan and cover them with the water. Add the cinnamon stick and place the pan over low heat. Cover the pan and gently poach the pears for 40 minutes, or until they are tender.

Remove the pan from the heat and strain the pears and poaching liquid into a medium-sized mixing bowl. Discard the cinnamon stick and push the pears through the strainer with a wooden

spoon. Return the pear purée to the saucepan and set it aside.

Drain the cherries, reserve the syrup and set them aside.

Add the cherry syrup to the pear purée in the saucepan with the red wine, sugar and lemon rind and juice. Return the pan to low heat and cook and stir the mixture until the sugar has dissolved. Increase the heat to moderate and bring the mixture to the boil. Reduce the heat to low again and stir in the cherries. Cook the soup for 2 to 3 minutes, stirring occasionally.

Remove the pan from the heat and pour the soup into a deep serving bowl. Allow the soup to cool to room temperature, then place the bowl in the refrigerator. Chill the soup for at least 1 hour before serving.

Gazpacho

A classic Spanish soup, cold Gazpacho makes a refreshing summer lunch served with croûtons, small bowls of chopped olives, cucumbers, hard-boiled eggs and onion. Each guest then sprinkles his soup with a little of these accompaniments. To make this soup most easily you will need an electric blender, although good results can be obtained from a food mill or mortar and pestle.

Preparation and cooking time: 25 minutes
4 SERVINGS

3 slices of brown bread, cut into
   1-inch cubes
10 fl. oz. [1¼ cups] canned tomato juice
2 garlic cloves, finely chopped
½ cucumber, peeled and finely
   chopped
1 green pepper, white pith
   removed, seeded and finely
   chopped
1 red pepper, white pith removed,
   seeded and finely chopped
1 large onion, finely chopped
1½ lb. tomatoes, blanched, peeled,
   seeded and chopped
3 fl. oz. [⅜ cup] olive oil
2 tablespoons red wine vinegar
½ teaspoon salt
¼ teaspoon black pepper
¼ teaspoon dried marjoram
¼ teaspoon dried basil
4 ice cubes (optional)

Place the bread cubes in a medium-sized mixing bowl and pour over the tomato juice. Leave the bread cubes to soak for 5 minutes, then squeeze them to extract the excess juice. Transfer them to a large mixing bowl. Reserve the tomato juice.

Add the garlic, cucumber, peppers, onion and tomatoes to the soaked bread cubes and stir to mix. Purée the ingredients by pounding them in a mortar with a pestle to a paste and then rubbing them through a strainer, or by putting them through a food mill. Stir in the tomato juice. If you are using a blender, purée the vegetables and bread cubes with the reserved tomato juice.

Add the oil, vinegar, salt, pepper, marjoram and basil to the purée and stir well. The soup should be the consistency of single [light] cream, so add more tomato juice if necessary.

Turn the soup into a deep serving bowl and place it in the refrigerator to chill for at least 1 hour. Just before serving, stir the soup well and drop in the ice cubes.

Vichyssoise

A classic soup, Vichyssoise is a superb blend of leeks, potatoes and cream and is equally good hot or cold.
Preparation and cooking time: 50 minutes
6 SERVINGS

1 tablespoon butter or margarine
1 onion, finely chopped
2 large leeks, white part only, finely chopped
3 medium-sized potatoes, peeled and thinly sliced
1¾ pints [4⅜ cups] Light Vegetable Stock
1 teaspoon salt
5 fl. oz. single cream [⅝ cup light cream]
⅛ teaspoon white pepper

In a large saucepan, melt the butter or margarine over moderate heat. When the foam subsides, add the onion and leeks. Fry them, stirring occasionally, for 8 to 10 minutes or until they are a light golden brown. Add the potatoes, stock and salt and bring the mixture to the boil.

Reduce the heat to moderately low and simmer the mixture for 15 to 20 minutes or until the potatoes are tender. Remove the pan from the heat and strain the mixture into a medium-sized mixing bowl, pushing the vegetables through the strainer with a wooden spoon. Alternatively, purée the mixture in a blender.

Return the purée to the pan and stir in the cream. Place the pan over low heat and heat the soup for 5 minutes, stirring occasionally. Do not let it boil. Taste the soup and add the pepper if necessary.

Turn the Vichyssoise into a warmed tureen or individual bowls and serve.

If the soup is to be served cold, allow it to cool to room temperature, then place it in the refrigerator to chill for 30 minutes.

Accompaniments
Sesame Seed and Honey Fingers

A rich and nourishing accompaniment for soups, Sesame Seed and Honey Fingers take very little time to prepare.
Preparation and cooking time: 20 minutes
4 SERVINGS

4 thick slices of bread, toasted and crusts removed
3 oz. [⅜ cup] butter
1 tablespoon sesame seeds
1 tablespoon thick honey

Preheat the grill [broiler] to high.

With a sharp knife, carefully split each piece of toasted bread in two to make eight thin slices of toast. Set aside.

In a small mixing bowl, cream the butter with a wooden spoon until it is soft and fluffy. Beat in the sesame seeds and honey.

Place the toast slices, untoasted side up, on the grill [broiler] rack. Liberally spread each slice with the sesame seed mixture. Place the rack under the grill [broiler] and cook for 5 to 6 minutes, or until the tops are brown and bubbling.

Remove the slices from the heat and cut each one into three fingers. Serve immediately.

Diablotins

Diablotins (dee-ah-bloh-tan) are circles of bread covered with a thick cheese sauce and browned under the grill [broiler]. They make a good accompaniment for soups, but may also be served as a hot snack.
Preparation and cooking time: 30 minutes
6 SERVINGS

6 slices of day-old bread, cut ½-inch thick
3 oz. [⅜ cup] butter or margarine
3 tablespoons flour
8 fl. oz. [1 cup] milk
½ teaspoon salt
¼ teaspoon white pepper
½ teaspoon cayenne pepper
4 oz. [1 cup] Cheddar cheese, grated
2 oz. [½ cup] Parmesan cheese, grated

Preheat the grill [broiler] to moderate.

With a 3-inch pastry cutter, cut a circle from the centre of each slice of bread. Using half of the butter or

margarine, butter the circles and set them aside.

In a medium-sized saucepan, melt the remaining butter or margarine over moderately low heat. Remove the pan from the heat and, with a wooden spoon, stir in the flour to make a smooth paste. Gradually add the milk, stirring constantly.

Return the pan to the heat and bring the sauce to the boil, stirring constantly. Cook for 2 to 3 minutes or until it is very thick and smooth. Add the salt, pepper, cayenne and Cheddar cheese and vigorously beat the sauce until the cheese has melted and the mixture is smooth.

Arrange the buttered circles of bread on the grill [broiler] rack. Spoon the cheese sauce on to the circles. Sprinkle the Parmesan cheese over the tops.

Place the rack under the grill [broiler] and cook the Diablotins for 3 to 4 minutes or until they are browned and bubbling. Serve at once.

Pine Kernel Dumplings

An excellent addition to any soup, Pine Kernel Dumplings have an unusual flavour that complements almost every vegetable.
Preparation and cooking time: 40 minutes
ABOUT 12 DUMPLINGS

3 oz. [¾ cup] flour
1 teaspoon salt
½ teaspoon black pepper
2 oz. [¼ cup] butter or margarine
3 tablespoons ground pine kernels
3 oz. [1½ cups] fresh brown breadcrumbs
1 teaspoon dried basil
1 egg, lightly beaten
2 fl. oz. [¼ cup] water

Sift the flour, salt and pepper into a medium-sized mixing bowl. Add the butter or margarine and cut it into small pieces with a table knife. With your fingertips, rub the fat into the flour until the mixture resembles coarse breadcrumbs.

Stir in the pine kernels, brown breadcrumbs and basil. Make a well in the centre of the flour mixture and pour in the egg and half of the water. Using your fingers or a spatula, gradually draw the flour mixture into the liquid and continue mixing until all the flour mixture has been incorporated. Add more water if the dough is too dry. It should be stiff.

Form the dough into small balls and drop them into boiling soup or stew. Cover the saucepan and simmer the dumplings for 15 minutes. Serve immediately.

Sauces

White Sauce

A basic White Sauce has innumerable uses, both as an ingredient and as a coating. It also forms the basis for a wide variety of other sauces, such as mustard, caper, egg and cheese. For a thick sauce, to coat vegetables such as cauliflower, double the quantities of fat and flour.

Preparation and cooking time: 10 minutes

1 PINT [2½ CUPS]

- 1 oz. [2 tablespoons] butter or margarine
- 2 tablespoons flour
- 1 pint [2½ cups] milk, warmed
- ½ teaspoon salt
- ¼ teaspoon white pepper

In a medium-sized saucepan, melt the butter or margarine over moderate heat. Remove the pan from the heat. With a wooden spoon, stir in the flour to make a smooth paste. Gradually add the milk, stirring constantly.

Return the pan to the heat and bring the sauce to the boil, still stirring. Reduce the heat to low and simmer the sauce, stirring constantly, for 2 to 3 minutes or until it is thick and smooth. Stir in the salt and pepper.

The sauce is now ready to serve.

Béchamel Sauce

Louis de Béchamel, Marquis de Nointel, who was steward of the household at the court of Louis XIV, is reputed to have introduced this sauce. Like White Sauce, Béchamel may be served plain or used as the base for other sauces. For a thick coating sauce, double the quantities of butter or margarine and flour.

Preparation and cooking time: 15 minutes

1 PINT [2½ CUPS]

- 1 pint [2½ cups] milk
- 1 bay leaf
- 1 mace blade
- 1 slice onion
- 6 black peppercorns
- ½ teaspoon salt
- 1 oz. [2 tablespoons] butter or margarine
- 2 tablespoons flour

Pour the milk into a medium-sized saucepan. Add the bay leaf, mace blade, onion slice, peppercorns and salt. Place the pan over low heat and warm the milk for 7 minutes so that it becomes infused with the flavours of the seasonings.

Remove the pan from the heat and strain the milk into a small bowl. Set aside. Discard the seasonings.

Rinse and thoroughly dry the saucepan. Put the butter or margarine in the pan and melt it over moderate heat. Remove the pan from the heat. With a wooden spoon, stir in the flour to make a smooth paste. Gradually add the milk, stirring constantly.

Return the pan to the heat and bring the sauce to the boil, still stirring. Reduce the heat to low and simmer the sauce, stirring constantly, for 2 to 3 minutes or until it is thick and smooth.

The sauce is now ready to serve.

Mustard Sauce

Stir 2 teaspoons of prepared French mustard into 1 pint [2½ cups] of hot White or Béchamel Sauce.

Caper Sauce

Stir 2 tablespoons of capers and 2 tablespoons of chopped fresh parsley into 1 pint [2½ cups] of hot White or Béchamel Sauce.

Egg Sauce

Stir 4 finely chopped hard-boiled eggs into 1 pint [2½ cups] of hot White or Béchamel Sauce.

Cheese Sauce

Stir 2 ounces [½ cup] grated Parmesan cheese, 2 ounces [½ cup] grated Gruyère cheese and 1 teaspoon prepared French mustard into 1 pint [2½ cups] of hot White or Béchamel Sauce.

Brown Sauce

Thick, rich Brown Sauce is the perfect accompaniment for a nut roast or savoury vegetable quiche.

Preparation and cooking time: 10 minutes

1 PINT [2½ CUPS]

- 1 oz. [2 tablespoons] butter or margarine
- 2 tablespoons flour
- 1 pint [2½ cups] hot Dark Vegetable Stock
- 1 tablespoon yeast extract

In a medium-sized saucepan, melt the butter or margarine over moderate heat. With a wooden spoon, stir in the flour

to make a smooth paste. Cook, stirring constantly, for 3 to 4 minutes, or until the paste (roux) turns light brown.

Remove the pan from the heat. Gradually add the stock, stirring constantly. Return the pan to the heat and bring the sauce to the boil, still stirring. Reduce the heat to low. Stir in the yeast extract. Simmer and stir the sauce for 2 to 3 minutes or until it is thick and smooth.

The sauce is now ready to serve.

Onion Sauce

Smooth Onion Sauce will beautifully complement any vegetable or egg dish, and is particularly good spooned over an omelet.

Preparation and cooking time: 15 minutes

1 PINT [2½ CUPS]

- 2 oz. [¼ cup] butter or margarine
- 3 medium-sized onions, finely chopped
- 2 tablespoons flour
- 1 pint [2½ cups] hot Light Vegetable Stock
- 1½ teaspoons yeast extract

In a medium-sized saucepan, melt the butter or margarine over moderate heat. Add the onions to the pan and fry them, stirring occasionally, for 5 to 7 minutes or until they are soft and translucent but not brown.

Remove the pan from the heat. With a wooden spoon, stir in the flour to make a smooth paste. Gradually add the stock, stirring constantly. Return the pan to the heat and bring the sauce to the boil, still stirring. Reduce the heat to low. Stir in the yeast extract. Simmer and stir the sauce for 2 to 3 minutes or until it is thick and smooth.

The sauce is now ready to serve.

Pepper Sauce

Particularly good with cauliflower or other delicately flavoured vegetables, Pepper Sauce is made from both red and green peppers.

Preparation and cooking time: 50 minutes

12 FLUID OUNCES [1½ CUPS]

- 3 tablespoons olive oil
- 1 medium-sized onion, finely chopped
- 1 garlic clove, crushed
- 1 green pepper, white pith removed, seeded and finely chopped
- 1 red pepper, white pith removed, seeded and finely chopped
- 1 celery stalk, finely chopped
- 10 fl. oz. [1¼ cups] Light Vegetable Stock

3 tablespoons tomato puree
½ teaspoon salt
½ teaspoon black pepper
⅛ teaspoon cayenne pepper

In a medium-sized saucepan, heat the oil over moderate heat. Add the onion and garlic and fry them, stirring occasionally, for 5 to 7 minutes or until the onion is soft and translucent but not brown.

Stir in the green and red peppers and celery and continue cooking and stirring for 10 minutes or until the vegetables are soft. Add the stock, stir to mix and bring the mixture to the boil. Reduce the heat to low and simmer for 15 minutes, stirring occasionally.

Remove the pan from the heat and strain the pepper mixture into a medium-sized mixing bowl, rubbing the vegetables through the strainer with a wooden spoon. Alternatively, purée the mixture in a blender.

Return the purée to the saucepan and stir in the tomato purée, salt, pepper and cayenne. Replace the pan on the heat and simmer the sauce for 5 minutes, stirring occasionally.

The sauce is now ready to serve.

Lemon Sauce

Smooth-textured with a fresh flavour, Lemon Sauce is very tasty with green vegetables such as courgettes [zucchini], artichokes or asparagus.
Preparation and cooking time: 20 minutes
12 FLUID OUNCES [1½ CUPS]
10 fl. oz. [1¼ cups] Light Vegetable Stock
2 tablespoons cornflour [cornstarch] dissolved in 2 fl. oz. [¼ cup] water
2 egg yolks
2 tablespoons lemon juice
2 teaspoons grated lemon rind
1 tablespoon butter or margarine, cut into small pieces

In a medium-sized saucepan, bring the stock to the boil over high heat. Reduce the heat to moderate and stir in the dissolved cornflour [cornstarch]. Simmer for 8 minutes, stirring constantly.

In a small bowl, beat the egg yolks and lemon juice together with a kitchen fork. Stir in 2 tablespoons of the hot stock mixture, then add the egg yolk mixture to the remaining stock in the saucepan with the lemon rind. Reduce the heat to low and gently cook the sauce for 5 minutes, stirring constantly.

Add the butter or margarine, one piece at a time, still stirring. When all the butter or margarine has been absorbed, the sauce is ready to serve.

Mushroom and Cheese Sauce

Poured over tender but still slightly crunchy leeks, carrots or courgettes [zucchini], Mushroom and Cheese Sauce will start your mouth watering.
Preparation and cooking time: 20 minutes
1 PINT [2½ CUPS]
1 oz. [2 tablespoons] butter or margarine
4 oz. button mushrooms, wiped clean and finely chopped
2 tablespoons flour
10 fl. oz. [1¼ cups] hot Light Vegetable Stock
10 fl. oz. [1¼ cups] milk, warmed
½ teaspoon salt
¼ teaspoon pepper
4 oz. [1 cup] Cheddar cheese, grated

In a medium-sized saucepan, melt the butter or margarine over moderate heat. Add the mushrooms to the pan and fry them, stirring constantly, for 6 to 8 minutes, or until the mushrooms are soft.

Remove the pan from the heat. With a wooden spoon, stir in the flour to make a smooth paste. Gradually add the stock and milk, stirring constantly. Stir in the salt and pepper.

Return the pan to the heat and bring the sauce to the boil, still stirring. Reduce the heat to low and simmer and stir the sauce for 2 to 3 minutes or until it is thick and smooth. Stir in the cheese. When all the cheese has been absorbed, the sauce is ready to serve.

Tomato Sauce I

The flavour and fragrance of a home-made Tomato Sauce can never be duplicated by that available in the shops. Very simple to make, this recipe produces a rich creamy tomato sauce that is superb with pasta or poured over almost any vegetable.
Preparation and cooking time: 40 minutes
8 FLUID OUNCES [1 CUP]
1 oz. [2 tablespoons] butter or margarine
1½ lb. tomatoes, blanched, peeled, seeded and chopped
2 teaspoons finely chopped fresh basil
5 fl. oz. single cream [⅝ cup light cream]
½ teaspoon black pepper

In a medium-sized saucepan, melt the butter or margarine over moderate heat. When the foam subsides, add the tomatoes and basil. Reduce the heat to low, cover the pan and cook the tomatoes, stirring occasionally, for 25 to 30 minutes or until they are soft and pulpy.

Stir in the cream and pepper and continue cooking gently, uncovered and stirring constantly, for 5 minutes.

The sauce is now ready to serve.

Tomato Sauce II

This Tomato Sauce is rich, thick and glossy in appearance and is ideal for coating vegetables such as French beans or aubergines [eggplants].
Preparation and cooking time: 1 hour
16 FLUID OUNCES [2 CUPS]
1½ oz. [3 tablespoons] butter or margarine
1 tablespoon flour
10 fl. oz. [1¼ cups] Dark Vegetable Stock
1 lb. tomatoes, halved and seeded
2 teaspoons tomato purée
bouquet garni, consisting of 2 parsley sprigs, 1 thyme spray and 1 bay leaf tied together
½ teaspoon salt
¼ teaspoon black pepper
¼ teaspoon dried basil
⅛ teaspoon sugar

In a medium-sized saucepan, melt 1 ounce [2 tablespoons] of the butter or margarine over moderate heat. Remove the pan from the heat. With a wooden spoon, stir in the flour to make a smooth paste. Gradually add the stock, stirring constantly.

Return the pan to the heat and bring the sauce to the boil, still stirring. Reduce the heat to low and add the tomatoes, tomato purée, bouquet garni, salt, pepper, basil and sugar. Stir to mix and cover the pan. Simmer the sauce for 25 to 30 minutes or until the tomatoes are reduced to a pulp.

Remove the pan from the heat. Remove and discard the bouquet garni. Strain the sauce into a medium-sized mixing bowl, pressing down on the tomato pulp and skins with a wooden spoon to extract all their juices. Discard the tomato pulp and skins left in the strainer.

Rinse and thoroughly dry the saucepan. Return the sauce to it and place the pan over moderate heat. Simmer the sauce for 4 to 6 minutes or until it is smooth and fairly thick. Stir in the remaining butter or margarine.

The sauce is now ready to serve.

Salads and Dressings

There are delightful surprises in store for all those who thought that salads could only be served on a hot summer's day! Salads have no special season – simple, easy-to-make green salads with vinaigrette dressing or mixed vegetable salads make wonderful accompaniments to savoury bakes, omelets or quiches at any time of the year. Splendid moulded salads may form part of a buffet or become a centrepiece for an elegant dinner party table.

Apart from being appetizing, most salad ingredients are rich in essential vitamins, calcium, iron and proteins. Agar-agar (a vegetable substitute for gelatine obtained from seaweed) is suggested for the moulded salad recipes, because it is tasteless, easy to use and a good source of iodine. However, if you prefer, gelatine may be used instead, but do remember that gelatine should be softened and completely dissolved before being added to the salad ingredients.

Salad dressings do not just enhance or complement taste and textures; the addition of vinegar or lemon juice – the basis of most dressings – helps to maintain the nutritional value of fresh cut fruit and vegetables. One point to remember, however, is that some salad ingredients – particularly lettuce – will become soggy and wilted if they are dressed too long before serving.

Summer Garden Salad

A beautiful crisp salad in varying shades of green does much to whet the appetite – especially when the weather is warm.
Preparation and cooking time: 20 minutes
6-8 SERVINGS
1 curly endive or escarole, separated into leaves
1 crisp head of lettuce, outer leaves removed, washed and separated into leaves
1 green pepper, white pith removed, seeded and cut into thin strips
3 celery stalks, finely chopped
1 cucumber, peeled and thinly sliced
4 spring onions [scallions], finely chopped
1 bunch of watercress, washed, shaken dry and stalks removed
2 tablespoons chopped fresh green herbs (basil, chervil, parsley, etc.)
4 to 6 fl. oz. [½ to ¾ cup] Vinaigrette Dressing I

Tear the curly endive or escarole and lettuce into small pieces and put them in a large salad bowl. Add the green pepper, celery, cucumber, spring onions [scallions], watercress and herbs.

Pour over the dressing and toss the salad well. Serve immediately.

Brazil Nut Salad

A nourishing first course, Brazil Nut Salad combines the smoothness of bananas with the crunchiness of Brazil nuts.
Preparation and cooking time: 20 minutes
4 SERVINGS
1 crisp head of lettuce, outer leaves removed, washed and separated into leaves
2 fl. oz. [¼ cup] French Dressing
3 bananas
1 tablespoon lemon juice
4 oz. [⅔ cup] Brazil nuts, finely chopped

Arrange half of the lettuce leaves in a shallow serving bowl. Set aside.

Shred the remaining lettuce into a medium-sized mixing bowl. Pour over the French dressing and toss the lettuce until it is well coated.

Peel the bananas and slice them into a small mixing bowl. Sprinkle over the lemon juice. Add half of the sliced bananas and the Brazil nuts to the shredded lettuce and toss the ingredients together.

Pile the nut and banana mixture on top of the lettuce leaves in the serving bowl. Arrange the remaining banana slices around the edge in a ring and serve.

Andalusian Rice Salad

One of the great classic salad dishes, Andalusian Rice Salad makes a stunning centrepiece for a summer buffet. And it's as good to eat as it looks!
Preparation and cooking time: 20 minutes
4-6 SERVINGS
8 oz. [1⅓ cups] long-grain brown rice, cooked and cooled
1 small onion, finely chopped
2 garlic cloves, crushed
1 tablespoon chopped fresh parsley
3 fl. oz. [⅜ cup] olive oil
2 tablespoons red wine vinegar
1 teaspoon paprika
½ teaspoon salt
½ teaspoon white pepper
1 lb. tomatoes, quartered
4 hard-boiled eggs, sliced
2 medium-sized red peppers, white pith removed, seeded and cut into thin strips
2 tablespoons chopped fresh chervil, or 1 teaspoon dried chervil

In a medium-sized mixing bowl, combine the rice with the onion, garlic, parsley, olive oil, vinegar, paprika, salt and pepper. Toss until all the ingredients are well blended. Arrange the rice mixture in the centre of a large serving dish.

Arrange the tomatoes, eggs and peppers decoratively around the rice and sprinkle the chopped chervil over the mixture.

Serve at once.

North African Salad

An exotic blend of sweet and sour, North African Salad makes a satisfying lunch or supper meal by itself.

Preparation and cooking time: 40 minutes

4 SERVINGS

12 oz. [2 cups] long-grain brown rice, cooked and cooled
1 small cucumber, halved lengthways and sliced
2 medium-sized bananas, sliced
2 tablespoons seedless raisins
1 tablespoon chopped almonds
4 tablespoons olive oil
1½ tablespoons lemon juice
1 tablespoon grated lemon rind
1 teaspoon salt
¼ teaspoon ground coriander
¼ teaspoon ground cumin
¼ teaspoon cayenne pepper
1 teaspoon clear honey

Arrange the rice, cucumber and bananas in a large salad bowl. Stir in the raisins and almonds.

In a small bowl, combine the oil, lemon juice and rind, salt, coriander, cumin, cayenne and honey together, beating with a fork until all the ingredients are well blended.

Pour the dressing over the rice mixture and stir well to mix. Chill in the refrigerator for 30 minutes before serving.

Brussels Sprout and Corn Salad

The flavours in this Brussels Sprout and Corn Salad complement each other very well. Served with a baked potato, you have a complete meal.

Preparation and cooking time: 15 minutes

4-6 SERVINGS

1 lb. Brussels sprouts, trimmed, cooked, cooled and halved
8 oz. carrots, scraped and grated
4 oz. canned sweetcorn, drained
5 fl. oz. [⅝ cup] Vinaigrette Dressing I
3 tablespoons chopped walnuts
watercress sprigs (to garnish)

In a medium-sized salad bowl, mix together the Brussels sprouts, carrots and sweetcorn. Pour over the dressing and toss the ingredients together throughly.

Sprinkle over the walnuts and garnish with the watercress. Serve immediately.

Apple and Celeriac Salad

A crunchy and fresh-tasting salad with a herb-flavoured mayonnaise dressing, Apple and Celeriac Salad would be a good accompaniment for a spicy main dish.

Preparation and cooking time: 45 minutes

4 SERVINGS

1½ lb. celeriac
1 teaspoon salt
3 fl. oz. [⅜ cup] mayonnaise
1 tablespoon finely chopped fresh chervil or borage
1 tablespoon finely chopped fresh parsley
2 crisp eating apples, cored and sliced
4 oz. [⅔ cup] salted cashew nuts, finely chopped

Put the celeriac in a medium-sized saucepan. Pour over enough water just to cover the celeriac and add the salt. Place the pan over high heat and bring the water to the boil.

Reduce the heat to moderate and cook the celeriac for 15 minutes. Drain the celeriac thoroughly in a colander and dry it on kitchen paper towels. Allow it to cool and then slice it thinly.

In a medium-sized serving bowl beat together the mayonnaise, chervil or borage and parsley. Add the apple and celeriac slices and stir to coat them with the mayonnaise dressing.

Sprinkle the nuts over the top and serve.

Tomatoes with Prune Cheese Stuffing

Tomatoes stuffed with a smooth cream cheese and prune mixture make a delicious first course or light luncheon dish with bread and butter.

Preparation and cooking time: 35 minutes

4 SERVINGS

4 large tomatoes
8 oz. cream cheese
4 canned and drained or dried and soaked prunes, stoned and chopped
2 spring onions [scallions], finely chopped
1 teaspoon finely chopped fresh basil or ½ teaspoon dried basil
¼ teaspoon salt
⅛ teaspoon white pepper
2 to 3 tablespoons milk
8 lettuce leaves
watercress sprigs (to garnish)

With a sharp knife, cut off about a ½-inch lid from the top of each tomato. Scoop out and discard the seeds and tomato centres. Set the shells and lids aside.

In a small mixing bowl, mash the cream cheese with a wooden spoon until it is soft. Add the prunes, onions [scallions], basil, salt and pepper and blend the ingredients thoroughly. Beat in enough milk to make the mixture the consistency of stiffly whipped double [heavy] cream.

Spoon the cheese and prune mixture into the tomato shells and replace the lids on a slant.

Arrange the lettuce leaves on four individual serving dishes. Place a stuffed tomato in the centre of each dish and garnish with the watercress.

Serve immediately.

Neapolitan Salad Bowl

A colourful blend of tastes and textures, Neapolitan Salad Bowl makes a refreshing light luncheon meal. Serve it with crusty wholemeal bread and a well-chilled white wine.

Preparation and cooking time: 35 minutes

4 SERVINGS

4 medium-sized tomatoes, quartered
1 small green pepper, white pith removed, seeded and thinly sliced
1 small red pepper, white pith removed, seeded and thinly sliced
1 small head of lettuce, outer leaves removed, washed and shredded
4 oz. canned sweetcorn, drained
2 oz. mozzarella cheese, chopped
3 hard-boiled eggs, sliced
3 spring onions [scallions], thinly sliced
6 black olives, halved and stoned
4 fl. oz. [½ cup] French Dressing
1 garlic clove, finely chopped
½ teaspoon dried oregano
1 tablespoon chopped fresh basil leaves

Arrange the tomatoes, green and red peppers, lettuce, sweetcorn, cheese, eggs, spring onions [scallions] and olives in a large salad bowl. Place the bowl in the refrigerator and chill the salad for 20 minutes.

In a screw-top jar, combine the French dressing with the garlic and oregano. Cover the jar and shake it vigorously for 10 seconds.

Pour the dressing over the salad and toss well to coat all the ingredients thoroughly.

Sprinkle the chopped basil leaves on top and serve.

Melon Boats

Serve these lovely Melon Boats as a first course or as a dessert. Any musk melon, such as cantaloupe, Charentais, honeydew or ogen, may be used.

Preparation and cooking time: 1 hour

4 SERVINGS

- 2 small musk melons
- 2 pears, peeled, cored and chopped
- 4 oz. black grapes, halved and seeded
- 2 teaspoons lemon juice
- 3 tablespoons clear honey
- 2 tablespoons chopped sweet cicely (optional)
- 4 mint sprigs

Cut the melons in half. With a spoon, remove the seeds from the centres. Using a round melon baller, scoop out the melon flesh in balls.

Transfer the melon balls to a medium-sized mixing bowl. Add the chopped pears and halved grapes. Stir in the lemon juice, honey and sweet cicely, if you are using it. Set the bowl aside while you finish the boats.

With a sharp-edged spoon, scoop out any flesh remaining in the melon shells. If you like, scallop the edges with a sharp knife.

Pile the fruit mixture into the melon boats. Place them in the refrigerator to chill for 20 minutes.

Just before serving, garnish each boat with a sprig of mint.

Avocado Pâté

Serve this creamy Avocado Pâté with thin slices of buttered black bread for an elegant appetizer.

Preparation and cooking time: 35 minutes

4 SERVINGS

- 2 avocados
- 4 hard-boiled eggs, finely chopped
- 2 tablespoons cider or red wine vinegar
- 1 garlic clove, finely chopped
- 2 teaspoons finely chopped lemon balm
- 1/4 teaspoon salt
- 1/8 teaspoon black pepper
- 8 lettuce leaves
- 4 lemon slices
- 4 parsley sprigs

With a sharp knife, cut the avocados in half and remove the stones. Carefully scoop out the avocado flesh, leaving the skins intact, and transfer the flesh to a medium-sized mixing bowl. Reserve the skins.

Using a kitchen fork or wooden spoon,

mash the avocado flesh with the eggs, vinegar, garlic, lemon balm, salt and pepper to a smooth paste. Alternatively, mash the ingredients in a mortar with a pestle.

Spoon the avocado mixture back into the avocado skins.

Arrange the lettuce leaves on four individual serving dishes. Place a stuffed avocado half on each dish. Garnish each portion with a slice of lemon and a sprig of parsley.

Serve immediately.

Creole Banana Salad

A joy to the eye as well as to the palate, Creole Banana Salad makes an attractive addition to any summer meal. Or, serve it with Onion and Herb Bread and a well-chilled white wine, for a light, refreshing lunch.

Preparation and cooking time: 20 minutes

4 SERVINGS

- 4 large bananas, sliced
- 1 tablespoon lemon juice
- 1 lb. [2 2/3 cups] long-grain rice, cooked and cooled
- 1 medium-sized red apple, cored and chopped
- 4 oz. small seedless green grapes
- 3 oz. canned pineapple, drained and chopped
- 2 tablespoons finely chopped walnuts
- 1 tablespoon snipped fresh chives
- 4 large lettuce leaves
- 2 tablespoons desiccated [shredded] coconut

DRESSING

- 4 fl. oz. [1/2 cup] mayonnaise
- 2 tablespoons lemon juice
- 1/4 teaspoon hot chilli powder
- 1/2 teaspoon dry English mustard

In a large mixing bowl, combine the bananas, lemon juice, rice, apple, grapes, pineapple, walnuts and chives and mix to blend.

In a small bowl, beat the mayonnaise, lemon juice, chilli powder and mustard together until they are well blended. Carefully stir the dressing into the banana and rice mixture, mixing well.

Arrange the lettuce leaves in a large, shallow serving dish. Pile the banana and rice mixture on top and sprinkle over the coconut. Serve at once.

Carrot and Fruit Salad

A deliciously light and healthy lunch dish, Carrot and Fruit Salad will delight slimmers with its low calorie ingredients.

Preparation and cooking time: 45 minutes

4 SERVINGS

- 4 medium-sized carrots, scraped and grated
- 1 medium-sized eating apple, peeled, cored and finely chopped
- 2 tablespoons lemon juice
- 1 small orange, peeled, pith removed and finely chopped
- 2 oz. cream cheese
- 1 tablespoon chopped fresh parsley
- 1/2 teaspoon salt
- 1/4 teaspoon white pepper
- 1/4 teaspoon paprika

In a medium-sized salad bowl, combine the carrots and apple. Sprinkle over 1 tablespoon of the lemon juice. Add the orange and mix well to blend the ingredients together. Chill in the refrigerator for 30 minutes.

In a small bowl, mix the cream cheese and the remaining lemon juice together with a fork until they are well blended. Stir in the parsley, salt, pepper and paprika.

Stir the dressing into the salad and serve at once.

Rice and Avocado Salad

Nourishing and satisfying, Rice and Avocado Salad makes an excellent summer lunch or supper dish.

Preparation and cooking time: 1 1/4 hours

4 SERVINGS

- 2 fl. oz. [1/4 cup] French Dressing
- 1 garlic clove, crushed
- 1 lb. [2 2/3 cups] long-grain brown rice, cooked and cooled
- 2 medium-sized avocados, peeled, stoned and chopped
- 3 medium-sized tomatoes, blanched, peeled, seeded and chopped
- 2 hard-boiled eggs, chopped
- 2 oz. mushrooms, wiped clean and sliced

Pour the French dressing into a screw-top jar and add the garlic clove. Set the dressing aside for 1 hour.

In a large salad bowl, combine the rice, avocados, tomatoes, eggs and mushrooms together.

Remove the garlic clove from the dressing and discard it. Pour the dressing over the rice mixture. Stir well to blend. Chill the salad in the refrigerator for 1 hour, stirring occasionally, before serving.

Grapefruit Stuffed with Cheese Balls

An unusual and nutritious first course for a dinner party, Grapefruit Stuffed with Cheese Balls may also be served as a light main meal.

Preparation and cooking time: 1¾ hours

4-8 SERVINGS

6 oz. Camembert cheese, or similar soft cheese
1 oz. crushed digestive biscuits [⅓ cup crushed graham crackers]
2 oz. [¼ cup] walnuts, crushed
4 grapefruit, halved
3 bananas, mashed
3 fresh peaches, peeled, stoned and mashed

Using a sharp knife, cut the rind from the cheese. Mash the cheese through a strainer into a small bowl. Stir in the digestive biscuit [graham cracker] crumbs and beat the mixture with a wooden spoon until it is smooth and firm. Working carefully, shape the mixture into small, walnut-sized balls. Place the balls in the refrigerator to chill for 30 minutes, or until they are very firm.

Remove the balls from the refrigerator and coat them generously with the crushed walnuts. Set aside.

Using a sharp knife, scoop out the grapefruit flesh and place it in a medium-sized mixing bowl. Reserve the skins.

Add the bananas and peaches to the grapefruit flesh and stir with a wooden spoon to blend the ingredients together.

Spoon the grapefruit and banana mixture into the grapefruit skins and top with the cheese balls. Chill in the refrigerator for 15 minutes before serving.

Caesar Salad

This crisp lettuce salad with Parmesan cheese and crunchy croûtons goes well with any egg or cheese dish, especially a savoury quiche.

Preparation and cooking time: 20 minutes

4-6 SERVINGS

4 fl. oz. [½ cup] Vinaigrette Dressing I
1 garlic clove, crushed
2 tablespoons vegetable oil
3 slices of bread, cut into small dice
2 crisp lettuces, outer leaves removed, washed and separated into leaves
2 oz. [½ cup] Parmesan cheese, grated

In a screw-top jar, combine the vinaigrette dressing and garlic. Cover the jar and set it aside for 1 hour.

In a medium-sized frying-pan, heat the oil over moderately high heat. When it is hot, add the diced bread to the pan. Fry for 3 to 4 minutes, turning constantly, or until the croûtons are crisp and lightly browned.

Remove the pan from the heat. With a slotted spoon transfer the croûtons to kitchen paper towels to drain and cool.

Tear the lettuce leaves into small pieces and put them in a medium-sized salad bowl.

Remove and discard the garlic clove from the dressing and pour it over the lettuce. Toss the lettuce until it is well coated.

Sprinkle over the cheese and top with the croûtons. Serve at once.

Tuscan Salad

An impressive and elegant rice salad, Tuscan Salad makes an attractive centre-piece for a cold summer buffet. The rice and beans combine to make the salad a well-balanced and nutritious meal on its own. If you prefer, serve it with a cheese omelet and wholemeal bread.

Preparation and cooking time: 1½ hours

4 SERVINGS

8 oz. [1⅓ cups] long-grain brown rice
1 pint [2½ cups] water
1 teaspoon salt
2 fl. oz. [¼ cup] dry white wine
1 green pepper, white pith removed, seeded and thinly sliced
1 red pepper, white pith removed, seeded and thinly sliced
4 oz. canned fagioli, or similar small white beans, drained
1 small cucumber, peeled and diced
10 stuffed green olives, halved
2 spring onions [scallions], thinly sliced
1 tomato, quartered

DRESSING
3 fl. oz. [⅜ cup] olive oil
3 tablespoons red wine vinegar
1 teaspoon dried basil
1 garlic clove, crushed
½ teaspoon black pepper
1 teaspoon salt

Put the rice in a medium-sized saucepan. Pour over the water and add the salt. Place the pan over moderately high heat and bring the water to the boil. Cover the pan, reduce the heat to very low and

simmer for 20 to 25 minutes, or until all the water has been absorbed and the rice is tender. If all the liquid has not been absorbed at the end of this cooking time, continue to cook, uncovered, for 2 to 3 minutes.

Remove the pan from the heat and transfer the rice to a medium-sized mixing bowl. Stir in the wine and leave the rice to cool.

In a large salad bowl, combine the green and red peppers, fagioli, cucumber, olives and spring onions [scallions] together.

When the rice is cold, add it to the vegetable mixture and stir well to blend.

In a small mixing bowl, combine all the dressing ingredients, beating with a fork until they are well blended. Add the dressing to the rice mixture and toss very well. Chill in the refrigerator for 30 minutes, tossing occasionally.

Garnish the salad with the tomato quarters and serve.

Sweet and Sour Salad

Light yet spicy Sweet and Sour Salad makes an exciting accompaniment to cheese or vegetable soufflés. Or serve it with cottage cheese to cheer up a diet.

Preparation and cooking time: 1½ hours

4 SERVINGS

4 medium-sized dessert apples, peeled, cored and chopped
1 medium-sized grapefruit, peeled, pith removed and finely chopped
1 pickled cucumber
3 oz. canned pineapple, drained and chopped
2 heads of chicory [French or Belgian endive], outer leaves removed and thinly sliced
1 tablespoon chopped fresh coriander leaves

DRESSING
1 tablespoon clear honey
1 tablespoon lemon juice
1 tablespoon grated lemon rind
2 tablespoons vegetable oil
1 tablespoon cider vinegar
1 teaspoon salt
½ teaspoon white pepper

Arrange the apples, grapefruit, cucumber, pineapple and chicory [endive] in a large salad bowl and mix well.

In a small bowl, combine all the dressing ingredients together, beating briskly until they are well blended. Pour the dressing over the salad and toss well to coat. Place the bowl in the refrigerator and chill the salad for 1 hour.

Just before serving, stir in the coriander leaves.

Beetroot [Beets] and Egg Salad

Beetroot [beets], onion rings and hard-boiled eggs make a refreshing combination. Serve this as a side salad with a vegetable casserole.
Preparation and cooking time: 30 minutes
4 SERVINGS

1 lb. beetroots [beets], cooked, peeled and cooled
1 medium-sized onion, sliced and pushed out into rings
4 hard-boiled eggs
4 fl. oz. [½ cup] French Dressing
2 tablespoons chopped fresh parsley

Grate the beetroots [beets] into a medium-sized serving bowl. Add the onion and stir to mix.

Slice the eggs in half and remove the yolks. Rub the yolks through a strainer into the bowl. Set the whites aside.

Pour the dressing over the beetroot [beet] mixture and toss the ingredients gently together.

Finely chop the egg whites and sprinkle them over the salad with the parsley. Serve immediately.

Mixed Salad

Any vegetable that you choose may be included in this basic mixed salad. If you like, top the salad with grated carrot.
Preparation and cooking time: 25 minutes
6-8 SERVINGS

1 crisp head of lettuce, outer leaves removed, washed and separated into leaves
4 tomatoes, roughly chopped
½ cucumber, roughly chopped
2 celery stalks, chopped
4 oz. mushrooms, wiped clean and sliced
1 green pepper, white pith removed, seeded and chopped
1 red pepper, white pith removed, seeded and chopped
4 spring onions [scallions], chopped
1 bunch of watercress, washed, shaken dry and stalks removed
6 radishes, sliced
4 to 6 fl. oz. [½ to ¾ cup] French Dressing
1 tablespoon chopped fresh basil

Tear the lettuce into small pieces and put the pieces into a large salad bowl. Add the tomatoes, cucumber, celery, mushrooms, green and red peppers, spring onions [scallions], watercress and radishes.

Pour over the dressing and sprinkle the basil on top. Toss the salad well and serve.

Bean Salad

This salad is a favourite dish in the southwestern part of the United States.
Preparation and cooking time: 1¾ hours
4-6 SERVINGS

8 oz. red kidney beans, soaked overnight and drained
8 oz. white beans, such as haricot or butter [dried lima] beans, soaked overnight and drained
4 oz. chick-peas, soaked overnight and drained
1 red pepper, white pith removed, seeded and coarsely chopped
1 small onion, finely chopped, or 3 spring onions [scallions], chopped
1 garlic clove, crushed
2 tablespoons snipped fresh chives
2 tablespoons white wine vinegar
1 tablespoon lemon juice
6 tablespoons olive oil
½ teaspoon salt
¼ teaspoon black pepper

Put the beans and peas in a large saucepan. Cover with water and bring to the boil over moderately high heat. Cover the pan, reduce the heat to moderate and simmer for 40 minutes, or until the beans and peas are tender. Drain the beans and peas in a colander and allow to cool.

In a large salad bowl, combine the beans, peas, red pepper, onion, crushed garlic and chives.

In a small bowl, combine the vinegar, lemon juice, oil, salt and pepper. Add the dressing to the bean mixture and toss well.

Place the bowl in the refrigerator and chill for 30 minutes before serving.

Brussels Sprouts and Chicory [French or Belgian Endive] Salad

The Brussels sprouts are blanched before they are added to the other salad ingredients to make them more digestible. The resulting salad is quite fantastic.
Preparation and cooking time: 45 minutes
4 SERVINGS

8 oz. Brussels sprouts
1 teaspoon salt
5 fl. oz. [⅝ cup] Thousand Island Dressing
2 heads of chicory [French or Belgian endive], sliced lengthways
1 tablespoon lemon juice

Place the Brussels sprouts in a medium-sized saucepan. Pour over enough water to cover the sprouts and add the salt. Place the pan over moderately high heat and bring the water to the boil.

Reduce the heat to moderate and cook the sprouts for 5 minutes. Drain the sprouts thoroughly in a colander and set them aside to cool.

When the sprouts are completely cold chop them into walnut-sized pieces. Transfer the pieces to a medium-sized mixing bowl and stir in the dressing. Set aside.

Arrange the slices of chicory [endive] decoratively on a shallow serving dish and sprinkle them with the lemon juice. Pile the Brussels sprouts mixture in the centre and serve.

Tomato Salad

Tomato Salad is simple to prepare and its clean fresh taste goes well with a savoury omelet or Sweetcorn and Asparagus Flan.
Preparation and cooking time: 15 minutes
4 SERVINGS

1 lb. tomatoes
1 medium-sized onion, thinly sliced and pushed out into rings
2 fl. oz. [¼ cup] French Dressing
1 tablespoon chopped fresh basil or 1 teaspoon dried basil
1 teaspoon capers (optional)

With a sharp knife, thinly slice the tomatoes. Arrange the tomato slices, overlapping, in circles on a shallow serving dish. Place the onion rings on top, overlapping, in a circle.

Spoon over the French dressing and sprinkle over the basil and capers (if you are using them). Serve at once.

Button Mushroom Salad

A very simple and classic first course or accompanying salad, Button Mushroom Salad has a strong garlic flavour. If you like, remove the crushed garlic clove before serving.
Preparation and cooking time: 1¼ hours
4 SERVINGS

6 fl. oz. [¾ cup] French Dressing
1 garlic clove, crushed
1 lb. button mushrooms, wiped clean and sliced
1 tablespoon chopped fresh parsley

In a screw-top jar, combine the dressing with the garlic clove. Cover the jar and set it aside for 1 hour so that the dressing becomes infused with the flavour of the garlic.

Put the mushrooms in a medium-sized serving dish. Pour over the dressing and toss the mushrooms so that they become well coated.

Sprinkle over the parsley and serve.

Pecan Peach Salad

Mild and pleasant-tasting pecans combine with ripe juicy peaches and cottage cheese in a filling and attractive main dish salad.

Preparation and cooking time: 20 minutes

4 SERVINGS

4 peaches
2 tablespoons lemon juice
8 oz. [1 cup] cottage cheese
4 oz. [⅔ cup] pecans, finely chopped
8 lettuce leaves

Peel the peaches. Cut them in half and remove the stones. Place the peach halves in a medium-sized mixing bowl and sprinkle over the lemon juice. Toss the peach halves so that they become well coated. Set aside.

In a small mixing bowl, thoroughly combine the cottage cheese and pecans.

Arrange the lettuce leaves on four individual serving dishes. Place two peach halves on each dish. Spoon the cottage cheese mixture into the centres of the peach halves and serve.

Kartoffel Salat

An adaptation of a German recipe, Kartoffel Salat blends potatoes, tomatoes and salted cashew nuts in a mustard flavoured dressing.

Preparation and cooking time: 1¼ hours

4 SERVINGS

2 lb. potatoes, scrubbed but not peeled
1 teaspoon salt
6 lettuce leaves
4 tomatoes, quartered
2 tablespoons salted cashew nuts
3 tablespoons finely chopped Cologne mint
DRESSING
3 tablespoons cider vinegar
8 tablespoons olive oil
1 tablespoon prepared mild French mustard
½ teaspoon salt
¼ teaspoon black pepper
3 tablespoons chopped spring onions [scallions]

Put the potatoes into a medium-sized saucepan. Pour over enough water to cover the potatoes and add the salt. Place the pan over moderately high heat and bring the water to the boil.

Reduce the heat to moderate and cook the potatoes for 15 to 20 minutes, or until they are tender when pierced with the point of a sharp knife.

Drain the potatoes in a colander. Slice them into a medium-sized mixing bowl. Set them aside to cool slightly.

While the potatoes are cooling, prepare the dressing. In a small mixing bowl, combine the vinegar, oil, mustard, salt, pepper and spring onions [scallions] with a fork or wire whisk.

Pour the dressing over the still warm potato slices and gently toss them so that they become well coated. Place the bowl in the refrigerator to chill for 30 minutes.

Arrange the lettuce leaves in a medium-sized salad bowl. Spoon the potato slices into the centre and arrange the tomato quarters around the sides. Sprinkle over the nuts and mint and serve

Asparagus Salad

A delicate and unusual way to serve asparagus, Asparagus Salad makes a particularly excellent first course.

Preparation and cooking time: 40 minutes

4 SERVINGS

8 oz. asparagus, cooked, cooled and chopped
1 small head of Webb [iceberg] lettuce, outer leaves removed and coarsely shredded
2 fl. oz. [¼ cup] French Dressing
1 small onion, sliced and pushed out into rings
1 tablespoon chopped fresh parsley

Arrange the asparagus and the lettuce in a medium-sized salad bowl.

Pour over the French dressing and toss to coat well. Chill in the refrigerator for 30 minutes, basting occasionally.

Toss the salad and arrange the onion rings on top. Sprinkle with the chopped parsley and serve.

Apricot Salad

This salad is made with fresh apricots and served with a tarragon cream dressing.

Preparation and cooking time: 30 minutes

4 SERVINGS

2 lb. ripe apricots, blanched and peeled
4 tablespoons sour cream
3 tablespoons tarragon vinegar
1 tablespoon sugar
½ teaspoon salt
¼ teaspoon black pepper
a few tarragon leaves, chopped

Cut each apricot in half and remove the stones. Arrange the apricot halves in a glass serving bowl. Crack the stones with a nutcracker or hammer. Take out the kernels, chop them and set aside.

To make the dressing, in a small

mixing bowl, combine the sour cream, vinegar, sugar, salt and pepper. When it is thoroughly mixed, taste the dressing and adjust the seasoning if necessary.

Pour the dressing over the apricots. Sprinkle with the tarragon leaves and chopped kernels and serve.

Mexican Sweetcorn Salad

This colourful, attractive salad will make a filling meal with a baked potato.

Preparation and cooking time: 40 minutes

6 SERVINGS

12 oz. canned sweetcorn, drained
½ medium-sized red pepper, white pith removed, seeded and finely chopped
½ medium-sized green pepper, white pith removed, seeded and finely chopped
2 oz. mushrooms, wiped clean and sliced
2 spring onions [scallions], finely chopped
1 green chilli, seeds removed and finely chopped
2 fl. oz. [¼ cup] Honey Dressing

In a large salad bowl combine the sweetcorn, red and green peppers and the mushrooms, mixing well to blend. Stir in the spring onions [scallions] and the chilli. Chill in the refrigerator for 30 minutes.

Stir in the dressing and coat well. Serve at once.

Winter Salad

This nutritious Winter Salad makes a tasty side salad when salad greens are not easily obtainable.

Preparation and cooking time: 15 minutes

4-6 SERVINGS

4 medium-sized potatoes, cooked, peeled and diced
1 large celery stalk, finely chopped
2 carrots, scraped and grated
1 small onion, finely chopped
½ small white cabbage, coarse outer leaves removed, washed and shredded
2 tablespoons chopped pickled gherkins
8 black olives, stoned and chopped
4 fl. oz. [½ cup] French Dressing
2 tablespoons chopped fresh parsley

In a large salad bowl, combine the potatoes, celery, carrots, onion, cabbage, gherkins and olives. Pour over the dressing and toss the salad thoroughly.

Sprinkle over the parsley and serve.

Fennel Salad

Fennel is a vegetable that is becoming increasingly popular. Its fresh, slightly liquorice-like taste makes it a particularly adaptable vegetable that blends well with other vegetables or fruit.

Preparation and cooking time: 1¼ hours

4 SERVINGS

    3 medium-sized heads of fennel,
      coarse outer leaves removed
    1 small eating apple, peeled, cored
      and finely chopped
    2 medium-sized tomatoes, chopped
    2 spring onions [scallions], chopped
    4 fl. oz. [½ cup] Vinaigrette Dressing I

Finely chop the fennel and arrange the pieces in a medium-sized salad bowl. Add the apple, tomatoes and spring onions [scallions] and stir well to mix.

   Pour in the vinaigrette dressing and toss to coat well. Chill in the refrigerator for 1 hour, stirring occasionally, before serving.

Carrot and Salted Soya Bean Split Salad

A healthy and tasty salad with a super crunchy texture, Carrot and Soya Bean Split Salad will be especially good with an omelet.

Preparation and cooking time: 2¾ hours

4 SERVINGS

    8 oz. soya bean splits
    1 teaspoon salt
   1½ pints [3¾ cups] water
    2 tablespoons vegetable oil
    2 teaspoons sea salt
    4 medium-sized carrots, scraped
      and grated
    2 fl. oz. [¼ cup] French Dressing

Put the soya bean splits in a medium-sized saucepan and add the salt. Pour over the water and place the pan over high heat. Bring the water to the boil. Reduce the heat to low and simmer the soya bean splits for 45 minutes, or until they are just chewable. Test by taking one split from the pan and eating it. Remove the pan from the heat and drain the splits in a colander.

   In a large frying-pan, heat the oil over moderate heat. When the oil is hot, add the soya bean splits and the sea salt and, stirring and turning frequently, cook for 15 minutes or until the splits turn golden brown at the edges.

   Remove the pan from the heat and, with a slotted spoon, transfer the splits to a shallow serving dish. Allow the splits to cool to room temperature, then place the bowl in the refrigerator to chill for 1 hour.

   Sprinkle the grated carrot over the soya bean splits and pour over the French dressing. Toss the ingredients together and serve.

Chicory [French or Belgian Endive] and Apple Salad

A refreshing and delicate dish, Chicory [French or Belgian endive] and Apple Salad makes an excellent accompaniment to vegetable flans or risottos.

Preparation and cooking time: 40 minutes

6 SERVINGS

    6 medium-sized heads of chicory
      [French or Belgian endive], outer
      leaves removed and thinly sliced
    2 medium-sized eating apples,
      peeled, cored and finely chopped
    2 tablespoons lemon juice
    2 fl. oz. [¼ cup] Vinaigrette
      Dressing I
    2 tablespoons chopped walnuts

Arrange the chicory [endive] and apple in a medium-sized salad bowl. Sprinkle with the lemon juice and chill in the refrigerator for 30 minutes.

   Pour the vinaigrette dressing over the salad and toss to coat well. Scatter with the chopped walnuts and serve at once.

Walnut, Orange and Chicory [French or Belgian Endive] Salad

An exotic and superb blend of flavours makes this salad a versatile accompaniment to any main dish.

Preparation and cooking time: 20 minutes

4-6 SERVINGS

    4 oranges
    4 heads of chicory [French or Belgian
      endive], sliced
    4 oz. [⅔ cup] walnuts, chopped
    5 fl. oz. [⅝ cup] Honey Dressing

Peel the oranges, removing as much of the white pith as possible. Using a serrated-edge knife, thinly slice the oranges into a medium-sized serving dish.

   Add the chicory [endive] and walnuts and pour over the dressing. Toss the ingredients together and serve.

Cucumber and Yogurt Salad

This traditional Middle Eastern salad is very cool and refreshing and is especially good served with a hot curry or spicy vegetable dish.

Preparation and cooking time: 45 minutes

6-8 SERVINGS

    4 large cucumbers, peeled
   10 fl. oz. [1¼ cups] yogurt
    2 tablespoons chopped fresh
      Cologne mint
    ½ teaspoon salt
    ½ teaspoon black pepper

Run the prongs of a kitchen fork down the cucumbers on all sides. Then slice them thinly and transfer them to a medium-sized serving dish.

   Stir in the yogurt, mint, salt and pepper. Place the bowl in the refrigerator and chill for at least 20 minutes before serving.

Coleslaw with Caraway

Caraway seeds provide the interesting variation in this crisp coleslaw salad.

Preparation and cooking time: 1¼ hours

6-8 SERVINGS

    1 large white cabbage, coarse outer
      leaves removed, washed and
      shredded
    1 medium-sized onion, finely
      chopped
    ½ green pepper, white pith removed,
      seeded and finely chopped
    ½ teaspoon lemon juice
    1 tablespoon caraway seeds
DRESSING
    6 fl. oz. double cream [¾ cup heavy
      cream]
    3 fl. oz. [⅜ cup] sour cream
    1 tablespoon French mustard
    3 tablespoons lemon juice
    1 tablespoon sugar
    ½ teaspoon salt
    ¼ teaspoon white pepper

Arrange the shredded cabbage in a large serving dish and sprinkle with the onion, green pepper and lemon juice. Set aside.

   In a medium-sized mixing bowl, combine the double [heavy] cream, sour cream, mustard and lemon juice, beating vigorously with a wooden spoon until the ingredients are thoroughly blended. Add the sugar, salt and pepper and mix well.

   Pour the dressing over the shredded cabbage and add the caraway seeds to the mixture. Using 2 large spoons or forks, toss the cabbage mixture until it is completely saturated with dressing. Place the bowl in the refrigerator and chill for at least 1 hour before serving.

Cabbage and Pepper Salad

Tasty and attractive, Cabbage and Pepper Salad is ideal to serve when salad greens are not available.

Preparation and cooking time: 20 minutes

8-10 SERVINGS

1 red pepper, white pith removed, seeded and thinly sliced
1 green pepper, white pith removed, seeded and thinly sliced
1 onion, thinly sliced and pushed out into rings
1 cucumber, cut into ½-inch cubes
2 tomatoes, thinly sliced
½ white cabbage, coarse outer leaves removed, washed and thinly sliced
2 tablespoons clear honey
   juice of 1 lemon
10 tablespoons olive oil
4 tablespoons red wine vinegar
2 teaspoons salt
1 teaspoon black pepper

Combine the peppers, onion rings, cucumber, tomatoes and cabbage in a large salad bowl.

Pour the honey, lemon juice, oil, vinegar, salt and pepper into a screw-top jar and shake it vigorously until the dressing is well mixed.

Pour the dressing over the salad and toss well. Serve immediately.

Marinated Pepper Salad

A Romanian salad, Marinated Pepper Salad may be served as an hors d'oeuvre or as an accompaniment. The peppers in the marinade, without the cheese and olives, can be kept in a jar with a tight fitting lid and stored in the refrigerator for a few days.

Preparation and cooking time: 1 day and 20 minutes

4 SERVINGS

4 green peppers, white pith removed, seeded and cut into large pieces
4 red peppers, white pith removed, seeded and cut into large pieces
6 tablespoons white or red wine vinegar
2 tablespoons medium dry sherry
1 tablespoon Worcestershire sauce
6 tablespoons olive oil
1 teaspoon salt
½ teaspoon black pepper
2 teaspoons sugar
1 teaspoon paprika
12 black olives, stoned
8 oz. cream cheese, cut into cubes

Half fill a large saucepan with water and bring it to the boil over high heat. Add the peppers and cook them for 3 minutes. Drain the peppers in a colander and dry them on kitchen paper towels. Allow the peppers to cool completely.

In a large mixing bowl, combine the vinegar, sherry, Worcestershire sauce, oil, salt, pepper, sugar and paprika. Stir well to mix. Taste and add more seasoning if necessary.

Put the peppers into the marinade and turn and mix until they are well coated. Cover the bowl and place it in the refrigerator. Leave the peppers to marinate for 24 hours.

To serve, place the peppers in a shallow bowl or dish. Spoon a little of the marinade over them. Place the olives and cheese on the top and serve.

Basic Dark Savoury Jelly [Gelatine] for Moulded Salads

This basic recipe for a savoury jelly [gelatine] is very easy to prepare. If you prefer to use gelatine, use the same quantity as for agar-agar and dissolve it in 2 tablespoons of the hot stock before adding the remaining stock and yeast extract. Be sure the gelatine is completely dissolved.

Preparation and cooking time: 2 hours

1 PINT [2½ CUPS]

1 pint [2½ cups] dark vegetable stock
1 tablespoon yeast extract
2 teaspoons agar-agar

In a medium-sized saucepan, bring the stock to the boil over high heat. Stir in the yeast extract.

With a wire whisk, beat in the agar-agar. Continue whisking for 3 minutes.

Pour the liquid jelly [gelatine] over the vegetables in the mould and leave to cool to room temperature. Then place the mould in the refrigerator and chill until the salad is set. This will take 1½ to 2 hours.

If you are making a moulded salad with layers of jelly [gelatine] and vegetables, place the mould in a bowl of iced water so that each layer of jelly [gelatine] will set more quickly.

Basic Light Savoury Jelly [Gelatine] for Moulded Salads

Substitute light vegetable stock. Omit the yeast extract and use 1 teaspoon of salt.

Basic Sweet Jelly [Gelatine] for Moulded Salads

Substitute fruit juice and omit the yeast extract.

Spicy Tomato Jelly [Gelatine] Salad

Serve this moulded salad of celery, corn and eggs, in a slightly spicy tomato jelly [gelatine], for an unusual luncheon dish.

Preparation and cooking time: 2¼ hours

6-8 SERVINGS

1 pint [2½ cups] tomato juice
2 teaspoons Worcestershire sauce
2 teaspoons agar-agar
4 celery stalks, finely chopped
8 oz. canned sweetcorn, drained
6 hard-boiled eggs, finely chopped
   parsley sprigs (to garnish)
4 fl. oz. [½ cup] mayonnaise

In a medium-sized saucepan, bring the tomato juice to the boil over moderately high heat. Stir in the Worcestershire sauce. With a wire whisk, beat in the agar-agar. Continue whisking for 3 minutes. Remove the pan from the heat.

Rinse a 2-pint [5-cup] plain or decorative mould in cold water. Place the celery, corn and eggs in the mould and pour in the liquid tomato jelly [gelatine]. Allow it to cool to room temperature, then place the mould in the refrigerator and chill for 1½ to 2 hours, or until the jelly [gelatine] is completely set.

Dip the mould quickly into hot water, then invert it over a serving dish. The salad should slide out easily.

Garnish with the sprigs of parsley and serve with the mayonnaise.

Moulded Fruit Salad

This attractive salad of grapes, bananas and satsumas or tangerines set in grape jelly [gelatine] is delicious as a first course or as a dessert served with vanilla ice-cream.

Preparation and cooking time: 3½ hours

4-6 SERVINGS

1 pint [2½ cups] white grape juice
2 teaspoons agar-agar
8 oz. black grapes, halved and pitted
3 bananas, peeled and sliced
2 satsumas or tangerines, peeled and separated into segments

In a medium-sized saucepan, bring the grape juice to the boil over moderately high heat. With a wire whisk, beat in the agar-agar. Continue whisking for 3 minutes. Remove the pan from the heat.

Rinse a 2-pint [5-cup] plain or decorative mould with cold water. Arrange a layer of grapes, cut sides down, on the bottom. Place a layer of banana slices on the grapes and top with a layer of satsuma or tangerine segments. Carefully pour in enough of the liquid grape jelly [gelatine] to make a 1-inch layer on top of the satsuma or tangerine segments.

Place the mould in a bowl of iced water. Allow the jelly [gelatine] to set and then arrange a layer of grapes on it, followed by a layer of banana slices and a layer of satsuma or tangerine segments. Pour in enough of the liquid jelly [gelatine] to make another 1-inch layer. If the jelly [gelatine] in the saucepan has set, melt it over moderate heat.

Continue making layers until all the ingredients are used, ending with a layer of jelly [gelatine].

Place the mould in the refrigerator and chill for 1½ to 2 hours, or until the salad is completely set.

Dip the mould quickly into hot water and invert it over a serving dish. The salad should slide out easily.

Serve immediately.

Moulded Grapefruit and Cucumber Salad

A decorative salad set in a grapefruit-flavoured jelly [gelatine], this moulded salad will be a welcome addition to a summer buffet.

Preparation and cooking time: 3¼ hours

4-6 SERVINGS

2 grapefruit
1 pint [2½ cups] grapefruit juice
2 teaspoons agar-agar
1 cucumber, finely chopped
6 lettuce leaves

Peel the grapefruit, removing as much of the white pith as possible. Separate the grapefruit into segments. Set aside.

In a medium-sized saucepan, bring the grapefruit juice to the boil over moderately high heat. With a wire whisk, beat in the agar-agar. Continue whisking for 3 minutes. Remove the pan from the heat.

Rinse a 2-pint [5-cup] plain or decorative mould with cold water. Pour in enough of the liquid grapefruit jelly [gelatine] to make a 1-inch layer on the bottom. Place the mould in a bowl of iced water. Allow the jelly [gelatine] to set and then arrange a layer of grapefruit segments on it.

Pour in enough of the liquid jelly [gelatine] to make a 1-inch layer on top of the grapefruit segments. If the jelly

28

[gelatine] in the saucepan has set, melt it over moderate heat. Allow the jelly [gelatine] to set and then arrange the chopped cucumber on it. Place the remaining grapefruit segments on the cucumber and pour over the remaining liquid jelly [gelatine].

Place the mould in the refrigerator and chill for 1½ to 2 hours, or until the salad is completely set.

Arrange the lettuce leaves on a serving dish. Dip the mould quickly into hot water and invert it over the dish. The salad should slide out easily.

Serve immediately.

Egg and Asparagus Moulded Salad

The time needed to prepare this moulded salad is certainly worth the effort.

Preparation and cooking time: 5 hours

4-6 SERVINGS

1 pint [2½ cups] basic dark savoury jelly [gelatine], cool but still liquid
12 asparagus spears, cooked
4 hard-boiled eggs, sliced
watercress sprigs (to garnish)

Rinse a 2-pint [5-cup] plain or decorative mould in cold water. Pour in enough of the liquid jelly [gelatine] to make a 1-inch layer on the bottom.

Place the mould in a bowl of iced water. When the jelly [gelatine] is almost set, arrange the asparagus spears standing upright around the sides of the mould, with their tips in the jelly [gelatine].

Allow the jelly [gelatine] to set completely and then place a layer of sliced eggs on it. Carefully pour in enough of the liquid jelly [gelatine] to make a 1-inch layer on top of the egg slices. If the jelly [gelatine] in the saucepan has set, melt it over moderate heat.

Continue making layers of egg slices and jelly [gelatine] until they are all used, ending with a layer of jelly [gelatine].

Place the mould in the refrigerator and chill for 1½ to 2 hours, or until the salad is completely set.

Dip the mould quickly into hot water and invert it over a serving dish. The salad should slide out easily. Garnish with the watercress and serve.

Salad Dressings

French Dressing

A very basic salad dressing, French Dressing has a myriad of uses. If you like a garlic flavour, add 1 crushed garlic clove to the dressing and leave it to infuse for 1 hour. Remove the garlic before serving.

Preparation and cooking time: 5 minutes

4 FLUID OUNCES [½ CUP]

2 tablespoons red wine vinegar
3 fl. oz. [⅜ cup] olive oil
½ teaspoon salt
¼ teaspoon black pepper

In a small mixing bowl, beat all the ingredients together with a kitchen fork until they are well combined.

Alternatively, put all the ingredients in a screw-top jar. Cover the jar and shake it for about 10 seconds.

Use the dressing as required.

Vinaigrette Dressing I

A basic dressing for vegetable salads, Vinaigrette Dressing I may be varied with the addition of any herbs you wish to use.

Preparation and cooking time: 10 minutes

6 FLUID OUNCES [¾ CUP]

3 hard-boiled egg yolks
1 teaspoon prepared mustard
½ teaspoon salt
5 fl. oz. [⅝ cup] olive oil
3 tablespoons cider or red wine vinegar
¼ teaspoon black pepper

In a small mixing bowl, mash the egg yolks, mustard and salt to a smooth paste with a kitchen fork. Gradually add the oil, beating constantly.

When all the oil has been incorporated, beat in the vinegar and pepper.

Use the dressing as required.

Vinaigrette Dressing II

Use this Vinaigrette dressing for fruit salads. If you prefer a sweeter dressing, increase the quantity of sugar.

Preparation and cooking time: 15 minutes

6 FLUID OUNCES [¾ CUP]

2 hard-boiled egg yolks
1 teaspoon prepared mustard
½ teaspoon sugar
5 fl. oz. [⅝ cup] olive oil
3 tablespoons lemon juice

In a small mixing bowl, mash the egg yolks, mustard and sugar to a smooth paste with a fork. Gradually add the oil, beating constantly.

When all the oil has been incorporated, beat in the lemon juice.

Use the dressing as required.

Mayonnaise

This basic recipe for Mayonnaise will produce a thick, smooth dressing. If you require a thin mayonnaise, whisk in 1 to 2 tablespoons of water to achieve the desired consistency.

Should the mayonnaise curdle while you are adding the oil, you must start again in another bowl with a new egg yolk. Whisk in the curdled mixture and when it is smooth, begin blending in the oil again.

Preparation and cooking time: 20 minutes
10 FLUID OUNCES [1¼ CUPS]

2 egg yolks, at room temperature
½ teaspoon salt
¾ teaspoon dry mustard
¼ teaspoon white pepper
8 fl. oz. [1 cup] olive oil, at room temperature
1 tablespoon white wine vinegar or lemon juice

Place the egg yolks, salt, mustard and pepper in a medium-sized mixing bowl. Using a wire whisk, beat the ingredients until they are thoroughly blended. Add the oil, a few drops at a time, whisking constantly. Do not add the oil too quickly or the mayonnaise will curdle. After the mayonnaise has thickened, the oil may be added a little more rapidly.

Beat in a few drops of lemon juice or vinegar from time to time to prevent the mayonnaise from becoming too thick. When all the oil has been added, stir in the remaining lemon juice or vinegar. Taste the mayonnaise and add more salt, mustard or vinegar if desired.

Use the mayonnaise as required.

Whole Egg Mayonnaise

Unlike the traditional basic mayonnaise which uses only egg yolks, this mayonnaise uses the whole egg. The resulting dressing is not as rich as the basic mayonnaise.

Preparation and cooking time: 20 minutes
12 FLUID OUNCES [1½ CUPS]

1 egg
½ teaspoon salt
1 teaspoon dry mustard
¼ teaspoon light brown sugar
5 fl. oz. [⅝ cup] olive oil
5 fl. oz. [⅝ cup] vegetable oil
2 tablespoons cider vinegar

Place the egg, salt, mustard and sugar

in a medium-sized mixing bowl. Using a wire whisk, beat the ingredients until they are thoroughly blended. Add the oils, a few drops at a time, whisking constantly. Do not add the oil too quickly or the mayonnaise will curdle.

After the mayonnaise has thickened, the oil may be added a little more rapidly. When all the oil has been incorporated, whisk in the vinegar.

Taste the mayonnaise and add more salt, mustard or sugar, if necessary.

Use the mayonnaise as required.

Honey Dressing

This delicately flavoured dressing may be varied by adding 2 tablespoons of chopped fresh Cologne mint.

Preparation and cooking time: 5 minutes
6 FLUID OUNCES [¾ CUP]

2 tablespoons clear honey
4 tablespoons lemon juice
6 tablespoons olive oil
½ teaspoon prepared French mustard
¼ teaspoon salt
⅛ teaspoon black pepper

In a small mixing bowl, beat all the ingredients together with a kitchen fork until they are well combined.

Alternatively, put all the ingredients in a screw-top jar. Cover the jar and shake it for 10 seconds.

Use the dressing as required.

Cardamom Honey Dressing

This nourishing and unusual dressing may be served with fresh fruit salad and melon or with waffles and pancakes. Use a blender or beat by hand with a wire whisk or rotary beater.

Preparation and cooking time: 15 minutes
10 FLUID OUNCES [1¼ CUPS]

½ teaspoon cardamom seeds
10 fl. oz. [1¼ cups] clear honey
2 tablespoons lemon juice
¼ teaspoon orange-flower water

Place the cardamom on a sheet of greaseproof or waxed paper and fold the paper over the cardamom, so that it is completely enclosed. With the back of a wooden spoon, coarsely crush the cardamom seeds.

In a blender, blend the honey at high speed until it is light in colour. Gradually add the lemon juice and orange-flower water to the honey, and then stir in the crushed cardamom.

Pour the dressing into a screw-top jar and use it as required.

Thousand Island Dressing

A rich, thick dressing that is delicious with green or mixed salads, Thousand Island Dressing may be made with mayonnaise or Whole Egg Mayonnaise.

Preparation and cooking time: 15 minutes
12 FLUID OUNCES [1½ CUPS]

10 fl. oz. [1¼ cups] mayonnaise
2 tablespoons chopped mango chutney
1 tablespoon chopped mixed pickles
2 tablespoons chopped stuffed olives
1 teaspoon minced onion
1 hard-boiled egg, finely chopped
2 fl. oz. [¼ cup] French dressing

In a medium-sized mixing bowl, combine all the ingredients, beating them with a wooden spoon until they are thoroughly mixed.

Use the dressing as required.

Yogurt Dressing

Yogurt enlivens the flavour of this creamy salad dressing, which is particularly good with coleslaw, but can accompany any green salad.

Preparation and cooking time: 5 minutes
12 FLUID OUNCES [1½ CUPS]

8 fl. oz. [1 cup] mayonnaise
4 tablespoons yogurt
1 teaspoon sugar
½ teaspoon salt
1 tablespoon grated onion
1 tablespoon finely chopped celery

In a medium-sized mixing bowl, blend the mayonnaise with the yogurt, mixing well with a wooden spoon. Add the remaining ingredients and beat for 1 minute. Use immediately.

Roquefort Dressing

This rich dressing may be made with mayonnaise or with French Dressing, depending on whether you want a heavy or light dressing. If you use mayonnaise, the dressing is delicious with a green salad. Made with French Dressing, it will beautifully complement a bean salad.

Preparation and cooking time: 10 minutes
8 FLUID OUNCES [1 CUP]

4 oz. Roquefort cheese
6 fl. oz. [¾ cup] mayonnaise or French dressing

Crumble the cheese into a small mixing bowl. Add the mayonnaise or dressing and mash the cheese and mayonnaise or dressing together with a kitchen fork.

Use the dressing as required.

Vegetables

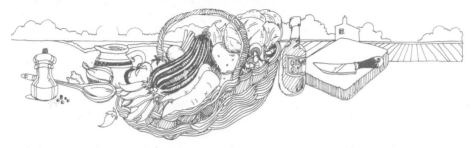

In this high-rise-instant-food age we live in, there are still some people lucky enough to have a garden in which to grow vegetables. For those of us who cannot just walk outside and pick compost grown fresh beans, peas, cabbages, celery and tomatoes, etc., it is important to make sure that all store-bought vegetables are absolutely fresh.

There are very few hard and fast rules about the cooking of vegetables, mainly because of the variety of ways in which they can be cooked. There are, however, two very important points to remember: never over-cook vegetables, and, if they are simmered in stock or water, *never* throw away the cooking liquid. Most of the vegetables' vitamin content is drawn out into the liquid, so, if possible, reserve the liquids for stock or for cooking rice and pastas.

The possibilities for vegetable combinations are endless. Two, three, four, or even five different vegetables can be combined, then sautéed, steamed, casseroled or baked. They can be covered with luscious melted cheeses or chopped nuts, or complemented by a rich, savoury sauce or custard.

So go ahead, choose an exciting, new recipe from this section and surprise your family. But do remember that if you are preparing a simple vegetable or vegetable and rice dish, such as Courgette [Zucchini] Casserole, to precede, accompany or follow it with a protein rich appetizer, salad or dessert.

Asparagus au Naturel
COOKED ASPARAGUS

Asparagus is one of the most delicate – and succulent – of vegetables. This recipe is the traditional, and basic, method of cooking asparagus. It is best served simply with a light White or Béchamel Sauce, which will enhance the flavour of the vegetable without overpowering it.

Preparation and cooking time: 30 minutes

4-6 SERVINGS

2 lb. asparagus
1½ pints [3¾ cups] water
¼ teaspoon salt

Peel or scrape the asparagus stalks with a sharp knife. (The peeling process should gradually become thinner towards the tip.)

Arrange the asparagus in bundles of 4 to 6 stalks and tie them securely together with string. Trim the ends of the stalks so that they form an even base.

Pour the water into a large saucepan and add the salt. Place the pan over moderately high heat and bring the water to the boil. Reduce the heat to moderate and carefully place the asparagus bunches in the pan, stalks down. The tips of the asparagus should be just above the water. Cook the asparagus for 14 minutes, or until they are just tender.

Remove the pan from the heat and drain the asparagus in a colander. Untie the bundles and serve at once.

Caponata
AUBERGINES [EGGPLANTS] IN SWEET AND SOUR SAUCE

A tangy vegetable dish, Caponata may be served as an appetizer or as an extra-special accompaniment. It is important that a good quality vinegar be used, otherwise the blend of flavours will not be so delicate. Caponata can be stored in the refrigerator for up to 2 weeks.

Preparation and cooking time: 3½ hours

4-6 SERVINGS

4 small aubergines [eggplants]
2 teaspoons salt
4 fl. oz. [½ cup] olive oil
4 celery stalks, finely chopped
2 large onions, thinly sliced
4 oz. tomato purée diluted in 2 fl. oz. [¼ cup] water
1 tablespoon capers
2 oz. green olives, stoned and chopped
3 fl. oz. [⅜ cup] red wine vinegar
1 tablespoon sugar

Peel and dice the aubergines [eggplants]. Place the pieces in a colander and sprinkle them with the salt. Leave them to dégorge for 30 minutes. Rinse the aubergines [eggplants] with cold water, drain them in a colander and pat them dry with kitchen paper towels.

In a large frying-pan, heat 3 fluid ounces [⅜ cup] of the oil over moderate heat. Add the diced aubergines [eggplants] and cook for 8 to 10 minutes, or until the pieces are soft and brown. With a slotted spoon, remove the pieces from the pan and drain them on kitchen paper towels. Set aside.

Pour the remaining oil into the frying-pan and add the celery and onions. Cook them for 8 to 10 minutes, or until they are lightly coloured. Pour in the tomato purée mixture and stir to coat the vegetables. Reduce the heat to low, cover the pan and simmer the mixture for 15 minutes.

Stir in the capers, olives, vinegar and sugar, mixing until all the ingredients are blended. Return the aubergine [eggplant] pieces to the pan and coat them thoroughly with the sauce. Reduce the heat to low and cook the mixture for 20 minutes.

Turn the caponata into a serving dish. Allow it to cool to room temperature. Then place the dish in the refrigerator. Chill the Caponata for at least 2 hours before serving.

Stuffed Aubergines [Eggplants] with Tomato Sauce

A delicious way in which to serve aubergines [eggplants], *Stuffed Aubergines* [Eggplants] *with Tomato Sauce may be served as a first course for a dinner party.*

Preparation and cooking time: 2½ hours

4-8 SERVINGS

4 oz. soya bean splits
1 pint [2½ cups] water
4 small aubergines [eggplants]
2½ teaspoons salt
4 oz. [½ cup] butter or margarine
2 medium-sized onions, sliced
1 garlic clove, crushed
4 mushrooms, wiped clean and sliced
½ teaspoon white pepper
½ teaspoon ground mace
2 tablespoons chopped fresh parsley
1 tablespoon vegetable oil
10 fl. oz. [1¼ cups] Tomato Sauce II

Put the soya bean splits in a medium-sized saucepan and pour in the water. Place the pan over moderately high heat and bring the water to the boil. Reduce the heat to moderate and cook the splits for 25 minutes or until they are chewy. (Test by removing a split from the pan and eating it.) Drain the soya bean splits in a colander and set them aside in a large mixing bowl.

Meanwhile, cut the aubergines [eggplants] in half, lengthways. With a sharp knife, scoop out the aubergine [eggplant] flesh and set it aside in a colander. Sprinkle the flesh with 2 teaspoons of the salt and leave it to dégorge for 30 minutes. Dry the hollowed out aubergine [eggplant] shells with kitchen paper towels and set them aside.

Preheat the oven to fairly hot 375°F (Gas Mark 5, 190°C).

Drain the aubergine [eggplant] flesh on kitchen paper towels.

In a large frying-pan, melt 2 ounces [¼ cup] of the butter or margarine over moderate heat. When the foam subsides, add the aubergine [eggplant] flesh to the pan. Cook it, stirring occasionally, for 5 minutes, or until it browns. Transfer the flesh to the mixing bowl containing the soya bean splits.

Add the remaining butter or margarine to the frying-pan and melt it over moderate heat. When the foam subsides, add the onions and garlic to the pan. Cook them, stirring occasionally, for 5 to 7 minutes, or until the onions are soft and translucent but not brown. Add the mushrooms, the remaining salt, the pepper, mace and parsley to the pan. Stirring constantly, cook for a further 3 minutes. Transfer the mushroom and onion mixture to the aubergine [eggplant] mixture in the mixing bowl and mash the ingredients together well.

Coat the bottom of a large roasting tin with the vegetable oil. Arrange the aubergine [eggplant] shells in the roasting tin. Spoon the aubergine [eggplant] flesh mixture into the shells. Pour the tomato sauce over and around the stuffed aubergine [eggplant] shells.

Place the tin in the oven and bake for 30 minutes.

Remove the tin from the oven and transfer the stuffed aubergine [eggplant] halves to individual serving plates. Spoon over any sauce in the tin and serve.

Broccoli Ring

A tasty and attractive dish, Broccoli Ring may be filled with tiny, new boiled potatoes or French-Fried Cauliflower.

Preparation and cooking time: 1½ hours

6 SERVINGS

1½ oz. [3 tablespoons] butter or margarine
2 oz. [½ cup] plus 1 tablespoon flour
10 fl. oz. [1¼ cups] water
1½ teaspoons salt
1½ lb. broccoli, trimmed, washed and cut into small pieces
1 garlic clove
8 fl. oz. double cream [1 cup heavy cream]
4 eggs, separated and the yolks lightly beaten
¼ teaspoon black pepper
2 oz. [½ cup] Parmesan cheese, grated

Grease a 2-pint [5-cup] ring mould with 1 tablespoon of the butter or margarine and lightly coat the mould with the tablespoon of flour. Knock out any excess flour and set the mould aside.

In a large saucepan, bring the water, with 1 teaspoon salt, to the boil over moderately high heat. Place the broccoli and garlic in the water. Bring the water back to the boil. Cover the pan, reduce the heat to moderately low and cook the broccoli for 15 minutes.

With a slotted spoon, remove the garlic clove and discard it.

Drain the broccoli in a colander. Chop it finely and set it aside in a large mixing bowl.

Preheat the oven to moderate 350°F (Gas Mark 4, 180°C).

In a medium-sized saucepan, melt the remaining butter or margarine over low heat. Remove the pan from the heat and, with a wooden spoon, stir in the remaining flour to make a smooth paste. Slowly add the cream, stirring constantly. Return the pan to the heat and cook, stirring constantly, for 2 to 3 minutes. When the sauce is thick and smooth, stir in the broccoli. Remove the pan from the heat and stir in the beaten egg yolks, the remaining ½ teaspoon of salt and the pepper.

In a medium-sized mixing bowl, beat the egg whites with a wire whisk or rotary beater until they will hold a stiff peak. With a metal spoon, carefully fold the egg whites into the broccoli mixture. Turn the mixture into the greased mould. Stand the mould in a roasting tin one-third full of boiling water and place it in the oven. Bake for 35 to 40 minutes, or until the mixture is puffed and set.

Remove the mould from the oven and loosen the ring with a knife. Place a serving platter, upside-down, on the mould and reverse the two. The ring should slide easily out of the mould. Sprinkle with the cheese and serve.

Broccoli with Black Olives

Try this unusual way of serving broccoli – with black olives and garlic and Parmesan cheese.

Preparation and cooking time: 35 minutes

4 SERVINGS

1½ lb. broccoli
10 fl. oz. [1¼ cups] water
1 teaspoon salt
3 tablespoons olive oil
1 garlic clove, finely chopped
½ teaspoon black pepper
2 oz. [¾ cup] black olives, halved and stoned
4 tablespoons grated Parmesan cheese

Wash the broccoli, remove the leaves and break the flowerets into fairly large bunches.

In a large saucepan, bring the water to the boil over moderately high heat. Add ½ teaspoon of salt and the broccoli. Reduce the heat to moderate, cover the pan and cook the broccoli for 10 minutes. Drain the broccoli. Reserve the water in which it was cooked.

In a large frying-pan, heat the oil over low heat. Add the garlic and fry it for 5 minutes. Add the broccoli and season with the remaining salt and the pepper. Cook the broccoli for 10 minutes, stirring frequently. Add some of the water in which the broccoli was cooked if the pan gets too dry.

Add the olives to the pan and cook for another 2 minutes. Turn the broccoli and olives into a warmed serving dish. Sprinkle with the Parmesan cheese and serve at once.

Artichoke Hearts in Butter

This is a simple, well-flavoured dish which can be served as a first course or as a vegetable accompaniment to egg or cheese dishes.

Preparation and cooking time: 30 minutes

4 SERVINGS

4 oz. [½ cup] butter
4 tablespoons chopped shallots or spring onions [scallions]
12 artichoke hearts, cooked and cut into quarters
½ teaspoon salt
¼ teaspoon white pepper
4 tablespoons finely chopped fresh parsley

Preheat the oven to warm 325°F (Gas Mark 3, 170°C).

In a medium-sized flameproof casserole, melt the butter over moderate heat. When the foam subsides, add the shallots or spring onions [scallions] and the artichoke hearts. Baste the vegetables with the butter and sprinkle them with the salt and pepper.

Cover the casserole and transfer it to the oven. Bake for 20 minutes.

Remove the casserole from the oven. Sprinkle the artichoke hearts with the parsley and serve.

Brussels Sprouts Creole

This simple recipe makes a colourful change from plain Brussels sprouts, and goes very well with an omelet.

Preparation and cooking time: 45 minutes

4 SERVINGS

1½ lb. Brussels sprouts
1½ oz. [3 tablespoons] butter or margarine
1 large onion, finely chopped
1 garlic clove, crushed
1 green pepper, white pith removed, seeded and chopped
1 lb. tomatoes, blanched, peeled and chopped
½ teaspoon black pepper
¼ teaspoon dried basil
1 teaspoon salt

With a sharp knife, trim any tough or discoloured leaves from the sprouts, and wash them thoroughly. Cut a cross in the base of each sprout.

In a medium-sized saucepan, melt the butter or margarine over moderate heat. When the foam subsides, add the onion, garlic and green pepper. Cook, stirring occasionally, for 8 minutes. Stir in the tomatoes, sprouts, pepper, basil and salt. Taste the mixture and add more salt and pepper if necessary.

Reduce the heat to low, cover the pan and cook for 15 to 20 minutes, or until the sprouts are tender. Turn the mixture into a warmed serving dish and serve.

Braised Brussels Sprouts with Chestnuts

Both Brussels sprouts and chestnuts have very high food values and this exceptional dish is therefore very good for you – as well as tasting marvellous!

Preparation and cooking time: 2 hours

6-8 SERVINGS

1 lb. chestnuts, blanched and peeled
2 celery stalks, chopped
3½ pints [8¾ cups] water
2 teaspoons salt
1½ teaspoons grated nutmeg
bouquet garni, consisting of 4 parsley sprigs, 1 thyme spray and 1 bay leaf tied together
2 lb. Brussels sprouts, washed and trimmed
2 oz. [¼ cup] butter or margarine, softened
1 teaspoon black pepper
10 fl. oz. [1¼ cups] dry red wine
1 tablespoon tomato purée
1 large tart apple, cored and chopped
2 oz. [¼ cup] beurre manié, made with 1½ oz. [3 tablespoons] butter mashed to a paste with 2 tablespoons flour

Put the peeled chestnuts and the celery into a large saucepan. Pour in 1½ pints [3¾ cups] of the water and add 1 teaspoon of the salt, ½ teaspoon of the nutmeg and the bouquet garni. Place the pan over moderately high heat and bring the water to the boil. Reduce the heat to low, cover the pan and simmer the chestnuts for 50 minutes, or until they are tender but still firm.

Remove the pan from the heat. Drain the chestnuts in a colander. Remove and discard the bouquet garni. Set the chestnuts aside.

Preheat the oven to moderate 350°F (Gas Mark 4, 180°C).

Put the Brussels sprouts into a large saucepan. Pour in the remaining 2 pints [5 cups] of water and add the remaining salt. Place the pan over moderately high heat and bring the water to the boil. Reduce the heat to moderate and cook the sprouts for 10 minutes. Remove the pan from the heat. Drain the sprouts in a colander and set them aside.

Spread the softened butter or margarine thickly over the bottom and sides of a large, shallow flameproof baking dish. Add the sprouts to the dish and sprinkle the remaining nutmeg and the black pepper on top.

In a small bowl, mix together the wine and tomato purée. Pour this over the sprouts and sprinkle the chopped apple on top. Cover the dish with greaseproof or waxed paper and place it in the oven. Bake for 15 to 20 minutes, or until the Brussels sprouts are tender but still firm.

Remove the dish from the oven and take off the greaseproof or waxed paper. With a slotted spoon, transfer the sprouts to a large mixing bowl and keep them warm.

Place the baking dish over moderately high heat and bring the cooking juices to the boil. Cook, stirring frequently, for 2 minutes, or until the liquid has reduced slightly. Reduce the heat to moderately low and stir in the beurre manié, a small piece at a time. Continue to cook gently, stirring constantly, until the sauce is smooth and fairly thick.

Return the Brussels sprouts to the baking dish and add the cooked chestnuts. Stir to coat the vegetables with the sauce. Cook the mixture, stirring occasionally, for 5 minutes, or until the vegetables are heated through.

Transfer the mixture to a heated serving dish and serve.

Brussels Sprouts with Yogurt Sauce

An unusual and subtle blend of flavours makes this vegetable dish a special one. Try yogurt sauce with cauliflower or other vegetables as well.

Preparation and cooking time: 25 minutes

4 SERVINGS

1½ teaspoons salt
1½ lb. Brussels sprouts
10 fl. oz. [1¼ cups] plain yogurt
½ teaspoon black pepper
1 tablespoon snipped fresh chives
1 tablespoon chopped fresh parsley

Half fill a large saucepan with water. Add 1 teaspoon of the salt and bring the water to the boil over high heat. Add the sprouts.

Reduce the heat to moderately low and simmer for 10 minutes, or until the sprouts are just tender. Drain the sprouts in a colander and transfer them to a warmed serving dish. Keep warm.

In a medium-sized saucepan, combine the yogurt, remaining salt, the pepper, chives and parsley over low heat. Cook, stirring occasionally, for 3 to 4 minutes or until the sauce is hot. Do not allow the sauce to boil.

Pour the yogurt sauce over the sprouts and serve.

Top For an attractive unusual-shaped loaf, Wholewheat Bread (page 6) may be baked in well-greased flower pots. This nutritious bread keeps fresh for a week.
Bottom A luscious Swiss Bread, Birnbrot (page 10) is filled with nuts, spices, dried fruit, kirsch and red wine. Serve it with steaming cups of hot chocolate.

This page top left Quick and easy-to-make Bran Bread (page 7) is ideal for slimmers *Top right*
Freshly baked Onion and Herb Loaf (page 9) has a superb aroma. *Centre left* Rich with candied fruit and
nuts, Stollen (page 9) is sweet and spicy. *Centre right* Little Raisin Drops (page 11) are nourishing and
chewy. *Bottom* Christmas Bread (page 8) deliciously combines stout, molasses, and orange rind.

This page top left Wholewheat Bread (page 6) is most delicious eaten freshly baked and spread with butter and honey. *Centre* Perfect with morning coffee, light Egg Bread (page 7) is plaited [braided] and sprinkled with poppy seeds. *Right* A Scottish speciality, crunchy Oatcakes (page 11) are lovely spread with butter and jam. *Bottom* Tempting Date and Walnut Loaf (page 10) is a moist tea bread.

This page top left A popular American soup, Corn Chowder (page 13) combines sweetcorn, onion, peppers and mushrooms. *Top right* The beautifully smooth taste of Creamed Spinach Soup (page 15) is enhanced by a swirl of fresh cream. *Centre* Elegant Vichyssoise (page 17) is a superb blend of leeks, potatoes and cream. *Bottom left* Winter Vegetable Soup (page 13) is perfect on winter's nights.

This page top A classic Spanish soup, chilled Gazpacho (page 16) makes a refreshing summer lunch, served with croûtons and small bowls of olives. Sprinkle the soup with a little chopped cucumber, hard-boiled eggs and onion. *Bottom* A traditional French recipe, French Onion Soup (page 14), topped with lots of grated cheese and grilled [broiled], is a very warming main dish.

Refreshing Cabbage and Pepper Salad (page 27) combines crunchy red and green peppers with white cabbage, tomatoes and cucumbers and is tossed in a piquant honey and vinegar dressing. Ideal to serve when salad greens are not available, it is a perfect accompaniment to a cheese quiche or flan.

Top A lovely summery salad, Apricot Salad (page 25) is ripe apricots covered in a cream and tarragon dressing. *Bottom* Crunchy Coleslaw with Caraway (page 26) is shredded cabbage, onion and green pepper topped with a sour cream, mustard, lemon juice and caraway seed dressing. Serve it with a savoury bake or rice dish.

This page top Beautifully crisp Summer Garden Salad (page 20), in varying shades of green, is so refreshing . *Centre* A basic dressing for most green and vegetable salads, Vinaigrette Dressing (page 28) may be varied with the addition of herbs. *Bottom* An elegant centrepiece for a summer buffet, Egg and Asparagus Moulded Salad (page 28) takes time to prepare but is well worth it.

This page top Bananas, rice, grapes, pineapple, walnuts and coconut are just some of the tempting ingredients in Creole Banana Salad (page 22). *Centre* This lovely Melon Boat (page 22) filled with black grapes, pears and melon is a refreshing first course or dessert. *Right* Creamy Avocado Pâté (page 22), served with thin slices of buttered toast, makes an elegant dinner party appetizer.

A tasty combination of Brussels sprouts, green pepper, tomatoes, garlic and basil, Brussels Sprouts Creole (page 32) makes a colourful vegetable accompaniment. Serve it with an omelet for a light family lunch or supper.

Top Quick and easy to prepare, Aniseed Carrots (page 50) is an unusual and delicately flavoured vegetable dish. *Bottom* Ideal to serve with salad or soup for a light family lunch, Stuffed Baked Potatoes (page 55) are filled with a luscious mixture of eggs, butter, cream and chives.

A very different way to serve celery, Chinese Celery (page 52) combines bean sprouts,
celery, pimiento and soy sauce and is topped with whole toasted almonds and
breadcrumbs. Serve it as part of a Chinese meal with steamed noodles and water
chestnuts or as a crunchy vegetable accompaniment to a soufflé or omelet.

44

Top Filled with tiny, new boiled potatoes, Broccoli Ring (page 31) is an elegant vegetable dish to serve for a dinner party. *Bottom* A classic French hors d'oeuvre, Tomatoes with Herbs (page 56) is a superb way to start a meal.

Left A nourishing winter vegetable stew, Ghuvetch (page 59) is an adaptation of a traditional Romanian dish. *Right* Bean and Fruit Stew (page 58) makes a very filling main dish and is as delicious cold as it is hot. Serve it with crusty Corn Bread and pitchers of cool cider for an excellent summer lunch or supper.

46

Top An ideal dish to serve for a simple family supper, golden Cheese Charlotte (page 68) is tasty served with tomato salad. *Bottom* An elegant dinner party hors d'oeuvre, Aubergines Farcies Duxelles (page 66) is aubergines [eggplants] filled with mushrooms, cottage cheese, herbs and topped with cheese and breadcrumbs.

An exotic yet simple to prepare dish, Moroccan Vegetable Couscous (page 66)
is a delicately spiced mixture of courgettes [zucchini], green peppers,
chick-peas, tomatoes, raisins and almonds served on a fluffy bed of couscous.

Dressed Beetroots [Beets]

Beetroots [beets] *in a piquant honey and vinegar dressing makes an unusual accompaniment to a savoury entrée.*

Preparation and cooking time: 2 hours

4-6 SERVINGS

1½ lb. beetroots [beets], trimmed and scrubbed
1 teaspoon salt
4 tablespoons cider vinegar
2 tablespoons olive oil
2 tablespoons clear honey

Put the beetroots [beets] into a large saucepan. Pour over enough water just to cover the beetroots [beets] and add the salt. Place the saucepan over moderately high heat and bring the water to the boil. Reduce the heat to moderate and cook the beetroots [beets] for about 1½ hours, or until they are cooked. (The cooking time will vary considerably according to the size and age.) To test if the beetroots [beets] are cooked, remove one from the pan and rub the skin gently with your fingers. If the skin comes away easily, the beetroot [beet] is cooked. Drain the beetroots [beets] in a colander and slice them thinly. Transfer the slices to a warmed serving dish.

In a small mixing bowl, combine the vinegar, olive oil and honey together, beating with a fork until they are well blended. Add this dressing to the warm beetroots [beets] and toss well to coat.

Serve at once.

Harvard Beets

A classic American vegetable dish, Harvard Beets makes an excellent accompaniment to egg dishes.

Preparation and cooking time: 2¼ hours

4 SERVINGS

3 large beetroots [beets], trimmed and scrubbed
2 pints 2 fl. oz. [5¼ cups] water
3 fl. oz. [⅜ cup] clear honey
1 teaspoon cornflour [cornstarch] dissolved in 1 teaspoon water
2 fl. oz. [¼ cup] white wine vinegar
1 tablespoon butter or margarine

Put the beetroots [beets] into a large saucepan and pour in 2 pints [5 cups] of the water. Place the pan over moderately high heat and bring the water to the boil. Reduce the heat to moderate, cover the pan and cook the beetroots [beets] for 1½ hours, or until they are cooked. (Cooking time will vary considerably according to size and age.) To test if the beetroots [beets] are cooked, remove one from the pan and rub the skin gently with your fingers. If the skin comes off easily, the beetroot [beet] is cooked. Remove the pan from the heat and drain the beetroots [beets] in a colander. Slice the beetroots [beets] and set them aside.

In a medium-sized saucepan, heat the honey over moderate heat, stirring constantly. Add the dissolved cornflour [cornstarch] and stir to blend. Add the vinegar and remaining water. Bring the mixture to the boil and cook, stirring constantly, for 5 minutes.

Remove the pan from the heat and stir in the beetroot [beet] slices. Cover the pan and set it aside for 20 minutes.

Return the pan to moderate heat, uncover and bring the mixture to the boil.

Remove the pan from the heat and gently stir in the butter or margarine.

Serve as soon as the butter or margarine has melted.

Latvian Red Cabbage

Red cabbage is a vegetable mainly associated with Northern and Middle Europe and the countries of Mittel Europa especially have come up with some wonderfully imaginative ways of cooking this sturdy and nutritious vegetable.

Preparation and cooking time: 2¼ hours

6-8 SERVINGS

1 tablespoon butter or margarine
1 large red cabbage, coarse outer leaves removed, washed and shredded
2 medium-sized onions, finely chopped
1 garlic clove, crushed
6 fl. oz. [¾ cup] red wine
3 tablespoons cider vinegar
1 tablespoon clear honey
½ teaspoon salt
2 teaspoons dried dill leaves
1 large cooking apple, cored and chopped

Preheat the oven to warm 325°F (Gas Mark 3, 170°C). Generously grease a fairly large, heavy flameproof casserole with the butter or margarine.

Arrange the cabbage, onions and garlic in the casserole.

In a small bowl, combine the red wine, vinegar, honey, salt and dill, mixing with a fork until the ingredients are well blended. Pour the wine mixture into the casserole and place it over moderately high heat. Bring the liquid to the boil. Cover the casserole and transfer it to the oven. Bake for 1 hour.

Remove the casserole from the oven and stir in the apple. Return the casserole to the oven and continue baking for another hour, or until the cabbage is very tender.

Remove the casserole from the oven and serve at once.

North Country Cabbage

A marvellously economical meal in itself, North Country Cabbage is as nutritious as it is good to eat. Serve it by itself for a healthful lunch, or as an accompaniment to an omelet or soufflé.

Preparation and cooking time: 1¾ hours

4-8 SERVINGS

1 x 3 lb. cabbage, coarse outer leaves removed, washed and shredded
2½ pints [6¼ cups] water
1½ teaspoons salt
3 tablespoons vegetable oil
2 medium-sized onions, thinly sliced
½ teaspoon black pepper
½ teaspoon ground allspice
1 tablespoon butter or margarine
3 medium-sized potatoes, scrubbed and cut into ¼-inch slices
2 small turnips, peeled and cut into ¼-inch slices
4 fl. oz. [½ cup] Dark Vegetable Stock

Put the cabbage into a large saucepan. Pour in the water and add 1 teaspoon of the salt. Place the saucepan over moderately high heat and bring the water to the boil. Reduce the heat to moderate and cook the cabbage for 10 minutes. Remove the pan from the heat. Drain the cabbage in a colander and set it aside in a large mixing bowl.

Preheat the oven to moderate 350°F (Gas Mark 4, 180°C).

In a medium-sized frying-pan, heat the oil over moderate heat. When the oil is hot, add the onions to the pan. Cook them, stirring occasionally, for 5 to 7 minutes, or until they are soft and translucent but not brown. Stir in the remaining salt, the pepper and allspice. Remove the pan from the heat and add the onion mixture to the cabbage, mixing well to blend.

Grease the bottom and sides of a large ovenproof casserole with the butter or margarine. Arrange half of the potato slices on the bottom of the casserole. Add half of the cabbage mixture, then all of the turnip slices. Top with the remaining cabbage, then the remaining potato slices. Pour in the stock. Cover the casserole and place it in the oven. Bake for 45 minutes. Uncover the casserole and continue to bake for a further 15 minutes.

Remove the casserole from the oven and serve at once.

Sautéed Courgettes [Zucchini]

Courgettes [zucchini] are becoming increasingly popular. This is one excellent and very easy method of cooking this delicious vegetable.

Preparation and cooking time: 30 minutes

6 SERVINGS

12 small courgettes [zucchini], washed and trimmed
2 pints [5 cups] water
1½ teaspoons salt
1½ teaspoons black pepper
4 oz. [½ cup] butter or margarine
1 large onion, sliced and pushed out into rings

Put the courgettes [zucchini] into a large saucepan. Pour in the water. Place the pan over moderately high heat and bring the water to the boil. Reduce the heat to moderate and cook the courgettes [zucchini] for 8 minutes. Drain the courgettes [zucchini] in a colander and cut them crossways, into ½-inch thick slices. Sprinkle the slices with the salt and pepper.

In a large frying-pan, melt 3 ounces [⅜ cup] of the butter or margarine over moderately high heat. When the foam subsides, add the courgette [zucchini] slices. Fry them, stirring occasionally, for 6 to 8 minutes, or until they are golden brown.

With a slotted spoon, transfer the courgette [zucchini] slices to a warmed serving dish and keep them warm.

Add the remaining butter or margarine to the frying-pan and melt it over moderate heat. When the foam subsides, add the onion to the pan. Cook it, stirring occasionally, for 5 to 7 minutes, or until it is soft and translucent but not brown.

With a slotted spoon, transfer the onion rings to the serving dish.

Serve at once.

Baked Courgettes [Zucchini]

Almost like a soufflé, this exciting dish of courgettes [zucchini], potatoes, tomatoes, turnip and onions is filling enough to be served as a meal in itself. It may be baked in a plain or ring mould. If you use a ring mould, the centre may be filled with French-Fried Cauliflower or canned cream-style sweetcorn.

Preparation and cooking time: 1¼ hours

4-6 SERVINGS

2 tablespoons vegetable oil
6 small courgettes [zucchini], washed, trimmed and peeled
2 medium-sized potatoes, cooked and mashed
1 small turnip, cooked and mashed
2 medium-sized tomatoes, blanched, peeled, seeded and finely chopped
2 small onions, minced
1 garlic clove, crushed
4 eggs, separated
3 oz. [¾ cup] Parmesan cheese, grated
½ teaspoon salt
½ teaspoon black pepper
1 teaspoon dried basil

Preheat the oven to moderate 350°F (Gas Mark 4, 180°C). Lightly grease a large, deep plain or ring mould with 1 tablespoon of the vegetable oil. Set aside.

Coarsely grate the courgettes [zucchini]. Squeeze out any excess moisture by drying the flesh with kitchen paper towels. Put the grated courgettes [zucchini] into a large mixing bowl.

Add the potatoes, turnip, tomatoes, onions and garlic. Stir in the egg yolks, remaining oil, one-third of the cheese, the salt, pepper and basil.

In a medium-sized mixing bowl, beat the egg whites with a wire whisk or rotary beater until they form stiff peaks. With a metal spoon, carefully fold the egg whites into the courgette [zucchini] mixture.

Spoon the mixture carefully into the mould and thickly sprinkle the remaining grated cheese over the top.

Place the mould in the oven and bake for 30 to 35 minutes, or until the mixture is cooked and the top is brown.

Remove the mould from the oven. Run a knife around the mixture to loosen it and place a serving dish, inverted, over the top. Holding the mould and dish firmly together, reverse them. The baked courgettes [zucchini] should slide out easily on to the dish.

Serve immediately.

Aniseed Carrots

This is an unusual combination of flavours and makes a most interesting vegetable dish.

Preparation and cooking time: 25 minutes

4 SERVINGS

1½ lb. carrots, scraped
2 oz. [¼ cup] butter or margarine
1 tablespoon soft brown sugar
1 heaped teaspoon aniseed
1 teaspoon salt
½ teaspoon white pepper

If you are using small carrots, leave them whole. Large carrots should be cut in quarters lengthways.

In a large saucepan, melt the butter or margarine over moderate heat. When the foam subsides, stir in the sugar, aniseed, salt and pepper. Add the carrots and stir to coat them with the sauce. Cover the pan, reduce the heat to low and cook for about 15 minutes, or until the carrots are tender when pierced with the point of a sharp knife.

Turn the carrots into a warmed serving dish and serve.

Creamed Carrots and Mushrooms in Potato Nests

A very decorative vegetable dish, these Creamed Carrots and Mushrooms in Potato Nests require care and attention, but they are not difficult to make.

Preparation and cooking time: 1¼ hours

4 SERVINGS

2 lb. potatoes, peeled
3 pints [7½ cups] water
1½ teaspoons salt
2½ oz. [¼ cup plus 1 tablespoon] butter or margarine
3 eggs, lightly beaten
1 teaspoon white pepper
¼ teaspoon ground mace
2 medium-sized carrots, scraped and sliced
4 medium-sized mushrooms, wiped clean and sliced
2 fl. oz. double cream [¼ cup heavy cream]
½ teaspoon prepared mustard
1 tablespoon vegetable oil

Put the potatoes into a large saucepan. Pour in 2 pints [5 cups] of the water and add 1 teaspoon of salt. Place the pan over moderately high heat and bring the water to the boil. Reduce the heat to moderate and cook the potatoes for 15 to 20 minutes, or until they are tender. Remove the pan from the heat and drain the poatoes in a colander.

Put the potatoes into a large mixing bowl and mash them with a fork or potato masher. Stir in 1½ ounces [3 tablespoons] of the butter or margarine, 2 of the eggs, the pepper and mace and beat briskly until all the ingredients are well blended. Spoon the potato mixture into a piping bag and set it aside.

Meanwhile, put the carrots into a medium-sized saucepan. Pour in the remaining water and add the remaining salt. Place the pan over moderately high heat and bring the water to the boil. Reduce the heat to moderate and cook the carrots for 10 to 12 minutes, or until they are tender. Remove the pan from the heat and drain the carrots in a colander. Put the carrots into a medium-sized mixing bowl. Mash them with a fork or potato masher. Set aside and keep warm.

Preheat the grill [broiler] to moderate.

In a small frying-pan, melt the remaining butter or margarine over moderate heat. When the foam subsides, add the mushrooms. Cook them, stirring occasionally, for 3 to 5 minutes, or until the mushrooms are very tender. Stir in the cream and mustard and coat the mushrooms well. Cook the mixture for a further 1 minute.

Remove the pan from the heat and add the mushroom mixture to the mashed carrots. Stir well to blend. Set aside and keep warm.

Lightly coat a baking sheet with the vegetable oil. Pipe round mounds of the potato mixture on to the baking sheet, allowing about a 1-inch space between each mound. With your fingertips, press a hollow in the centre of each mound. With a pastry brush, glaze the 'nests' with the remaining beaten egg and place them under the grill [broiler]. Cook for 2 minutes, or until the 'nests' start to turn brown.

Remove the nests from the heat and spoon the carrot and mushroom mixture into the centre of each one. Serve at once.

Honey-Glazed Carrots with Celery and Onions

This is a very good combination of baked vegetables lightly covered with a sweet honey glaze.

Preparation and cooking time: 1 hour

8 SERVINGS

2 oz. [¼ cup] plus 1 teaspoon butter or margarine, melted
2 lb. carrots, scraped and sliced
3 celery stalks, chopped
12 small white onions, peeled and left whole
3 pints [7½ cups] water
1½ teaspoons salt
3 fl. oz. [⅜ cup] clear honey
1½ teaspoons dried rosemary
1 teaspoon black pepper

Preheat the oven to moderate 350°F (Gas Mark 4, 180°C). Lightly grease a medium-sized flameproof casserole with the teaspoon of butter or margarine. Set aside.

Put the carrots, celery and onions in a large saucepan. Pour over the water and add 1 teaspoon of the salt. Place the pan over high heat and bring the water to the boil. Reduce the heat to moderate and cook the vegetables for 10 minutes.

Remove the pan from the heat and drain the vegetables in a colander. Arrange the vegetables in the casserole.

In a small mixing bowl, combine the remaining melted butter or margarine with the honey. Stir in the remaining salt, the rosemary and the pepper. Pour the honey mixture over the vegetables in the casserole.

Place the casserole in the oven and bake for 15 minutes, or until the carrots are tender. Remove the casserole from the oven. With a slotted spoon, transfer the vegetables to a warmed serving dish. Keep them warm.

Place the casserole over moderately high heat and bring the cooking juices to the boil. Simmer, stirring occasionally, for 5 minutes, or until the liquid has reduced slightly.

Pour the liquid over the vegetables and serve.

Oven-Baked Carrots

A simple yet delicious accompaniment, Oven-Baked Carrots may be served with omelets or soufflés.

Preparation and cooking time: 1 hour

4 SERVINGS

1½ oz. [3 tablespoons] butter or margarine
1½ lb. carrots, scraped
3 tablespoons water
1 tablespoon cider vinegar

Preheat the oven to moderate 350°F (Gas Mark 4, 180°C). Grease a medium-sized baking dish with one-third of the butter or margarine.

Coarsely grate the carrots into the baking dish. Stir in the water and vinegar. Cut the remaining butter or margarine into small pieces and dot them over the top of the grated carrots.

Cover the dish with a lid or aluminium foil and place it in the oven. Bake for 40 minutes, or until the carrots are tender.

Remove from the oven and serve at once.

Watercress and Cauliflower Purée

Both watercress and cauliflower are high in Vitamin C, which makes this exotic purée, topped with cheese and breadcrumbs, nourishing as well as attractive.

Preparation and cooking time: 1½ hours

4-6 SERVINGS

1 teaspoon butter or margarine
3 pints [7½ cups] water
1 cauliflower
2 teaspoons salt
1 bunch of watercress, washed, shaken dry and stalks removed
10 fl. oz. [1¼ cups] Béchamel Sauce
4 fl. oz. double cream [½ cup heavy cream]
4 oz. [1 cup] Gruyère cheese, grated

¼ teaspoon white pepper
2 tablespoons dry breadcrumbs
2 tablespoons melted butter or margarine

Preheat the oven to fairly hot 375°F (Gas Mark 5, 190°C). Lightly grease a medium-sized baking dish with the teaspoon of butter or margarine. Set the baking dish aside.

In a large saucepan, bring the water to the boil over high heat. Add the cauliflower and salt. Reduce the heat to moderate, half cover the pan and cook the the cauliflower gently for 6 minutes.

Add the watercress leaves and cook for a further 5 minutes, or until the cauliflower is tender when pierced with the point of a sharp knife.

Remove the pan from the heat and thoroughly drain the cauliflower and watercress in a colander.

Purée the cauliflower and watercress with the béchamel sauce in a blender or put the vegetables through a food mill and then mix in the sauce. Place the purée in a medium-sized mixing bowl and stir in the cream. When the cream is thoroughly blended in, the mixture should be stiff enough to hold its shape when lifted on a spoon. Fold in three-quarters of the cheese and the pepper.

Turn the purée into the greased baking dish. Mix the remaining cheese with the breadcrumbs. Sprinkle the top of the purée with the breadcrumb-and-cheese mixture and then with the melted butter or margarine.

Place the dish in the oven and bake for about 30 minutes, or until the top is golden brown.

Remove the dish from the oven and serve.

French-Fried Cauliflower

This is an interesting and different way to cook cauliflower.

Preparation and cooking time: 1¼ hours

4 SERVINGS

1 large cauliflower, washed, trimmed and broken into flowerets
2 pints [5 cups] water
1 teaspoon salt
2 eggs
1 teaspoon grated nutmeg
3 oz. [1 cup] fine dry breadcrumbs sufficient vegetable oil for deep-frying

Put the cauliflower flowerets into a large saucepan. Pour in the water and add the salt. Place the pan over moderately high heat and bring the water to the boil. Reduce the heat to moderate, half cover the pan and cook the cauliflower for 15 minutes, or until it is just tender. Remove the pan from the heat. Drain the cauliflower in a colander.

In a large shallow bowl, lightly beat the eggs and nutmeg together with a kitchen fork. Spread out the breadcrumbs on a sheet of greaseproof or waxed paper.

Dip the cauliflower flowerets, one by one, into the egg mixture and then into the breadcrumbs, make sure that each floweret is well coated on all sides. Place the flowerets on a sheet of greaseproof or waxed paper and put them in the refrigerator to chill for 10 minutes.

Half fill a large saucepan or deep-frying pan with the oil. Place the pan over moderate heat and heat until the oil reaches 360°F on a deep-fat thermometer, or until a cube of stale bread dropped in the oil turns brown in 50 seconds.

Drop the flowerets, a few at a time, into the oil and fry them for 5 minutes, or until they are golden brown. With a slotted spoon, remove the flowerets from the pan and drain them on kitchen paper towels. Keep them warm while you fry the remaining flowerets in the same way.

Serve piping hot.

Cucumber and Tomato Cooked Salad

The fresh, clean tastes of cucumber and tomato make this cold, cooked salad an appetizing summer vegetable dish.
Preparation and cooking time: 2 hours
4 SERVINGS

2 large cucumbers, peeled, cut in half lengthways, seeded and cut into ½-inch pieces
1¼ teaspoons salt
4 tablespoons olive oil
1 medium-sized onion, quartered and sliced
1 large garlic clove, finely chopped
8 oz. tomatoes, blanched, peeled, seeded and roughly chopped
2 tablespoons tomato purée
2 tablespoons red wine vinegar
¼ teaspoon dried basil
½ teaspoon black pepper

Place the cucumber pieces in a large saucepan. Pour in enough water just to cover them and add 1 teaspoon of the

salt. Bring the water to the boil over moderate heat and cook the cucumbers for 3 minutes. Drain the cucumbers in a colander and rinse them under cold running water. Dry the cucumber pieces on kitchen paper towels. Set aside.

In a large frying-pan, heat the oil over moderate heat. Add the onion and garlic and cook for 3 to 4 minutes, or until the onion is tender but still crisp. Remove the pan from the heat and mix in the chopped tomatoes, tomato purée, vinegar, basil, pepper and the remaining salt. Add the cucumber and mix well.

Turn the salad into a serving dish. Place the dish in the refrigerator and chill the salad for at least 1½ hours before serving.

Chinese Celery

A very different way to cheer up a delicious vegetable, Chinese Celery may be served as part of a Chinese meal or as a vegetable accompaniment to a soufflé or omelet.
Preparation and cooking time: 1 hour
4 SERVINGS

3 oz. [⅜ cup] butter or margarine
1 large head of celery, trimmed, washed and coarsely chopped
4 oz. canned bean sprouts, drained
4 oz. canned mange touts [snow peas], drained
2 oz. canned pimiento, drained and chopped
2 teaspoons soy sauce
¼ teaspoon salt
¼ teaspoon black pepper
1 oz. [½ cup] fresh breadcrumbs
1 oz. [¼ cup] whole almonds, toasted

Preheat the oven to moderate 350°F (Gas Mark 4, 180°C).

In a large frying-pan, melt 2 ounces [¼ cup] of the butter or margarine over moderate heat. When the foam subsides, add the celery to the pan. Cook, stirring occasionally, for 5 minutes, or until the the celery becomes slightly translucent.

Add the bean sprouts, mange touts [snow peas], pimiento, soy sauce, salt and pepper and stir to mix. Continue cooking for 2 minutes.

Transfer the celery mixture to a medium-sized ovenproof casserole. Spread the breadcrumbs over the top of the mixture. Cut the remaining butter or margarine into small pieces and dot them on top of the breadcrumbs.

Place the casserole in the oven and bake for 40 minutes, or until the top of the celery mixture is crisp and very brown.

Remove the casserole from the oven, sprinkle the almonds on top and serve at once.

Braised Celery with Béchamel Sauce

Celery is just as good cooked as it is raw, and one of the many delicious methods of cooking celery is braising. This recipe is a basic one for braising on top of the stove. Serve Braised Celery with Béchamel Sauce as a light accompaniment.
Preparation and cooking time: 2 hours
4 SERVINGS

2 medium-sized heads of celery, trimmed and washed
1½ pints [3¾ cups] water
½ teaspoon salt
1 tablespoon butter or margarine
1 large carrot, scraped and sliced
1 large onion, sliced
bouquet garni, consisting of 4 parsley sprigs, 1 thyme spray and 1 bay leaf tied together
1 teaspoon white pepper
½ teaspoon grated nutmeg
10 fl. oz. [1¼ cups] Light Vegetable Stock
8 fl. oz. [1 cup] hot Béchamel Sauce

Put the celery into a large saucepan (cut the stalks to fit, if necessary). Pour in the water and add the salt. Place the saucepan over moderately high heat and bring the water to the boil. Reduce the heat to moderate and cook the celery for 10 minutes. Drain the celery in a colander and set it aside.

Grease the bottom and sides of a large saucepan or flameproof casserole with the butter or margarine. Arrange the carrot and onion on the bottom. Place the celery on top. Add the bouquet garni, pepper and nutmeg to the mixture and pour in the stock. Place the pan over moderately high heat and bring the stock to the boil. Cover the pan tightly, reduce the heat to low and simmer the celery for 45 minutes, or until it is very tender.

Remove the pan from the heat and, with a slotted spoon, transfer the celery to a warmed serving dish. Keep the cooking liquid and vegetables for stock or soup.

Slice the celery in half, lengthways, then in half crosswise. Pour the béchamel sauce over the celery and serve at once.

Endive Farcie
CHICORY [FRENCH OR BELGIAN ENDIVE] LEAVES STUFFED WITH CREAM CHEESE

Endive Farcie (on-deeve phar-see) is a delectable dish of chicory [French or Belgian endive] leaves stuffed with a mixture of cream cheese, cream, mustard and mixed nuts. The leaves are rolled and fastened, and served cold as an appetizer or as a snack with drinks.

Preparation and cooking time: 1 hour

6-8 SERVINGS

6 oz. cream cheese
3 fl. oz. double cream [⅜ cup heavy cream]
⅛ teaspoon cayenne pepper
¼ teaspoon salt
¼ teaspoon black pepper
½ teaspoon prepared French mustard
1 teaspoon Worcestershire sauce
2½ oz. [½ cup] walnuts, finely chopped
2½ oz. [½ cup] hazelnuts, finely chopped
20 medium-sized to large chicory [French or Belgian endive] leaves, washed and shaken dry

In a medium-sized mixing bowl, mash the cream cheese with a fork until it is smooth. Add the cream, cayenne, salt, pepper, mustard and Worcestershire sauce and beat well to blend the ingredients thoroughly. Stir in the nuts.

Lay the chicory [endive] leaves on a clean flat surface. Put about 1 tablespoon of the cheese mixture on the base end of each leaf. Roll up the leaves and fasten each roll with a cocktail stick.

Arrange the stuffed leaves on a serving platter and place it in the refrigerator to chill for at least 30 minutes before serving.

French Beans Hungarian-Style

A spicy and pungent vegetable dish, French Beans Hungarian-Style makes an excellent accompaniment to soufflés.
Preparation and cooking time: 40 minutes

4 SERVINGS

1 lb. French beans, trimmed and washed
1½ pints [3¾ cups] water
½ teaspoon salt
2 fl. oz. [¼ cup] vegetable oil
2 medium-sized onions, sliced
1 garlic clove, crushed
1 teaspoon paprika
4 fl. oz. [½ cup] sour cream

Put the French beans into a large saucepan. Pour in the water and add the salt. Place the pan over moderately high heat and bring the water to the boil. Reduce the heat to moderate and cook the beans for 15 minutes, or until they

are just tender. Drain the beans in a colander and set them aside.

In a large frying-pan, heat the oil over moderate heat. When the oil is hot, add the onions and garlic. Cook them, stirring occasionally, for 5 to 7 minutes, or until the onions are soft and translucent but not brown. Remove the pan from the heat and stir in the paprika and sour cream, mixing well to blend.

Return the pan to low heat and mix in the French beans. Cook, stirring occasionally, for 5 minutes, or until the beans and sauce are heated through.

Turn the beans and sauce into a warmed serving dish and serve.

French Beans Italian-Style

A subtle yet very tasty accompaniment to pasta dishes or casseroles, French Beans Italian-Style is simple and economical to make.
Preparation and cooking time: 50 minutes

6 SERVINGS

1 lb. French beans, trimmed and washed
1½ pints [3¾ cups] water
1½ teaspoons salt
3 fl. oz. [⅜ cup] olive oil
2 small onions, sliced
1 garlic clove, crushed
1 small green pepper, white pith removed, seeded and thinly sliced
8 oz. canned peeled tomatoes, chopped
4 oz. mushrooms, wiped clean and sliced
¼ teaspoon cayenne pepper
1 teaspoon dried basil

Put the French beans into a large saucepan. Pour in the water and add 1 teaspoon of the salt. Place the pan over moderately high heat and bring the water to the boil. Reduce the heat to moderate and cook the beans for 10 minutes, or until they are just tender. Drain the beans in a colander and set them aside.

In a large frying-pan, heat the oil over moderate heat. When the oil is hot, add the onions, garlic and green pepper. Cook the vegetables, stirring occasionally, for 5 to 7 minutes, or until the onions are soft and translucent but not brown.

Add the tomatoes with their can juice, the mushrooms, the remaining salt, the cayenne and the basil and stir to mix. Continue cooking for 2 minutes.

Add the French beans to the pan. Reduce the heat to low, cover the pan and simmer for 15 minutes, or until the beans are very tender but still firm.

Turn the vegetables and sauce into a warmed serving dish and serve.

Fennel Baked in Foil

A delicious way in which to cook this exotic and delicate vegetable, Fennel Baked in Foil makes an excellent accompaniment to savoury flans or pasta.
Preparation and cooking time: 1 hour

4 SERVINGS

2 large heads of fennel, trimmed, washed and halved
2 oz. [¼ cup] butter or margarine, softened
1 teaspoon salt
½ teaspoon white pepper
¼ teaspoon cayenne pepper

Preheat the oven to fairly hot 375°F (Gas Mark 5, 190°C).

Place the fennel halves on a flat surface. With a knife, spread the cut sides of the fennels with the softened butter or margarine. Sprinkle two halves with the salt, pepper and cayenne. Place the unseasoned fennel halves on top, sandwiching in the seasoning and butter or margarine. Wrap the fennel sandwiches in aluminium foil.

Place the foil-wrapped fennel in the oven and bake them for 45 minutes, or until they are tender when pierced with the point of a sharp knife.

Remove the fennel from the oven, unwrap and serve immediately.

Onions in Madeira

A distinctive and most unusual dish, Onions in Madeira makes an excellent accompaniment to any savoury bake.
Preparation and cooking time: 1 hour

4-6 SERVINGS

12 medium-sized onions, sliced
2 pints [5 cups] water
1 teaspoon salt
2 oz. [¼ cup] plus 1 teaspoon butter or margarine
4 medium-sized mushrooms, wiped clean and sliced
½ teaspoon black pepper
½ teaspoon grated nutmeg
5 fl. oz. single cream [⅝ cup light cream]
2 tablespoons Madeira

Put the onions into a large saucepan. Pour in the water and add the salt. Place the pan over moderately high heat and bring the water to the boil. Reduce the heat to moderate and cook the onions for 10 to 15 minutes, or until they are just tender. Drain the onions in a colander and set them aside.

Preheat the oven to moderate 350°F (Gas Mark 4, 180°C). Lightly grease an ovenproof casserole with the teaspoon of butter or margarine. Set aside.

In a small frying-pan, melt the remaining butter or margarine over moderate heat. When the foam subsides, add the mushrooms, pepper and nutmeg to the pan. Cook the mushrooms, stirring constantly, for 3 minutes. Remove the pan from the heat and set it aside.

In a small bowl, combine the cream and the Madeira together, mixing well to blend. Stir the Madeira mixture into the mushrooms in the frying-pan.

Put the onions into the greased casserole and pour the Madeira and mushroom mixture over them. Cover the casserole and place it in the oven. Bake for 30 minutes.

Remove the casserole from the oven and serve at once.

Pepper Ragoût

A delicious and spicy mixture of red and green peppers and onions, this ragoût will best complement a bland entrée.

Preparation and cooking time: 45 minutes
4-6 SERVINGS

2 oz. [¼ cup] butter or margarine
2 red peppers, white pith removed, seeded and cut into strips
2 green peppers, white pith removed, seeded and cut into strips
2 celery stalks, chopped
1 medium-sized onion, sliced
2 garlic cloves, crushed
1 teaspoon dried oregano
1 teaspoon salt
½ teaspoon black pepper
¼ teaspoon red pepper flakes
6 fl. oz. [¾ cup] Dark Vegetable Stock
1 tablespoon flour dissolved in 1 tablespoon water

In a large, deep frying-pan, melt the butter or margarine over moderate heat. When the foam subsides, add the red and green peppers, celery, onion and garlic to the pan. Cook them, stirring occasionally, for 8 to 10 minutes, or until the vegetables are just beginning to turn brown.

Stir in the oregano, salt, pepper and red pepper flakes and mix well. Pour in the stock and bring it to the boil. Reduce the heat to low, cover the pan and simmer the ragoût, stirring occasionally, for 20 to 25 minutes, or until the vegetables are tender.

Stir in the flour and continue cooking for 2 to 3 minutes or until the liquid thickens slightly. Remove the pan from the heat and turn the ragoût into a warmed serving dish.

Serve immediately.

Party Mushrooms

A simple yet spectacular dish, Party Mushrooms are an exquisite vegetable accompaniment or first course.

Preparation and cooking time: 15 minutes
4 SERVINGS

1½ oz. [3 tablespoons] butter or margarine
1 lb. mushrooms, wiped clean and sliced
1 teaspoon salt
½ teaspoon black pepper
½ teaspoon ground cloves
2 fl. oz. [¼ cup] brandy
2 fl. oz. double cream [¼ cup heavy cream]

In a large frying-pan, melt the butter or margarine over moderate heat. When the foam subsides, add the mushrooms, salt, pepper and cloves. Cook, stirring constantly, for 5 minutes. Remove the pan from the heat and set it aside.

In a small saucepan, heat the brandy over low heat. When it is warm, pour it over the mushroom mixture. Set the brandy alight.

When the flames die down, stir in the cream, mixing until all the ingredients are well blended.

Turn the mushrooms and sauce into warmed serving dish and serve.

Petits Pois à la Francaise

One of the great vegetable dishes of French cuisine, Petits Pois à la Française (peh-tee pwah ah lah frahn-sehz) is surprisingly easy to prepare. It goes particularly well with cheese omelets.

Preparation and cooking time: 45 minutes
4 SERVINGS

1 lb. fresh green peas, shelled
heart of 1 lettuce, shredded
8 to 10 small white onions, peeled and left whole
3 oz. [⅜ cup] butter or margarine
bouquet garni, consisting of 4 parsley sprigs, 1 thyme spray and 1 bay leaf tied together
1½ teaspoons salt
2 teaspoons clear honey
4 fl. oz. [½ cup] water
½ teaspoon white pepper

Put the peas, lettuce, onions, half of the butter or margarine, the bouquet garni, salt and honey into a large saucepan. Pour in the water and place the pan over moderately high heat. Bring the water to the boil, stirring occasionally. Reduce the heat to moderate and cover the pan tightly. Cook for 20 minutes, or until the peas are tender.

Remove the pan from the heat and stir in the remaining butter or margarine and the pepper.

When the butter or margarine has melted, turn the petits pois into a warmed serving dish and serve.

Peas with Fennel

A delicious and simple dish, Peas with Fennel particularly complements heavier stews and bakes.

Preparation and cooking time: 40 minutes
4 SERVINGS

1 lb. fresh green peas, shelled
1 pint [2½ cups] water
1 teaspoon salt
1 head of fennel, trimmed, outer leaves removed and chopped
¼ teaspoon cayenne pepper
1 oz. [2 tablespoons] butter or margarine

Put the peas into a large saucepan. Pour in the water and add the salt. Place the pan over moderately high heat and bring the water to the boil. Reduce the heat to moderate. Stir in the chopped fennel and cayenne. Cover the pan and cook the mixture for 20 minutes, or until the peas are just tender.

Remove the pan from the heat and drain the peas and fennel in a colander. Transfer them to a warmed medium-sized serving dish.

Stir the butter or margarine into the peas and fennel. When the butter or margarine has melted, serve.

Petits Pois Garnis

Tiny tender peas with celery, mushrooms, tomatoes and garlic make this a tasty and colourful dish.

Preparation and cooking time: 45 minutes
4 SERVINGS

12 oz. frozen petits pois, thawed, or 14 oz. canned petits pois, drained
3 celery stalks, sliced
1 medium-sized onion, sliced
1 garlic clove, crushed
2 tomatoes, blanched, peeled, seeded and chopped
4 fl. oz. [½ cup] Light Vegetable Stock
2 oz. [¼ cup] butter or margarine
4 oz. mushrooms, wiped clean and sliced
1 teaspoon salt
½ teaspoon black pepper
1 teaspoon finely chopped fresh tansy (optional)
1 tablespoon cornflour [cornstarch] dissolved in 2 tablespoons single [light] cream

Put the petits pois, celery, onion, garlic and tomatoes into a large saucepan. Pour in the vegetable stock. Place the saucepan over moderately high heat and bring the stock to the boil. Reduce the heat to low, cover the pan and simmer the mixture, stirring occasionally, for 20 minutes, or until the vegetables are tender. Remove the pan from the heat and set it aside.

In a small frying-pan, melt the butter or margarine over moderate heat. When the foam subsides, add the mushrooms. Cook them, stirring frequently, for 3 minutes. Remove the pan from the heat and transfer the mushrooms and their cooking liquid to the petits pois mixture.

Stir in the salt, pepper and tansy if you are using it. Blend in the cornflour [cornstarch] mixture.

Return the pan to moderate heat and cook for a further 2 minutes, stirring constantly, until the vegetables are heated through. Remove the pan from the heat and turn the vegetables into a warmed serving dish. Serve immediately.

Rosti
FRIED POTATO CAKE

Almost a national dish in Switzerland, Rosti makes an elegant and absolutely marvellous accompaniment to almost any main dish.
Preparation and cooking time: 30 minutes
4-6 SERVINGS
2 lb. potatoes, cooked and cooled
1 oz. [2 tablespoons] butter or margarine
2 tablespoons olive oil
1 teaspoon salt
½ teaspoon black pepper

Coarsely grate the potatoes and set them aside.

In a large, heavy frying-pan, melt the butter or margarine with the oil over moderate heat. When the foam subsides, place the grated potatoes in the pan and spread them out, taking care not to press them down too much. Sprinkle with the salt and pepper.

Cover the pan and cook for 8 to 10 minutes, or until the underside of the potato mixture begins to turn brown. Shake the pan from time to time to make sure that the mixture does not stick.

Gently turn the potato mixture over. Fry for a further 5 to 6 minutes, or until the other side turns brown.

Remove the pan from the heat and slide the potato cake out of the pan on to a warmed serving dish. Serve at once.

Pommes de Terre aux Pruneaux
POTATOES WITH PRUNES

Yet another example of the French "way" with vegetables, Pommes de Terre aux Pruneaux (pohm d'tair oh proo-noh) combines potatoes with prunes. The result is not only an exciting and exotic vegetable dish, but it may be served as a beautifully balanced meal in itself.
Preparation and cooking time: 1½ hours
4 SERVINGS
1½ lb. potatoes, scrubbed
2 pints [5 cups] water
2 teaspoons salt
2 fl. oz. [¼ cup] vegetable oil
2 medium-sized onions, sliced
1 garlic clove, crushed
8 oz. dried prunes, soaked overnight and drained
3 oz. canned pineapple, drained and chopped
8 juniper berries, crushed
10 fl. oz. [1¼ cups] white wine
1 tablespoon grated lemon rind
1 tablespoon soy sauce
2 tablespoons clear honey

Put the potatoes into a large saucepan. Pour in the water and add 1 teaspoon of the salt. Place the pan over moderately high heat and bring the water to the boil. Reduce the heat to moderate and cook the potatoes for 10 minutes. Drain the potatoes in a colander and chop them into large cubes.

In a large frying-pan, heat the oil over moderate heat. When the oil is hot, add the onions and garlic to the pan. Cook them, stirring occasionally, for 5 to 7 minutes, or until the onions are soft and translucent but not brown. Add the potatoes, prunes and pineapple and continue cooking, stirring occasionally, for a further 5 minutes.

Stir in the juniper berries and the wine and increase the heat to high. Bring the wine to the boil. Reduce the heat to very low and cook, stirring occasionally, for 15 minutes. Add the lemon rind, soy sauce and honey and stir to mix. Cover the pan and continue to simmer the mixture, stirring occasionally, for 30 minutes, or until the potatoes are well glazed and very tender.

Turn the potato mixture into a warmed serving dish and serve.

Stuffed Baked Potatoes

A delicious and filling dish suitable for a light informal lunch or dinner, these baked potatoes are stuffed with a mixture of eggs, butter, cream and chives.
Preparation and cooking time: 2¼ hours
4 SERVINGS
4 large potatoes, scrubbed and dried
1 tablespoon butter
1 tablespoon snipped chives
1 teaspoon salt
¼ teaspoon black pepper
⅛ teaspoon grated nutmeg
4 tablespoons double [heavy] cream
4 eggs, lightly beaten

Preheat the oven to fairly hot 375°F (Gas Mark 5, 190°C).

Prick the potatoes lightly with a fork. Place the potatoes on the centre shelf in the oven and bake them for 1½ hours.

Remove the potatoes from the oven and cut off a 1-inch lid from the top of each one. Using a teaspoon, scoop out the potato flesh, taking care not to break the skin.

In a medium-sized mixing bowl, mash the potato flesh and butter together, using a fork or potato masher. Add the chives, salt, pepper and nutmeg. Stir in the cream and beat until the ingredients are thoroughly combined. Gradually beat in the eggs.

Stuff equal amounts of the egg and cream filling into each potato. Place the potatoes in a baking dish and return them to the oven. Bake for 10 to 12 minutes, or until the tops of the fillings are lightly browned.

Remove the potatoes from the oven and serve at once.

Potatoes Stuffed with Corn

Baked potatoes are especially popular in the United States, where the Idaho potato is particularly suitable for this form of cooking. This dish is an interesting and different way of serving this popular vegetable, and the potatoes may be topped with strips of pimiento, walnut halves or grated cheese.
Preparation and cooking time: 2 hours
6 SERVINGS
6 large baking potatoes, scrubbed
12 oz. canned cream-style sweetcorn
3 tablespoons finely chopped walnuts
1 teaspoon salt
½ teaspoon white pepper

Preheat the oven to fairly hot 400°F (Gas Mark 6, 200°C).

Prick the potatoes in two or three

places with a kitchen fork. Place them directly on the centre shelf in the oven and bake for 1 hour, or until the potatoes feel soft when squeezed.

Remove the potatoes from the oven. With a sharp knife cut a cross in the top of each potato and press it gently so that it opens. Scoop out the potato flesh, leaving only about a $\frac{1}{8}$-inch thick potato shell. Set the shells aside. Put the potato flesh in a medium-sized mixing bowl and mash it well with a fork or potato masher.

Reduce the oven temperature to moderate 350°F (Gas Mark 4, 180°C).

Add the sweetcorn, nuts, salt and pepper to the potato flesh and beat the mixture until all the ingredients are well blended.

Spoon the sweetcorn mixture back into the potato shells. Place the stuffed potatoes on a baking sheet and bake in the oven for a further 15 to 20 minutes.

Remove from the oven and garnish each stuffed potato with a parsley sprig, strips of pimiento, a walnut half or grated cheese. Serve at once.

New Potatoes in Cream

A delicate blend of tender young potatoes in a thick creamy sauce makes this a superb accompaniment to literally any savoury dish.

Preparation and cooking time: 1 hour
4 SERVINGS

1 lb. new potatoes, scrubbed
2 pints [5 cups] water
2 teaspoons salt
8 fl. oz. double cream [1 cup heavy cream]
$\frac{1}{2}$ teaspoon white pepper
$\frac{1}{2}$ teaspoon grated nutmeg
1 tablespoon snipped fresh chives

Put the potatoes into a large saucepan. Pour in the water and add 1 teaspoon of the salt. Place the pan over moderately high heat and bring the water to the boil. Reduce the heat to moderate and cook the potatoes for 15 to 20 minutes, or until they are just tender. Remove the pan from the heat and drain the potatoes in a colander.

Place the potatoes in the top half of a double saucepan or in a heatproof bowl placed over a saucepan half full of boiling water. Pour the cream over the potatoes and gently stir in the remaining salt, the pepper and nutmeg.

Cook the potatoes gently over low heat for 10 minutes, stirring occasionally.

Turn the potatoes into a warmed serving dish. Sprinkle over the chives and serve at once.

Pommes de Terre Lyonnaise
LYONNAISE POTATOES

French cuisine is not just rich sauces and elegant pastries – it is a special attitude towards food. Pommes de Terre Lyonnaise (pohm d'tair lee-oh-nayz) is an excellent example of this French 'magic' which can transform a simple, homely dish into a delicious vegetable accompaniment.

Preparation and cooking time: 45 minutes
4 SERVINGS

6 medium-sized potatoes, scrubbed
1$\frac{1}{2}$ pints [3$\frac{3}{4}$ cups] water
1$\frac{1}{2}$ teaspoons salt
2 oz. [$\frac{1}{4}$ cup] butter or margarine
1 medium-sized onion, sliced
1 teaspoon black pepper

Put the potatoes into a large saucepan. Pour in the water and add 1 teaspoon of the salt. Place the pan over moderately high heat and bring the water to the boil. Reduce the heat to moderate and cook for 10 minutes. Drain the potatoes in a colander and cut them into cubes.

In a large frying-pan, melt the butter or margarine over moderate heat. When the foam subsides, add the potato cubes and, turning occasionally, cook them for 8 to 10 minutes, or until they begin to brown.

Add the onion, the remaining salt and the pepper to the pan. Continue to cook, stirring occasionally, for a further 8 minutes, or until the onion is soft and translucent but not brown.

Turn the potatoes and onion into a warmed serving dish and serve.

Sweetcorn and Mushrooms

A super blend of tastes, Sweetcorn and Mushrooms may be served as an unusual first course for a dinner party, or as a vegetable accompaniment.

Preparation and cooking time: 30 minutes
4 SERVINGS

4 large 'umbrella' mushrooms, wiped clean
1 oz. [2 tablespoons] butter or margarine, cut into 4 pieces
5 oz. canned sweetcorn, drained
$\frac{1}{2}$ teaspoon salt
$\frac{1}{2}$ teaspoon black pepper

Preheat the grill [broiler] to moderate.

Remove the stalks from the mushrooms. Chop the stalks and set them aside in a small mixing bowl. Grill [broil] the mushroom caps, skin sides up, for 5 to 7 minutes. Remove from the grill [broiler] and turn the mushrooms over. Dot each one with a piece of butter or margarine. Set aside.

Add the sweetcorn, salt and pepper to the chopped mushroom stalks and mix well to blend. Spoon approximately one-quarter of the sweetcorn mixture on to each mushroom cap.

Return the mushrooms to the grill [broiler] and cook for a further 5 to 7 minutes, or until the stuffing turns brown.

Remove from the heat and serve.

Buttered Spinach

Spinach is a vegetable rich in Vitamin C. This is a simple and basic method of preparation.

Preparation and cooking time: 20 minutes
4 SERVINGS

2 lb. spinach, washed, drained and chopped
2 pints [5 cups] water
1$\frac{1}{2}$ teaspoons salt
$\frac{1}{2}$ teaspoon black pepper
$\frac{1}{2}$ teaspoon grated nutmeg
1$\frac{1}{2}$ oz. [3 tablespoons] butter

Put the spinach into a large saucepan. Pour in the water and add 1 teaspoon of the salt. Place the pan over moderately high heat and bring the water to the boil. Reduce the heat to moderate and cook the spinach for 10 minutes or until it is tender. Remove the pan from the heat and drain the spinach in a colander.

Using the back of a wooden spoon, press the spinach to extract all excess liquid.

Put the spinach into a warmed serving dish. Stir in the remaining salt, the pepper, nutmeg and butter.

Serve as soon as the butter has melted.

Tomatoes with Herbs

This classic and aromatic French vegetable dish is superb served with a bean casserole.

Preparation and cooking time: 40 minutes
4 SERVINGS

8 medium-sized tomatoes
1 teaspoon salt
1 teaspoon white pepper
2 oz. [$\frac{1}{4}$ cup] butter or margarine
2 tablespoons fresh breadcrumbs
2 teaspoons chopped fresh parsley
$\frac{3}{4}$ teaspoon dried chervil
$\frac{1}{4}$ teaspoon dried tarragon

Halve the tomatoes and sprinkle them with the salt and pepper. Set aside.

In a medium-sized frying-pan, melt 1$\frac{1}{2}$ ounces [3 tablespoons] of the butter or margarine over moderate heat. When the foam subsides, place the tomatoes in the pan, cut sides down. Reduce the heat to low and cook the tomatoes gently for 4 minutes. Using a slotted spoon, turn the tomato halves over and cook them for a further 3 minutes. With the slotted spoon transfer the tomatoes to a warmed, shallow serving dish. Keep them warm.

Put the remaining butter or margarine into the frying-pan and melt it over low heat. When the foam subsides, add the breadcrumbs. Cook gently, stirring constantly, for 2 minutes. Stir in the parsley, chervil and tarragon.

Remove the pan from the heat and spoon the breadcrumbs and herb mixture on top of the tomatoes. Serve at once.

Caramelized Tomatoes

A colourful and slightly sweet dish, Caramelized Tomatoes may be served as an accompaniment or as a light first course.
Preparation and cooking time: 20 minutes
4 SERVINGS

4 large tomatoes
8 teaspoons dark brown sugar
1 oz. [2 tablespoons] butter or margarine, cut into 8 small pieces
1 bunch of watercress, washed and shaken dry

Preheat the grill [broiler] to high.

Cut the tomatoes in half and squeeze them gently to remove a little of the liquid. Place them, cut sides down, on kitchen paper towels to drain for 2 minutes.

Arrange the tomatoes, cut sides up, on the grill [broiler] rack. Place a teaspoon of sugar on each tomato half and top with a piece of butter or margarine.

Place the tomatoes under the grill [broiler] and cook for 6 to 8 minutes or until the butter has melted and the sugar has caramelized.

Remove from the heat and transfer the tomatoes to a warmed serving dish. Garnish with the watercress and serve.

Pumpkin with Green Beans

An unusual and colourful dish, Pumpkin with Green Beans makes an excellent accompaniment to risottos or omelets.
Preparation and cooking time: 45 minutes
4-6 SERVINGS

1½ lb. pumpkin, peeled and cut into 2-inch cubes
4 pints [5 pints] water
2 teaspoons salt
1 lb. green beans, trimmed
4 fl. oz. [½ cup] vegetable oil

Put the pumpkin into a large saucepan. Pour over half of the water and add 1

teaspoon of salt. Place the pan over moderately high heat and bring the water to the boil. Reduce the heat to moderate and cook the pumpkin for 20 minutes, or until it is just tender. Remove the pan from the heat and drain the pumpkin in a colander. Set aside.

Meanwhile, put the green beans into a large saucepan. Pour in the remaining water and add the remaining salt. Place the pan over moderately high heat and bring the water to the boil. Reduce the heat to moderate and cook the green beans for 20 minutes, or until they are tender. Remove the pan from the heat. Drain the beans in a colander. Arrange them on the bottom of a large, warmed serving dish and keep warm. Set aside.

In a large frying-pan, heat the oil over moderate heat. When the oil is hot, add the pumpkin cubes. Cook them, stirring and turning occasionally, for 12 to 15 minutes, or until they are lightly browned. With a slotted spoon, transfer the pumpkin cubes to the serving dish with the green beans. Serve at once.

Turnips in Sour Cream

Sour cream and paprika turn this rather ordinary vegetable into something special.
Preparation and cooking time: 1 hour
6 SERVINGS

1½ lb. small turnips, peeled and quartered
1 small onion, sliced
2 pints [5 cups] water
2 teaspoons salt
1 oz. [2 tablespoons] butter or margarine, softened
1 teaspoon black pepper
1 teaspoon paprika
3 fl. oz. [⅜ cup] sour cream
1 oz. [¼ cup] fine dry breadcrumbs
1 oz. [¼ cup] Cheddar cheese, grated

Put the turnips and onion into a large saucepan. Pour in the water and add 1 teaspoon of salt. Place the pan over moderately high heat and bring the water to the boil. Reduce the heat to moderate and cook the turnips and onion for 20 to 25 minutes or until the turnips are tender.

Remove the pan from the heat and drain the vegetables in a colander. Put the turnips and onion into a large mixing bowl and set aside.

Preheat the grill [broiler] to moderate. Grease a flameproof baking dish with 1 tablespoon of the butter or margarine. Set aside.

Add the remaining salt, the pepper and paprika to the turnips and mash the mixture with a fork or potato masher.

Stir in the sour cream and mix well to blend. Transfer the turnip mixture to the baking dish, spreading it out evenly.

In a small bowl, combine the remaining butter or margarine, the breadcrumbs and cheese, rubbing them together with your fingertips. Sprinkle the mixture on top of the turnip mixture.

Put the baking dish under the grill [broiler] and grill [broil] for 8 to 10 minutes, or until the topping is brown.

Remove from the heat and serve.

Steamed Mixed Vegetables

This mixture of courgettes [zucchini], red and green peppers, potatoes, mushrooms and onion may be served as a light luncheon dish or as an accompaniment to an omelet.
Preparation and cooking time: 35 minutes
8 SERVINGS

4 fl. oz. [½ cup] olive oil
2 small courgettes [zucchini], trimmed, washed and cut into ¼-inch slices
1 red pepper, white pith removed, seeded and cut into strips
1 green pepper, white pith removed, seeded and cut into strips
1 medium-sized onion, sliced
1 garlic clove, crushed
1 green chilli, seeds removed and chopped
2 medium-sized potatoes, cooked and cut into ¼-inch slices
3 large mushrooms, wiped clean and sliced
1 teaspoon dried tarragon
½ teaspoon dried thyme
1 teaspoon salt
½ teaspoon black pepper
1 tablespoon chopped fresh parsley

In a large frying-pan, heat the oil over moderate heat. When the oil is hot, add the courgette [zucchini] slices, red and green peppers, onion, garlic, chilli and potatoes to the pan. Cook them, stirring occasionally, for 10 minutes or until the vegetables are lightly and evenly browned.

Add the mushrooms, tarragon, thyme, salt and pepper to the pan and stir to mix. Continue cooking for 2 minutes.

Transfer the vegetable mixture to the top half of a steamer or to a large heat-proof bowl. Place the pan or bowl over a saucepan half full of boiling water. Cover the pan or bowl with a lid or aluminium foil and steam the vegetable mixture for 10 minutes or until the vegetables are tender.

Turn the vegetable mixture into a warmed serving dish. Sprinkle the parsley over the top and serve.

Stews, Casseroles and Savoury Bakes

There are a whole new range of superb recipes in this section to tempt you – why not make a Mixed Cheese Pie, a wholemeal pizza, a delicious ratatouille with eggs, a versatile vegetable flan or a trayful of miraculous bouchées!

Most of the main dishes in this section have protein content derived from eggs, nuts, cheese and pulses – all familiar foods. One ingredient which may not be so familiar, but which is well worth trying, is Textured Vegetable Protein (T.V.P.). It can be bought in health food stores, in different meat flavours. It is also available hydrated (reconstituted) in cans or dried in packages. You will find it a very tasty and interesting substitute for meat.

Wholemeal flour is suggested for pastry-making, although you may, of course, use ordinary plain flour. If you do use wholemeal flour, remember to sift out the tiny bran particles before use.

There are plenty of delicious recipes here to delight all creative cooks – especially those who have always thought that a sustaining main dish *had* to include meat.

Pisto

MIXED VEGETABLE STEW

This vegetable stew has no liquid added to it because there should be sufficient juices in the vegetables themselves to keep it moist; however, should the stew be too dry, add 2 to 3 tablespoons of vegetable stock or red wine.

Preparation and cooking time: 1 hour

6 SERVINGS

3 fl. oz. [⅜ cup] olive oil
3 medium-sized onions, thinly sliced
2 garlic cloves, crushed
2 medium-sized potatoes, scrubbed and finely chopped
3 medium-sized courgettes [zucchini], trimmed, washed and cut into ¼-inch slices
1 medium-sized red pepper, white pith removed, seeded and sliced
1 medium-sized green pepper, white pith removed, seeded and sliced
6 tomatoes, blanched, peeled, seeded and chopped
½ teaspoon salt
½ teaspoon black pepper
2 teaspoons dried basil

In a large saucepan, heat the oil over moderate heat. When the oil is hot, add the onions, garlic, potatoes and cour-gette [zucchini] slices. Cook them, stirring occasionally, for 10 minutes, or until the courgette [zucchini] slices are very light brown. Add the red and green peppers, tomatoes, salt, pepper and basil and stir to mix. Reduce the heat to very low. Cover the pan and simmer for 30 minutes, or until all the vegetables are very tender.

Remove the pan from the heat and turn the stew into a warmed serving dish. Serve immediately.

Bean and Fruit Stew

A delicious yet light main dish, Bean and Fruit Stew is as good cold as it is hot. Serve with crusty bread and pitchers of cool cider for an excellent summer lunch.

Preparation and cooking time: 1½ hours

6 SERVINGS

8 oz. dried white haricot beans, soaked overnight and drained
4 pints [5 pints] Dark Vegetable Stock
1 lb. French beans, trimmed and washed
1 lb. carrots, scraped and sliced
2 medium-sized potatoes, scrubbed and quartered
3 oz. [⅜ cup] butter or margarine
2 medium-sized onions, sliced
8 fl. oz. [1 cup] cider
½ teaspoon black pepper
½ teaspoon grated nutmeg
½ teaspoon dried marjoram
½ teaspoon dried basil
1 lb. tart apples, peeled, cored and cut into large cubes
1 banana, sliced
2 oz. fresh or canned and drained pineapple, chopped
6 oz. canned prunes, stoned and drained

Put the haricot beans into a large saucepan. Pour over half of the stock. Place the pan over moderately high heat and bring the stock to the boil. Reduce the heat to moderate and cook the beans for 45 minutes, or until they are just tender.

Add the French beans, carrots and potatoes to the beans in the saucepan. Pour over the remaining stock. Increase the heat to moderately high and bring the stock back to the boil. Reduce the heat to moderate and cook the vegetables for 15 to 20 minutes, stirring occasionally, or until they are tender.

Meanwhile, in a small saucepan, melt the butter or margarine over moderate heat. When the foam subsides, add the onions. Fry them, stirring occasionally, for 5 to 7 minutes, or until they are soft and translucent but not brown. Add the onions to the beans and vegetables, stir to mix, and continue cooking, stirring occasionally, for a further 5 minutes. Pour in the cider and the pepper, nutmeg, marjoram and basil. Taste and add salt if necessary. Stir well to mix and bring the liquid to the boil. Reduce the heat to low and stir in the apples. Cover the casserole and simmer, stirring occasionally, for 10 minutes.

Stir in the banana, pineapple and prunes and continue simmering the stew for 5 minutes.

Remove the casserole from the heat and serve at once. If you wish to serve the stew cold, allow it to cool to room temperature. Then place the casserole in the refrigerator and chill the stew for 30 minutes before serving.

Family Hotpot

This is a sustaining dish for a family supper and you may substitute other vegetables if you wish.
Preparation and cooking time: 1¾ hours
4-6 SERVINGS

1 oz. [2 tablespoons] plus 1 teaspoon butter or margarine
2 oz. [½ cup] T.V.P. mince
2 teaspoons yeast extract dissolved in 10 fl. oz. [1¼ cups] boiling water
2 lb. potatoes, scrubbed and thinly sliced
1 teaspoon salt
½ teaspoon black pepper
6 oz. red lentils, soaked in cold water for 3 hours and drained
2 large onions, sliced and pushed out into rings
1 pint [2½ cups] boiling Dark Vegetable Stock
1 oz. [⅓ cup] dry breadcrumbs
1 oz. [¼ cup] Cheddar cheese, grated

Preheat the oven to moderate 350°F (Gas Mark 4, 180°C). Grease a medium-sized baking dish with the teaspoon of butter or margarine. Set aside.

Put the T.V.P. mince into a medium-sized saucepan and stir in the yeast extract liquid. Place the pan over moderate heat, cover and hydrate the T.V.P. for 5 minutes.

Arrange about one-third of the potato slices on the bottom of the baking dish and sprinkle them with half of the salt and pepper. Cover with half of the lentils, half of the onions and half of the T.V.P. Add a second layer of potato slices and the remaining salt and pepper, then the remaining lentils, onions and T.V.P. Top with the remaining potato slices. Pour the stock into the baking dish.

In a small mixing bowl, combine the breadcrumbs and cheese together and

sprinkle the mixture on top of the potato slices. Cut the remaining butter or margarine into small pieces and dot them on top of the breadcrumb-and-cheese mixture.

Put the dish in the oven and bake for 1 to 1¼ hours, or until the potatoes are very tender when pierced with the point of a sharp knife.

Remove the dish from the oven and serve at once.

Golden Corn Bake

Golden Corn Bake is delicious hot or cold. If you want to serve it cold, glaze it with a white grape juice jelly [gelatine] (see the Salads Section). Let the jelly [gelatine] set and then serve the bake surrounded by a green salad.
Preparation and cooking time: 1½ hours
6 SERVINGS

1 teaspoon butter or margarine
2 oz. [1 cup] plus 1 tablespoon fresh wholemeal breadcrumbs
12 oz. canned sweetcorn, drained
8 oz. [1⅓ cups] ground cashew nuts
3 oz. [1½ cups] millet flakes
2 medium-sized onions, finely chopped
2 medium-sized apples, peeled, cored and grated
1 teaspoon dried marjoram
1 teaspoon dried thyme
2 eggs
1 teaspoon prepared English mustard
½ teaspoon garlic powder
½ teaspoon salt
¼ teaspoon black pepper
10 fl. oz. [1¼ cups] Light Vegetable Stock

Preheat the oven to fairly hot 375°F (Gas Mark 5, 190°C). Lightly grease a baking dish with the teaspoon of butter or margarine. Coat the inside of the dish with the tablespoon of breadcrumbs, pressing them on with your fingertips, and shake out any excess. Set aside.

In a large mixing bowl, combine the sweetcorn, cashew nuts, remaining breadcrumbs, the millet flakes, onions, apples, marjoram and thyme, beating well to blend.

In a small mixing bowl, beat the eggs, mustard, garlic powder, salt, pepper and vegetable stock together with a fork. Add the stock mixture to the sweetcorn mixture, beating well until the ingredients are thoroughly blended.

Pour the sweetcorn mixture into the baking dish and place it in the oven. Bake for 1 hour, or until the mixture is 'set'.

Remove from the oven and serve at once.

Ghuvetch

This hearty vegetable stew is an adaptation of a traditional Romanian dish. Other vegetables may be substituted if you wish.
Preparation and cooking time: 1½ hours
6 SERVINGS

1 small cauliflower, trimmed, washed and broken into flowerets
3 medium-sized potatoes, scrubbed and quartered
2 medium-sized carrots, scraped and quartered
1 small turnip, peeled and cut into 2-inch cubes
2 pints [5 cups] Dark Vegetable Stock
2½ teaspoons salt
4 fl. oz. [½ cup] vegetable oil
2 medium-sized onions, thinly sliced
2 garlic cloves, crushed
1 green or red pepper, white pith removed, seeded and sliced
3 celery stalks, cut into 1-inch pieces
8 oz. fresh green beans, cut into 2-inch pieces
4 oz. fresh or frozen and thawed green peas
14 oz. canned peeled tomatoes
1 tablespoon dried dill leaves
½ teaspoon black pepper
1 teaspoon cornflour [cornstarch] dissolved in 1 tablespoon water

Put the cauliflower, potatoes, carrots and turnip into a large saucepan. Pour over the stock and add 2 teaspoons of the salt. Place the pan over moderately high heat and bring the stock to the boil. Reduce the heat to moderate, cover the pan and cook the vegetables for 8 to 10 minutes or until they are just tender. Drain the vegetables, reserving 8 fluid ounces [1 cup] of the cooking liquid. Return the vegetables to the saucepan with the reserved cooking liquid. Set aside and keep warm.

In a large frying-pan, heat the oil over moderate heat. When the oil is hot, add the onions, garlic, green or red pepper and celery. Fry them, stirring occasionally, for 5 to 7 minutes, or until the onions are soft and translucent but not brown. Add the beans, peas, tomatoes and their can juice, the dill, remaining salt and the pepper to the pan. Stir well and bring the mixture to the boil. Stir the pepper and tomato mixture into the vegetables in the saucepan.

Cover the pan and simmer the stew for 10 to 15 minutes, or until all of the vegetables are very tender. Stir in the dissolved cornflour [cornstarch] and continue simmering, stirring frequently, for 3 minutes, or until the sauce thickens.

Remove from the heat and serve at once.

Chestnut Loaf

A bake with a difference, rich Chestnut Loaf is delicious when coated with a Tomato Sauce and served with a green vegetable. The result will please the eye as well as the palate.

Preparation and cooking time: 1½ hours

4 SERVINGS

1 teaspoon butter or margarine
5 oz. [2½ cups] fresh brown bread-crumbs
10 oz. canned, unsweetened chestnut purée
1 small onion, finely chopped
1 large potato, cooked and mashed
1 small turnip, cooked and mashed
2 eggs, lightly beaten
½ teaspoon salt
½ teaspoon black pepper
½ teaspoon dried sage
½ teaspoon dried basil

Preheat the oven to moderate 350°F (Gas Mark 4, 180°C). Lightly grease a 1-pound loaf tin with the teaspoon of butter or margarine. Set aside.

In a large mixing bowl, combine all the remaining ingredients, beating them well together.

Spoon the mixture into the loaf tin.

Put the loaf tin in the oven and bake for 50 minutes to 1 hour, or until the loaf is brown and firm.

Remove the tin from the oven and allow to cool slightly. Place a warmed serving dish, inverted, over the top of the tin. Reverse the two—the loaf should slide out easily. Serve immediately.

Wholewheat and Vegetable Roast

This Wholewheat and Vegetable Roast may be made with any seasonal vegetable. Serve it with a Mixed Salad or Cabbage and Pepper Salad for a nourishing and filling meal.

Preparation and cooking time: 1¼ hours

6 SERVINGS

2 fl. oz. [¼ cup] plus 1 teaspoon vegetable oil
1 large onion, finely chopped
8 oz. carrots, scraped and finely chopped
8 oz. turnips, peeled and finely chopped
2 celery stalks, finely chopped
8 oz. [2 cups] wholewheat, soaked overnight and drained
4 oz. [1 cup] soya flour
¾ teaspoon dried thyme
½ teaspoon salt
¼ teaspoon black pepper
2 oz. [½ cup] Cheddar cheese, grated

Preheat the oven to fairly hot 400°F (Gas Mark 6, 200°C). Lightly grease a 1-pound loaf tin with the teaspoon of oil. Set aside.

In a large frying-pan, heat the remaining oil over moderate heat. When it is hot, add the onion. Fry it, stirring occasionally, for 5 to 7 minutes, or until it is soft and translucent but not brown.

Add the carrots, turnips and celery and stir to mix. Continue frying, stirring occasionally, for 12 to 15 minutes, or until the vegetables are just tender.

Remove the pan from the heat and transfer the vegetables to a large mixing bowl. Add the wholewheat, soya flour, thyme, salt and pepper and blend the ingredients together thoroughly until a sticky batter is formed.

Spoon the batter into the greased tin and sprinkle the cheese on top. Place the tin in the oven and bake for 45 minutes or until a knife inserted into the centre of the roast comes out clean.

Remove the tin from the oven and turn the roast out on to a warmed serving dish. Cool slightly before serving.

Savoury Hazel Bake

Serve this nourishing hazel bake hot with Petits Pois à la Française or cold with a Mixed Salad—either way it is delicious.

Preparation and cooking time: 1 hour 50 minutes

6 SERVINGS

2 oz. [½ cup] T.V.P. mince
2 teaspoons yeast extract, dissolved in 10 fl. oz. [1¼ cups] boiling Dark Vegetable Stock
2 teaspoons butter or margarine
2 fl. oz. [¼ cup] corn oil
2 medium-sized onions, chopped
3 tablespoons flour
2 medium-sized carrots, scraped and grated
½ small turnip, peeled and grated
4 oz. [⅔ cup] hazelnuts, ground
4 oz. [2 cups] fresh brown bread-crumbs
2 tablespoons rolled oats
1 egg, lightly beaten
2 teaspoons dried thyme
2 teaspoons ground mace
8 fl. oz. [1 cup] hot Onion or Mush-room and Cheese Sauce

Put the T.V.P. mince into a medium-sized saucepan. Stir in the yeast extract and stock mixture. Place the pan over moderate heat and hydrate the mince for 5 minutes. Remove the pan from the heat and transfer the mince to a large mixing bowl. Set aside.

Preheat the oven to moderate 350°F (Gas Mark 4, 180°C). Lightly grease a 2-pound loaf tin with 1 teaspoon of the butter or margarine. Line the tin with greaseproof or waxed paper and grease the paper with the remaining butter or margarine. Set aside.

In a small frying-pan, heat the corn oil over moderate heat. When the oil is hot, add the onions. Fry them, stirring occasionally, for 5 to 7 minutes, or until they are soft and translucent but not brown. Remove the pan from the heat and, with a wooden spoon, stir in the flour, mixing until it is absorbed. Add the onion mixture to the mince.

Add all of the remaining ingredients except the sauce to the mince mixture and beat well until they are blended.

Spoon the mixture into the loaf tin and put the tin in the oven. Bake for 1 hour 10 minutes, or until the top is crisp and brown and a knife inserted into the centre of the loaf comes out clean.

Remove the tin from the oven and allow to cool slightly. Turn the loaf out of the tin on to a heated serving dish. Pour over the sauce and serve at once.

Brazil Ring Bake

Serve this nutty bake with baked potatoes and a green salad for a nutritious and interesting meal.

Preparation and cooking time: 1½ hours

4-6 SERVINGS

1 teaspoon butter or margarine
2 tablespoons fine dry breadcrumbs
6 medium-sized tomatoes, blanched, peeled, seeded and chopped
8 oz. [1⅓ cups] Brazil nuts, ground
5 oz. [2½ cups] fresh brown breadcrumbs
2 tablespoons soya flour
4 tablespoons skimmed milk powder
2 tablespoons rolled oats
3 fl. oz. [⅜ cup] canned or bottled tomato juice
2 teaspoons dried basil
1 teaspoon dried thyme
1 teaspoon salt
4 oz. hot cooked broccoli

Preheat the oven to fairly hot 375°F (Gas Mark 5, 190°C). Grease a medium-sized ring mould with the butter or margarine. Lightly coat the inside of the mould with the dry breadcrumbs, pressing them on with your fingertips and shaking out any excess. Set aside.

In a large mixing bowl, mash the tomatoes with a wooden spoon. Add all of the other ingredients, except the broccoli, and beat well to blend.

Spoon the mixture into the ring mould

pressing it down well. Place the mould in the oven and bake for 50 minutes, or until a knife inserted into the centre comes out clean. Remove the mould from the oven and allow it to cool.

Run a knife around the inside of the ring to loosen it. Place a warmed serving dish, inverted, over the top. Holding the two firmly together, reverse them. The ring should slide out easily. Fill the centre with the hot broccoli and serve.

Tajin Naboul

A spicy Tunisian dish, Tajin Naboul may be accompanied by a crisp, cool salad such as Cucumber and Yogurt.
Preparation and cooking time: 1½ hours
4 SERVINGS

3 fl. oz. [⅜ cup] olive oil
2 large onions, sliced
2 medium-sized courgettes [zucchini], trimmed and cut into ¼-inch slices
1 large green pepper, white pith removed, seeded and chopped
1 large red pepper, white pith removed, seeded and chopped
5 tomatoes, blanched, peeled, seeded and chopped
½ teaspoon ground cinnamon
¼ teaspoon cayenne pepper
½ teaspoon ground cumin
½ teaspoon salt
4 fl. oz. [½ cup] water
2 oz. [½ cup] Parmesan cheese, grated
6 eggs, lightly beaten

In a large frying-pan, heat the oil over moderate heat. When the oil is hot, add the onions and courgettes [zucchini]. Cook them, stirring occasionally, for 5 to 7 minutes, or until the onions are soft and translucent but not brown. Add the green and red peppers, tomatoes, cinnamon, cayenne, cumin and salt and stir well to mix. Pour in the water and increase the heat to high. Bring the mixture to the boil. Reduce the heat to low and simmer, stirring occasionally, for 20 minutes, or until most of the liquid has been absorbed. Remove the pan from the heat and transfer the mixture to a large baking dish.

Preheat the oven to moderate 350°F (Gas Mark 4, 180°C).

Stir the cheese into the courgette [zucchini] mixture. When the cheese is incorporated, stir in the eggs.

Put the baking dish in the oven and bake for 40 to 50 minutes, or until the top is brown and the vegetables are tender.

Remove from the oven and serve.

Cauliflower Mould

This attractive and nourishing Cauliflower Mould is steamed like a pudding. Serve it with a flavourful sauce, such as Pepper or Tomato Sauce I or II.
Preparation and cooking time: 2¼ hours
4–6 SERVINGS

4 oz. [½ cup] plus 2 teaspoons butter or margarine
2 tablespoons fine dry breadcrumbs
1 large cauliflower, trimmed, washed and broken into flowerets
2 pints [5 cups] water
1½ teaspoons salt
3 oz. [1½ cups] fresh breadcrumbs
3 fl. oz. single cream [⅜ cup light cream]
4 eggs, separated
½ teaspoon white pepper
½ teaspoon grated nutmeg

Grease a 2-pint [5-cup] pudding basin with 1 teaspoon of butter or margarine. Coat the inside of the mould with the dry breadcrumbs, pressing them on with your fingertips, and shake out any excess. Set aside.

Put the cauliflower flowerets into a large saucepan. Pour in the water and add 1 teaspoon of the salt. Place the pan over moderately high heat and bring the water to the boil. Reduce the heat to moderate, cover the pan and cook the cauliflower for 15 minutes, or until it is just tender. Remove the pan from the heat and drain the cauliflower in a colander. Set aside.

In a small mixing bowl, soak the breadcrumbs in the cream for 5 minutes.

In a medium-sized mixing bowl, cream the 4 ounces [½ cup] of butter or margarine with the egg yolks, beating with a wooden spoon until the mixture is pale and fluffy. Stir in the breadcrumb mixture, the remaining salt, the pepper and nutmeg.

In a large mixing bowl, beat the egg whites with a wire whisk or rotary beater until they form stiff peaks. With a metal spoon, carefully fold the egg whites into the egg yolk mixture.

Arrange the cauliflower in the pudding basin and then pour in the egg mixture.

Cut out a circle of greaseproof or waxed paper 4 inches wider than the basin. Grease the paper with the remaining teaspoon of butter or margarine. Cut out a circle of aluminium foil the same size as the paper circle and place them together, the greased side of the paper away from the foil. Holding them firmly together, make a 1-inch pleat across the centre. Place the pleated circle, foil uppermost, over the basin and tie it on securely with string.

Put the pudding basin into a very large

saucepan. Pour in enough boiling water to come halfway up the sides of the basin. Cover the saucepan and place it over moderately low heat. Steam for 1 hour, adding more boiling water when necessary.

Remove the pan from the heat and remove the pudding basin from the pan. Uncover the basin. Place a serving dish, inverted, over the basin and reverse them. The mould should slide out easily.

Serve at once.

Stuffed Cabbage Leaves in Coconut Sauce

A main dish with a Chinese flavour, cabbage leaves stuffed with a mixture of onions, mushrooms, rice, cheese and ginger and baked in coconut sauce is extremely tasty. Try a crunchy salad with bean sprouts or Chinese Celery to carry out the motif.
Preparation and cooking time: 2¼ hours
4–6 SERVINGS

1 large cabbage, coarse outer leaves removed and washed
3 pints [7½ cups] water
2 teaspoons salt
2 oz. [¼ cup] butter or margarine
2 small onions, sliced
1 garlic clove, crushed
6 oz. mushrooms, wiped clean and sliced
8 oz. [3 cups] cooked long-grain brown rice
4 oz. [1 cup] Cheddar cheese, grated
½ teaspoon ground ginger
10 fl. oz. [1¼ cups] boiling Light Vegetable Stock
4 oz. dessicated coconut [1 cup shredded coconut]

Put the cabbage into a large saucepan. Pour in the water and add the salt. Place the pan over moderately high heat and bring the water to the boil. Reduce the heat to moderate, cover the pan and cook the cabbage for 10 to 15 minutes, or until it is tender. Remove the pan from the heat and drain the cabbage in a colander. Put the cabbage on a plate and remove the larger leaves. Set them aside. Keep the smaller leaves for stock.

Preheat the oven to cool 300°F (Gas Mark 2, 160°C).

In a large frying-pan, melt the butter or margarine over moderate heat. When the foam subsides, add the onions and garlic. Fry them, stirring occasionally, for 5 minutes. Add the mushrooms to the pan and continue to cook, stirring occasionally, for 3 minutes.

Remove the pan from the heat and transfer the mushroom and onion mixture to a large mixing bowl. Stir in the rice, cheese and ginger.

Spread the cabbage leaves out on a flat surface. Spoon 2 or 3 tablespoons of the stuffing on to the end of one leaf and roll it up, envelope fashion, making sure the filling is completely enclosed. Stuff the remaining leaves in the same way.

Arrange the stuffed leaves in a large, shallow baking dish.

In a small mixing bowl, combine the vegetable stock with the coconut, beating with a fork until the mixture is smooth and slightly thick.

Pour the coconut mixture carefully around the stuffed cabbage leaves. Cover the dish with aluminium foil and place it in the oven. Bake for 1 hour.

Remove from the oven and serve at once.

Eggs Ratatouille

An unusual dish for a light supper, Eggs Ratatouille needs no accompaniment other than crusty Wholewheat or Spicy Cheese Bread.

Preparation and cooking time: 1½ hours
4 SERVINGS

2 aubergines [eggplants]
1 tablespoon plus ½ teaspoon salt
1 lb. courgettes [zucchini], trimmed and sliced
2 fl. oz. [¼ cup] olive oil
1 large onion, sliced and pushed out into rings
1 large garlic clove, crushed
1 green pepper, white pith removed, seeded and chopped
1 lb. tomatoes, blanched, peeled, seeded and chopped
¼ teaspoon black pepper
8 oz. mushrooms, wiped clean and sliced
1 oz. [2 tablespoons] butter or margarine
4 eggs

Cut the aubergines [eggplants] into thin slices and place them in a colander. Sprinkle over 1 teaspoon of the salt and leave the aubergines [eggplants] to dégorge for 30 minutes.

Meanwhile, place the courgette [zucchini] slices on a plate and sprinkle over 2 teaspoons of the salt. Leave them to dégorge for 30 minutes.

Rinse the aubergine [eggplant] and courgette [zucchini] slices and dry them with kitchen paper towels.

In a very large saucepan, heat the oil over moderate heat. When the oil is hot, add the onion and garlic. Fry for 2 minutes, stirring occasionally. Stir in the aubergine [eggplant] slices, courgette

[zucchini] slices, green pepper and tomatoes. Sprinkle over the remaining salt and the pepper.

Reduce the heat to moderately low and simmer the vegetables, stirring occasionally, for 20 minutes. Stir in the mushrooms and continue simmering for 20 minutes.

Five minutes before the ratatouille is ready, cook the eggs. In a large frying-pan, melt the butter or margarine over moderate heat. When the foam subsides, break the eggs into the pan. Fry them for 3 to 5 minutes, or until the whites are set.

Spoon the ratatouille on to four individual serving dishes and top each portion with a fried egg. Serve immediately.

Gratin de Fonds d'Artichauts
ARTICHOKES WITH CHEESE SAUCE

An elegant main dish for a dinner party, Gratin de Fonds d'Artichauts (gra-tan d'fohn dahr-tee-shoh) may be served with potatoes and Aniseed Carrots.

Preparation and cooking time: 50 minutes
4–6 SERVINGS

1 teaspoon butter or margarine
1 lb. canned artichoke bottoms, drained
2 tablespoons lemon juice
16 fl. oz. [2 cups] hot Béchamel Sauce
4 oz. [1 cup] Gruyère cheese, grated
1 oz. [¼ cup] Parmesan cheese, grated
½ teaspoon salt
½ teaspoon white pepper
½ teaspoon grated nutmeg

Preheat the oven to moderate 350°F (Gas Mark 4, 180°C). Lightly grease a large baking dish with the butter or margarine.

Arrange the artichoke bottoms in the baking dish and sprinkle them with the lemon juice.

In a large bowl, combine the béchamel sauce with the Gruyère and Parmesan cheeses, salt, pepper and nutmeg, beating with a wooden spoon until the mixture is smooth and thick. Pour the sauce over the artichokes.

Put the dish in the oven and bake for 15 to 20 minutes, or until the artichokes are heated through and the top is lightly browned.

Remove from the oven and serve at once.

Spinach Timbale

A new idea for a vegetable that is often taken for granted, Spinach Timbale is a mixture of spinach, onions, cream and eggs topped with crunchy hazelnuts.

Preparation and cooking time: 1¼ hours
6 SERVINGS

3 lb. spinach, trimmed, washed, drained and chopped
3 pints [7½ cups] water
1½ teaspoons salt
1 oz. [2 tablespoons] plus 1 teaspoon butter or margarine
2 medium-sized onions, finely chopped
1 garlic clove, crushed
6 fl. oz. single cream [¾ cup light cream]
5 eggs, lightly beaten
½ teaspoon white pepper
½ teaspoon grated nutmeg
3 tablespoons finely chopped hazel-nuts

Put the spinach into a large saucepan. Pour in the water and add 1 teaspoon of the salt. Place the pan over moderately high heat and bring the water to the boil. Reduce the heat to moderate and cook the spinach for 7 to 12 minutes, or until it is just tender.

Remove the pan from the heat and drain the spinach in a colander, pressing down on the spinach with the back of a wooden spoon to extract all excess liquid. Put the spinach into a large mixing bowl and set aside.

Preheat the oven to moderate 350°F (Gas Mark 4, 180°C). Lightly grease a deep medium-sized mould with the teaspoon of butter or margarine. Set the mould aside.

In a medium-sized frying-pan, melt the remaining butter or margarine over moderate heat. When the foam subsides, add the onions and garlic. Fry them, stirring occasionally, for 5 to 7 minutes, or until the onions are soft and translucent but not brown. Remove the pan from the heat. Add the mixture to the spinach and mix well.

In a medium-sized mixing bowl, beat the cream and eggs together with a fork. Stir in the remaining salt, the pepper and nutmeg. Stir the egg mixture into the spinach mixture, blending well.

Pour the spinach mixture into the mould. Place the mould in a deep roasting tin. Pour enough boiling water into the tin to come halfway up the sides of the mould. Put the tin in the oven and bake the timbale for 20 to 25 minutes, or until the top has risen and is set.

Remove from the oven, sprinkle the top with the hazelnuts and serve at once.

Green Vegetable Casserole

This casserole of spinach, cabbage, leeks and courgettes [zucchini], coated with an egg and cream custard and topped with a golden layer of cheese and breadcrumbs, needs no accompaniment. Any green vegetables in season may be substituted.

Preparation and cooking time: 1¾ hours

4 SERVINGS

1 lb. spinach, trimmed, washed, drained and chopped
3 pints [7½ cups] water
2 teaspoons salt
1 lb. green cabbage, coarse outer leaves removed, washed and quartered
2 leeks, trimmed, washed and halved
1 teaspoon butter or margarine
3 fl. oz. [⅜ cup] olive oil
3 small courgettes [zucchini], trimmed, washed and cut into ¼-inch slices
2 garlic cloves, crushed
3 eggs, lightly beaten
2 fl. oz. single cream [¼ cup light cream]
½ teaspoon white pepper
¼ teaspoon cayenne pepper
2 oz. [½ cup] Gruyère or Cheddar cheese, grated
1 oz. [½ cup] fresh brown breadcrumbs

Put the spinach into a large saucepan. Pour in half of the water and add half of the salt. Place the saucepan over moderately high heat and bring the water to the boil. Reduce the heat to moderate and cook the spinach for 7 to 12 minutes, or until it is just tender.

Remove the pan from the heat and drain the spinach in a colander, pressing down on the spinach with a wooden spoon to extract any excess liquid. Set the spinach aside in a large mixing bowl.

Meanwhile, put the cabbage and leeks into a large saucepan. Pour in the remaining water and salt. Place the pan over moderately high heat and bring the water to the boil. Reduce the heat to moderate and cook the vegetables for 10 minutes. Remove the pan from the heat and drain the vegetables in a colander. Add the cabbage and leeks to the spinach in the mixing bowl.

Preheat the oven to moderate 350°F (Gas Mark 4, 180°C). Lightly grease a large baking dish with the butter or margarine. Set aside.

In a large frying-pan, heat the olive oil over moderate heat. When the oil is hot, add half of the courgette [zucchini] slices and the garlic. Fry them, turning occasionally, for 8 to 10 minutes, or until the courgettes [zucchini] are lightly browned on both sides. With a slotted spoon, transfer the courgettes [zucchini] to the spinach mixture. Fry the remaining courgette [zucchini] slices in the same way and add them to the spinach mixture.

Chop all of the vegetables very finely and mix them well together. Arrange the mixed vegetables in the baking dish.

In a small mixing bowl, beat the eggs and cream together with a fork. Beat in the pepper and cayenne. Pour the egg mixture over the vegetables in the baking dish.

In another small mixing bowl, combine the cheese and breadcrumbs. Sprinkle this mixture over the vegetables.

Put the dish in the oven and bake for 30 to 35 minutes, or until the topping is melted and brown and the vegetables are very tender.

Remove the dish from the oven and serve at once.

Courgette [Zucchini] Casserole

Serve this colourful casserole of courgettes [zucchini], mushrooms, tomatoes and sour cream with wholemeal noodles or spaghetti.

Preparation and cooking time: 1 hour

4 SERVINGS

4 oz. [½ cup] butter or margarine
6 medium-sized courgettes [zucchini], trimmed, washed and cut into ¼-inch slices
2 garlic cloves, crushed
8 oz. mushrooms, wiped clean and sliced
14 oz. canned peeled tomatoes, drained and chopped
2 oz. [1 cup] fresh brown breadcrumbs
8 fl. oz. [1 cup] sour cream
1 tablespoon chopped almonds
1 teaspoon paprika
2 oz. [½ cup] Parmesan cheese, grated

Preheat the oven to moderate 350°F (Gas Mark 4, 180°C).

In a large frying-pan, melt 3 ounces [⅜ cup] of the butter or margarine over moderate heat. When the foam subsides, add as many courgette [zucchini] slices to the pan as it will hold in one layer. Cook them, stirring occasionally, for 8 to 10 minutes, or until they are brown. With a slotted spoon, remove the courgettes [zucchini] from the pan and place them in a large mixing bowl. Keep them warm while you fry the remaining slices in the same way. Set the courgettes [zucchini] aside.

Add the remaining butter or margarine to the frying-pan and melt it over moderate heat. When the foam subsides, add the garlic and mushrooms to the pan. Fry them, stirring frequently, for 3 minutes. Add the tomatoes and continue cooking, stirring occasionally, for 3 minutes.

Stir in the breadcrumbs, sour cream, almonds and paprika and mix well. Cook for 1 minute. Remove the pan from the heat and add the tomato mixture to the courgettes [zucchini]. Mix well and spoon the mixture into a large casserole.

Sprinkle the top generously with the grated cheese. Place the casserole in the oven and bake for 30 minutes.

Remove the casserole from the oven and serve.

Stuffed Green Peppers

Serve Stuffed Green Peppers with Green Beans Hungarian-Style or Mushrooms and Carrots in Potato Nests for a substantial meal.

Preparation and cooking time: 1½ hours

4 SERVINGS

4 large green peppers
2½ pints [6¼ cups] water
2 teaspoons salt
2 oz. [¼ cup] butter or margarine
2 medium-sized onions, finely chopped
2 garlic cloves
4 oz. mushrooms, wiped clean and sliced
1 large apple, peeled, cored and chopped
2 oz. [1 cup] fresh brown breadcrumbs
6 oz. canned cream-style sweetcorn
½ teaspoon black pepper
½ teaspoon paprika
1 tablespoon olive oil
2 tablespoons melted butter or margarine

Slice off about a ½-inch lid from the stem end of each pepper. Scoop out the white pith and seeds and dry the insides with kitchen paper towels.

In a large saucepan, bring the water to the boil over high heat. Reduce the heat to moderate and add the salt and the green peppers. Cook for 15 minutes. Remove the pan from the heat and drain the peppers in a colander. Set aside.

Preheat the oven to moderate 350°F (Gas Mark 4, 180°C).

In a large frying-pan, melt the butter or margarine over moderate heat. When the foam subsides, add the onions and garlic. Fry them, stirring occasionally, for 5 to 7 minutes, or until the onions are soft and translucent but not brown. Add the mushrooms and apple and continue to cook, stirring occasionally, for 3 minutes. Stir in the breadcrumbs, sweetcorn, remaining salt, the pepper and paprika. Cook for 1 minute. Remove the pan from the heat.

Coat a shallow baking dish, large enough to hold the four peppers, with the olive oil. Place the peppers in the dish and stuff each one generously with the mushroom and sweetcorn filling. Sprinkle the melted butter or margarine over the stuffed peppers.

Put the dish in the oven and bake the stuffed peppers for 15 to 20 minutes, or until the filling is brown and crisp.

Remove from the oven and serve at once.

Cheese and Sweetcorn Bake

Try this filling and tasty main dish with a Summer Garden Salad, or a Tomato Salad, and black olives for a colourful and delicious meal.

Preparation and cooking time: 1 hour 10 minutes

4–6 SERVINGS

2 teaspoons vegetable oil
2 oz. [1 cup] millet flakes
2 eggs, lightly beaten
4 tablespoons milk
2 teaspoons paprika
½ teaspoon salt
4 oz. [1 cup] Lancashire or any hard white cheese, grated
1½ lb. canned and drained or frozen and thawed sweetcorn
1 medium-sized onion, finely chopped

Preheat the oven to fairly hot 375°F (Gas Mark 5, 190°C). Lightly grease a medium-sized baking dish with the oil. Set aside.

In a large mixing bowl, beat together the millet flakes, eggs, milk, paprika and salt with a wire whisk or rotary beater. Add the cheese, sweetcorn and onion and blend the ingredients together thoroughly.

Spoon the mixture into the baking dish and cover it with aluminium foil. Place the dish in a roasting tin one-quarter full of hot water. Put the tin, with the dish, in the oven and bake for 50 minutes.

Remove from the oven and serve immediately, straight from the baking dish.

Aubergines [Eggplants] Parmesan

The aubergine [eggplant] is very popular in southern Europe and forms the basis of many southern French and Italian dishes. This recipe is adapted from perhaps the most famous Italian aubergine [eggplant] recipe and makes a warmly satisfying meal accompanied only by crusty bread and a light red Chianti wine.

Preparation and cooking time: 2½ hours

3 small aubergines [eggplants]
2½ teaspoons salt
6 fl. oz. [¾ cup] olive oil
2 medium-sized onions, sliced
2 garlic cloves, crushed
14 oz. canned peeled tomatoes
4 teaspoons chopped fresh basil, or 2 teaspoons dried basil
½ teaspoon black pepper
6 oz. mozzarella cheese, thinly sliced
2 oz. [½ cup] Parmesan cheese, grated

Cut the aubergines [eggplants] into slices. Place them in a colander and sprinkle them with 2 teaspoons of the salt. Leave them to dégorge for 30 minutes. Dry the aubergine [eggplant] slices on kitchen paper towels and set aside.

Meanwhile, in a medium-sized saucepan, heat 1½ fluid ounces [3 tablespoons] of the oil over moderate heat. When the oil is hot, add the onions and garlic to the pan. Fry them, stirring occasionally, for 5 to 7 minutes, or until the onions are soft and translucent but not brown. Add the tomatoes, with the can juice, half of the basil, the remaining salt and the pepper. Stir well to mix and bring the liquid to the boil. Reduce the heat to low and simmer the sauce, stirring occasionally, for 40 minutes.

Remove the pan from the heat and keep the sauce warm.

Preheat the oven to moderate 350°F (Gas Mark 4, 180°C).

In a large frying-pan, heat 1½ fluid ounces [3 tablespoons] of the olive oil over moderate heat. When the oil is hot, add about one-third of the aubergine [eggplant] slices to the pan. Fry them, turning occasionally, for 8 to 10 minutes, or until they are evenly browned on both sides. With a slotted spoon, remove the aubergine [eggplant] slices from the pan. Keep them warm while you fry the remaining slices in the same way, using the rest of the olive oil.

Arrange about one-third of the aubergine [eggplant] slices on the bottom of a medium-sized, deep baking dish. Top with half of the mozzarella slices and sprinkle with one-quarter of the grated Parmesan and half of the remaining basil. Make a second layer of aubergine [eggplant] slices and top with the remaining mozzarella, another quarter of the Parmesan and the rest of the basil. Top with the remaining aubergine [eggplant] slices. Pour the tomato sauce into the casserole and sprinkle the remaining grated Parmesan on top.

Place the baking dish in the oven and bake for 45 minutes, or until the aubergines [eggplants] are cooked and tender and the cheese has completely melted.

Remove from the oven and serve.

Cheddar and Potato-Turnip Pie

Layers of potato and turnip purée and Cheddar cheese with a crisp topping of Parmesan cheese and breadcrumbs make this a sustaining main dish. Serve it with a green vegetable such as spinach.

Preparation and cooking time: 1½ hours

4–6 SERVINGS

1½ lb. potatoes, scrubbed and quartered
2 small turnips, peeled and quartered
2 pints [5 cups] water
2½ teaspoons salt
1 teaspoon black pepper
¼ teaspoon dried thyme
1 large onion, finely grated
1 oz. [2 tablespoons] plus 1 teaspoon butter or margarine
8 oz. Cheddar cheese, thinly sliced
1 oz. [¼ cup] Parmesan cheese, grated
1 oz. [½ cup] fresh brown bread-crumbs

Put the potatoes and turnips into a large saucepan. Pour in the water and add 2 teaspoons of the salt. Place the pan over moderately high heat and bring the water to the boil. Reduce the heat to moderate, half cover the pan and cook the vegetables for 15 to 20 minutes, or until they are tender.

Remove the pan from the heat and drain the vegetables in a colander. Transfer the vegetables to a large mixing bowl.

Add the remaining salt, the pepper, thyme, onion and 1 tablespoon of the butter or margarine. Mash the ingredients together with a fork or potato masher until they are smooth. Set the purée aside.

Preheat the oven to fairly hot 375°F (Gas Mark 5, 190°C). Lightly grease a deep 9-inch pie dish with the teaspoon of butter or margarine.

Spoon half of the potato and turnip purée into the pie dish and spread it out over the bottom. Top with half of the Cheddar slices. Spoon over the remaining potato and turnip purée and cover it with the rest of the Cheddar slices.

In a small mixing bowl, combine the grated cheese and breadcrumbs together. Sprinkle them over the Cheddar slices. Cut the remaining butter or margarine into small pieces and scatter them over the breadcrumb topping.

Put the pie dish into the oven and bake for 35 minutes, or until the topping is golden.

Remove the pie from the oven and serve at once.

Lentil Loaf

Lentils are packed with protein and consequently this delicious loaf is very nutritious. Serve it with a colourful and piquant sauce, baked potatoes and a salad.

Preparation and cooking time: 1½ hours

6 SERVINGS

- 1 oz. [2 tablespoons] **butter or margarine**
- **12 oz. lentils, cooked until the skins split and drained**
- **8 oz.** [2 cups] **Cheddar cheese, grated**
- **2 medium-sized onions, minced**
- **2 oz. mushrooms, wiped clean and thinly sliced**
- **½ teaspoon salt**
- **½ teaspoon black pepper**
- **½ teaspoon ground cloves**
- **1 tablespoon finely chopped fresh parsley**
- **3 oz.** [1 cup] **dry brown breadcrumbs**
- **1 egg, lightly beaten**
- **3 tablespoons double** [heavy] **cream**
- **parsley sprigs (to garnish)**

Preheat the oven to moderate 350°F (Gas Mark 4, 180°C). Grease a 1-pound loaf tin with 1 tablespoon of the butter or margarine. Set aside.

In a large mixing bowl, combine the lentils, cheese, onions and mushrooms, mixing until they are well blended. Stir in the salt, pepper, cloves and parsley. Add the breadcrumbs, egg and cream and beat until all the ingredients are well blended.

Pour the mixture into the loaf tin. Cut the remaining butter or margarine into small pieces and dot them over the top. Place the tin in the oven and bake for 45 to 50 minutes, or until the loaf is firm and a skewer inserted into the centre comes out clean.

Remove the tin from the oven and turn the loaf out on to a warmed serving dish. Garnish with the parsley and serve.

Aubergine [Eggplant] and Courgette [Zucchini] Bake

Aubergines [eggplants] *and courgettes* [zucchini] *complement each other so well, and in this recipe they are combined with tomato sauce and Gruyère cheese to make a delicious bake.*

Preparation and cooking time: 2 hours

6 SERVINGS

- **1 large aubergine** [eggplant]
- **2 teaspoons salt**
- **3 large courgettes** [zucchini], **trimmed, washed and sliced**
- **1 teaspoon vegetable oil**
- **8 fl. oz. [1 cup] olive oil**
- **2 tablespoons dried basil**
- **1 garlic clove, finely chopped**
- **5 oz. tomato purée mixed with 3 fl. oz. [⅜ cup] water, or 8 fl. oz. [1 cup] Tomato Sauce II**
- **8 oz. Gruyère cheese, thinly sliced**
- **1 oz.** [¼ cup] **Parmesan cheese, grated**

Slice the aubergine [eggplant] and place the slices in a colander. Sprinkle over 1 teaspoon of the salt and leave the aubergine [eggplant] to dégorge for 30 minutes.

Meanwhile, place the courgette [zucchini] slices on a plate and sprinkle them with the remaining salt. Leave to dégorge for 30 minutes.

Rinse the aubergine [eggplant] and courgette [zucchini] slices and dry them with kitchen paper towels.

Preheat the oven to fairly hot 375°F (Gas Mark 5, 190°C). Lightly grease a large, deep baking dish with the vegetable oil. Set aside.

In a large frying-pan, heat 2 fluid ounces [¼ cup] of the olive oil over moderate heat. When the oil is hot, add about half of the aubergine [eggplant] slices. Fry them, turning occasionally, for 10 minutes, or until they are lightly browned on both sides. With a slotted spoon, transfer the aubergine [eggplant] slices to the baking dish. Keep them warm while you fry the remaining slices in the same way, using another 2 fluid ounces [¼ cup] of the olive oil. Add them to the baking dish. Sprinkle over 1 tablespoon of the basil and half of the garlic. Set aside.

Add another 2 fluid ounces [¼ cup] of olive oil to the frying-pan and heat it over moderate heat. When the oil is hot, add half of the courgette [zucchini] slices to the pan. Fry them, turning occasionally, for 8 to 10 minutes, or until they are lightly browned on both sides. With a slotted spoon, transfer the courgette [zucchini] slices to the baking dish. Fry the remaining slices in the same way, using the rest of the olive oil, and add them to the baking dish. Sprinkle over the remaining basil and garlic.

Pour the tomato purée mixture or tomato sauce into the baking dish. Top with the Gruyère slices and sprinkle the grated Parmesan on top.

Place the dish in the oven and bake for 30 to 35 minutes, or until the cheese has melted and the top is golden brown.

Remove from the oven and serve at once.

Mushrooms and Almonds with Egg Rolls

This adaptation of a popular Chinese dish is surprisingly simple to prepare. The recipe for basic Savoury Crêpe Batter is in the section on Soufflés, Omelets, Crêpes and Pancakes.

Preparation and cooking time: 2 hours

4 SERVINGS

- **3 tablespoons vegetable oil**
- **1 medium-sized onion, thinly sliced**
- **6 oz. mushrooms, wiped clean and sliced**
- **1 tablespoon soy sauce**
- **1 tablespoon cold water**
- **1 tablespoon cider vinegar**
- **4 oz. canned and drained bean sprouts**
- **2 tablespoons blanched almonds, toasted**

EGG ROLLS

- **sufficient vegetable oil for deep-frying**
- **4 oz. [1 cup] Savoury Crêpe Batter**
- **4 oz. canned and drained bean sprouts, chopped**
- **1 small onion, very finely chopped**
- **3 celery stalks, very finely chopped**
- **¼ teaspoon ground ginger**
- **2 egg whites**

First make the egg rolls. With a pastry brush, lightly coat a small frying-pan with a little of the vegetable oil. Place the pan over moderate heat. When the pan is hot, drop 3 to 4 tablespoons of the crêpe batter into the pan and quickly tilt the pan so that the batter spreads out evenly. Cook for 2 to 3 minutes, or until the underside of the crêpe is brown. Remove the crêpe from the pan and set it aside on a flat lightly floured surface, browned side up. Cook the remaining seven crêpes in the same way.

In a medium-sized mixing bowl, combine the bean sprouts, onion, celery and ginger and mix well. Spoon about 1 tablespoon of the stuffing on to the centre of each crêpe and roll them up, making sure that the filling is completely enclosed.

With a pastry brush, generously coat each rolled-up crêpe with the egg white and set aside.

Fill a large deep-frying pan one-third full of vegetable oil. Place the pan over moderate heat and heat the oil until it reaches a temperature of 360°F on a deep-fat thermometer, or until a cube of stale bread dropped into the oil browns in 50 seconds. Place a few of the egg rolls in a deep-frying basket and lower them into the oil. Fry them for 3 minutes, or until they are deeply browned. Remove the cooked rolls from the pan and drain them on kitchen paper towels. Keep them warm while you fry the remaining rolls in the same way.

When all the egg rolls are cooked, keep them warm.

In a large frying-pan, heat the oil over moderate heat. When the oil is hot, add the onion. Cook it, stirring occasionally, for 5 minutes. Add the mushrooms and, stirring frequently, cook the mushrooms and onion for 3 minutes.

Stir in the soy sauce, mixing briskly until the onion and mushrooms are well coated. Add the water and vinegar and cook, stirring constantly, for 1 minute. Stir in the bean sprouts and bring to the boil.

Remove the pan from the heat and transfer the mushroom mixture to a warmed serving dish. Sprinkle the toasted almonds on top. Arrange the egg rolls decoratively around the mushroom mixture and serve.

Aubergines Farcies Duxelles

BAKED AUBERGINES [EGGPLANTS] STUFFED WITH MUSHROOMS

Aubergines Farcies Duxelles (oh-bair-j-een FAHR-see dook-sell) *may be served with a tomato sauce as a first course or as an accompaniment.*

Preparation and cooking time: 2¼ hours
6 SERVINGS

3 large aubergines [eggplants]
1¼ teaspoons salt
4 tablespoons olive oil
1½ oz. [3 tablespoons] plus 1 teaspoon butter or margarine
1 onion, finely chopped
1 garlic clove, crushed
1 lb. mushrooms, wiped clean and chopped
¼ teaspoon black pepper
6 oz. [¾ cup] cottage cheese
3 tablespoons chopped fresh parsley
¼ teaspoon dried thyme
2 tablespoons grated Parmesan cheese
4 tablespoons dry breadcrumbs parsley sprigs (to garnish)

Cut the aubergines [eggplants] in half, lengthways. With a sharp knife, make cuts in the flesh to within ¼-inch of the skin. Sprinkle the aubergines [eggplants] with 1 teaspoon of the salt and place them, cut sides down, on kitchen paper towels. Leave them to dégorge for 30 minutes.

Preheat the grill [broiler] to moderate.

Squeeze the aubergines [eggplants] to remove as much liquid as possible and dry them on kitchen paper towels. Put the aubergines [eggplants], skin sides down, in a flameproof baking dish. Sprinkle each half with 1 teaspoon of the olive oil. Pour a little water into the dish to cover the bottom.

Place the dish under the grill [broiler] and cook the aubergines [eggplants] for 10 minutes or until they are soft. Remove the dish from the heat.

With a spoon, scoop out the flesh, leaving the skins intact. Roughly chop the flesh and place it in a medium-sized mixing bowl. Set the aubergine [eggplant] skins and flesh aside.

Preheat the oven to fairly hot 400°F (Gas Mark 6, 200°C). Lightly grease a large baking dish with the teaspoon of butter or margarine. Set aside.

In a large frying-pan, heat the remaining oil over moderate heat. Add the onion and garlic. Fry them, stirring occasionally, for 5 to 7 minutes, or until the onion is soft and translucent but not brown.

Add the remaining butter or margarine to the frying-pan. When it has melted, stir in the mushrooms and continue cooking, stirring frequently, for 4 to 5 minutes, or until the mushrooms are tender.

Remove the pan from the heat. Stir the reserved aubergine [eggplant] flesh, remaining salt and the pepper into the onion and mushroom mixture. Set the mixture aside.

In a small mixing bowl, mash the cottage cheese with a kitchen fork. Stir the mashed cottage cheese into the aubergine [eggplant] and mushroom mixture with the parsley and thyme.

Fill the aubergine [eggplant] shells with the cottage cheese and mushroom mixture. Sprinkle over the grated cheese and breadcrumbs. Place the stuffed aubergine [eggplant] shells in the greased baking dish and cover it tightly with aluminium foil.

Place the dish in the oven and bake for 20 minutes. Remove the foil and continue baking for 10 minutes, or until the tops are crisp and golden brown.

Remove the dish from the oven and transfer the aubergines [eggplants] to a warmed serving dish. Garnish with the parsley and serve.

Moroccan Vegetable Couscous

An exotic yet simple to prepare dish, Moroccan Vegetable Couscous will be a delightful centrepiece for a dinner party meal. Serve it with a light salad, crusty brown bread and lots of cool beer or white wine. If you do not have a couscoussier, you can construct a temporary one by placing a cheesecloth-lined colander on top of a saucepan, sealing the space between the colander and the rim of the pan with a twisted, damp cloth. But the best results will be obtained with a couscoussier.

Preparation and cooking time: 3¼ hours
6 SERVINGS

1 lb. couscous
18 fl. oz. [2¼ cups] lukewarm salted water
6 medium-sized courgettes [zucchini], trimmed, washed and sliced in half crosswise, then sliced in half lengthways
2 large green peppers, white pith removed, seeded and sliced
2 large onions, quartered
3 medium-sized potatoes, scrubbed and sliced
1 small turnip, peeled and sliced
4 large carrots, scraped and quartered
3 pints [7½ cups] cold water
3 oz. [⅜ cup] butter or margarine, melted
1 lb. canned chick-peas, drained
4 oz. [⅔ cup] seedless raisins
2 oz. [⅓ cup] blanched almonds
1 lb. tomatoes, quartered
3 garlic cloves, crushed
3 green chillis, seeds removed and finely chopped
2 teaspoons salt
1 teaspoon black pepper
½ teaspoon cayenne pepper
2 teaspoons ground cumin
2 teaspoons paprika
½ teaspoon ground saffron, dissolved in 1 teaspoon hot water
3 teaspoons turmeric
2 teaspoons ground coriander

Put the couscous grains into a large mixing bowl. Pour over 16 fluid ounces [2 cups] of the lukewarm salted water. Leave the couscous to soak for 1 hour, or until it swells slightly. Drain the grains in a fine strainer and set them aside.

Meanwhile, put the courgettes [zucchini], green peppers, onions, potatoes, turnip and carrots into the bottom half of the couscoussier. Pour in 2 pints [5 cups] of the cold water and bring the water to the boil over moderately high heat. Reduce the heat to low, cover the pan and simmer the vegetables for 30 minutes.

Fit the top half, or steamer, on to the

couscoussier and pour the couscous grains into the steamer. Cover the pan and cook the mixture for 40 minutes.

Remove the top half, or steamer, from the couscoussier and transfer the couscous grains to a large mixing bowl. Pour on the melted butter or margarine and remaining lukewarm salted water. Leave the mixture to soak for 15 minutes.

Meanwhile, add the chick-peas, raisins, almonds and tomatoes to the bottom half of the couscoussier and pour in the remaining 1 pint [2½ cups] of cold water. Stir in the garlic, chillis, salt, pepper, cayenne, cumin, paprika, saffron, turmeric and ground coriander and bring the liquid to the boil over moderately high heat. Reduce the heat to low and simmer the mixture for 15 minutes.

Stir the couscous grains, breaking up any lumps that have formed and return the couscous to the top part, or steamer, of the couscoussier. Fit this attachment to the couscoussier again, cover and cook the mixture for a further 20 minutes.

Remove the couscoussier from the heat and remove the top half. Arrange the vegetable mixture in a large, deep serving dish and spoon on some of the cooking liquid. Reserve about 4 fluid ounces [½ cup] of the cooking liquid and discard the rest.

Put the couscous grains into a second serving dish and pour over the reserved cooking liquid. Serve at once.

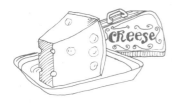

Oeufs de Fromage en Cocotte
BAKED CHEESE EGGS

A delicate and quite delicious snack lunch or supper, Oeufs de Fromage en Cocotte (euf d'froh-mahj on kaw-kaht) may be served with Honey-Glazed Carrots.
Preparation and cooking time: 30 minutes
4 SERVINGS

1 oz. [2 tablespoons] butter or
   margarine
4 eggs
½ teaspoon salt
½ teaspoon black pepper
2 oz. [½ cup] Cheddar cheese, grated

Preheat the oven to fairly hot 400°F (Gas Mark 6, 200°C). Lightly grease four individual ramekins with the butter or margarine.

Break one egg into each ramekin and sprinkle about ⅛ teaspoon of salt and pepper on each egg. Spread one-quarter of the grated cheese over the top of each egg. Place the ramekins in a deep roasting tin and pour in enough boiling water to come halfway up the sides of the ramekins. Put the tin in the oven.

Bake for 15 minutes, or until the eggs have set.

Remove the tin from the oven and serve the eggs at once, in the ramekins.

Stuffed Vine Leaves

This adaptation of a traditional Greek dish has an exotic and subtle flavour. Serve Stuffed Vine Leaves with a mixed salad and a bottle of Roditys to make the occasion a special one.
Preparation and cooking time: 2 hours
4-6 SERVINGS

3 oz. [½ cup] long-grain brown rice,
   washed, soaked in cold water for
   30 minutes and drained
7 fl. oz. [⅞ cup] water
1 teaspoon salt
2 fl. oz. [¼ cup] olive oil
2 medium-sized onions, finely
   chopped
2 garlic cloves, crushed
4 large tomatoes, blanched, peeled,
   seeded and chopped
3 tablespoons crushed toasted pine
   kernels
1 tablespoon cider vinegar
2 teaspoons dried basil
¼ teaspoon red pepper flakes
15 oz. canned vine leaves, drained
4 fl. oz. [½ cup] Tomato Sauce II

Put the rice into a medium-sized saucepan. Pour in the water and add the salt. Place the pan over high heat and bring the water to the boil.

Cover the pan, reduce the heat to low and simmer for 20 to 25 minutes, or until all the water has been absorbed and the rice is tender. Remove the pan from the heat and transfer the rice to a large mixing bowl. Set aside.

Preheat the oven to moderate 350°F (Gas Mark 4, 180°C).

In a medium-sized frying-pan, heat the oil over moderate heat. When the oil is hot, add the onions and garlic. Fry them, stirring occasionally, for 5 to 7 minutes, or until the onions are soft and translucent but not brown. Add the tomatoes, pine kernels, vinegar, basil and red pepper flakes and stir well to blend. Cook the mixture for 3 minutes. Remove the pan from the heat and add the tomato mixture to the rice, stirring well to mix. Set the stuffing aside.

Separate the vine leaves and spread them out on a flat surface. Spoon about 1 tablespoon of the stuffing on to the end of a leaf and roll it up envelope-fashion, making sure the filling is completely enclosed. Stuff the remaining vine leaves in the same way until all of the stuffing has been used up. You should have about five or six leaves left over.

Line a medium-sized baking dish with the leftover leaves and arrange the stuffed leaves on top. Pour over the tomato sauce.

Cover the dish with aluminium foil and place it in the oven. Bake for 20 minutes.

Remove from the oven and serve at once.

Courgettes Farcies aux Amandes
COURGETTES [ZUCCHINI] STUFFED WITH ALMONDS

An elegant vegetable dish, Courgettes Farcies aux Amandes (koor-jet fahr-see oh-zah-mohn) will really impress your guests.
Preparation and cooking time: 1½ hours
4 SERVINGS

4 large or 8 small courgettes
   [zucchini], trimmed
2 oz. [¼ cup] butter or margarine,
   melted
3 tablespoons olive oil
1 medium-sized onion, finely
   chopped
3 oz. [½ cup] ground almonds
4 fl. oz. double cream [½ cup heavy
   cream]
3 oz. [1 cup] fine dry breadcrumbs
3 oz. [¾ cup] Gruyère cheese, grated
½ teaspoon salt
¼ teaspoon pepper
¼ teaspoon mixed herbs
1 egg, lightly beaten

With a sharp knife, cut the courgettes [zucchini] in half lengthways and carefully hollow out the flesh, leaving boat-shaped shells of skin. Set the courgette [zucchini] shells aside.

Chop the courgette [zucchini] flesh. Wrap the flesh in kitchen paper towels and wring it to extract as much liquid as possible. Set the flesh aside.

Preheat the oven to fairly hot 400°F (Gas Mark 6, 200°C). Grease a large shallow baking dish with 1 teaspoon of the melted butter or margarine. Set aside.

In a large frying-pan, heat the oil over moderate heat. Add the onion. Fry it, stirring occasionally, for 5 to 7 minutes, or until it is soft and translucent but not brown. Stir in the chopped courgette [zucchini] flesh and continue to cook, stirring occasionally, for 5 minutes, or until the courgette [zucchini] flesh is lightly browned.

Transfer the mixture to a medium-sized mixing bowl. Add the almonds, cream and half of the breadcrumbs. Using a wooden spoon, beat the ingredients together until they are thoroughly blended. Stir in two-thirds of the cheese, the salt, pepper, mixed herbs and the egg and mix thoroughly. The mixture should be of a thick and firm consistency, so if it is too soft, add more breadcrumbs.

Arrange the courgette [zucchini] shells, skin sides down, in the baking dish. Stuff the courgette [zucchini] shells with the almond-and-cheese mixture and sprinkle the remaining cheese and the rest of the breadcrumbs on top. Spoon the remaining melted butter over the stuffed courgettes [zucchini].

Place the dish in the oven and bake for 25 minutes, or until the top is bubbling and brown.

Remove the dish from the oven and serve.

Cheese Charlotte

This savoury charlotte makes a light and tasty supper dish. Serve it with a crunchy salad and crusty Onion and Herb Loaf.
Preparation and cooking time: 1½ hours
4 SERVINGS

1 teaspoon vegetable oil
1 thick slice of bread, cut into cubes
7 fl. oz. [⅞ cup] milk
8 slices of bread, crusts removed
1½ oz. [3 tablespoons] butter or
    margarine
3 eggs, separated
1½ tablespoons flour
8 oz. [2 cups] Cheddar cheese, grated
½ teaspoon salt
¼ teaspoon grated nutmeg
4 fl. oz. single cream [½ cup light
    cream]

Preheat the oven to moderate 350°F (Gas Mark 4, 180°C). Lightly grease a straight-sided deep baking dish or casserole with the vegetable oil. Set aside.

Put the bread cubes in a shallow dish and sprinkle over half of the milk. In another dish, spread out the bread slices and sprinkle them with the remaining milk. Leave the cubes and slices to soak.

In a large mixing bowl, cream the butter or margarine with a wooden spoon until it is soft. Mix in the egg yolks, one at a time. Stir in the flour. Add the soaked bread cubes, cheese, salt and nutmeg. Blend well and stir in the cream.

In a medium-sized mixing bowl, beat the egg whites with a wire whisk or rotary beater until they form stiff peaks. With a metal spoon, carefully fold them into the cheese mixture.

Line the dish or casserole with the soaked bread slices. Pour the cheese mixture into the dish.

Place the dish in the oven and bake for 35 to 40 minutes, or until the charlotte is puffed up and lightly browned.

Remove the dish from the oven and serve.

Wholemeal Pizza

Pizzas are always popular—both with the family and to serve for an informal supper party. This simple tomato and cheese pizza is very easy to make, and goes well with a tomato salad and red wine.
Preparation and cooking time: 2½ hours
4 SERVINGS

PASTRY
¼ oz. fresh yeast
¼ teaspoon sugar
5 fl. oz. [⅝ cup] lukewarm water
7 oz. [1¾ cups] wholemeal flour
1 teaspoon salt
½ tablespoon olive oil
FILLING
14 oz. canned, peeled tomatoes,
    drained and sliced
½ teaspoon salt
½ teaspoon white pepper
1 tablespoon dried basil
½ teaspoon garlic salt
6 oz. Mozzarella cheese, sliced
8 black olives
1 tablespoon capers

Crumble the yeast into a small mixing bowl and mash in the sugar with a kitchen fork. Add 2 tablespoons of the water and cream the water and yeast together. Set the bowl aside in a warm, draught-free place for 20 minutes, or until the yeast mixture is puffed up and frothy.

Put the flour and salt into a large mixing bowl. Make a well in the centre and pour in the yeast mixture, olive oil and the remaining water. Using your fingers, gradually draw the flour into the liquid. Continue mixing until all the flour is incorporated.

Turn the dough out on to a lightly floured board or marble slab, and knead it for 5 minutes or until it is soft and elastic.

Rinse, thoroughly dry and lightly grease the mixing bowl. Form the dough into a ball and return it to the bowl. Cover with a clean cloth and set aside for 20 to 30 minutes, or until the dough has risen and almost doubled in bulk.

Turn the risen dough out of the bowl

on to a floured surface and knead it for 5 minutes. Roll out the dough to a large circle, about 9- or 10-inches in diameter. Lift the dough on your rolling pin and transfer it to a baking sheet. Leave to rest for 10 minutes.

Preheat the oven to fairly hot 375°F (Gas Mark 5, 190°C).

Push up the edges of the dough so that the filling will not run off.

Arrange the tomato slices over the dough. Sprinkle on the salt, pepper, basil and garlic salt. Spread the cheese slices over the top and sprinkle with the olives and capers.

Place the baking sheet in the oven and bake the pizza for 30 minutes, or until the cheese is melted and lightly browned and the pastry is crisp.

Remove from the oven and serve at once.

Vegetable Bouchées

Light puff pastry cases filled with cashew nuts and mushrooms in a creamy tomato-flavoured sauce, Vegetable Bouchées make a superb luncheon dish.
Preparation and cooking time: 4 hours
12 BOUCHEES

PUFF PASTRY CASES
8 oz. [2 cups] flour
⅛ teaspoon salt
8 oz. [1 cup] butter
1 teaspoon lemon juice
5 fl. oz. [⅝ cup] water
1 egg, lightly beaten with ½
    teaspoon salt
FILLING
8 oz. unsalted cashew nuts
2 tablespoons vegetable oil
2 large onions, sliced
2 garlic cloves, crushed
8 oz. mushrooms, wiped clean and
    sliced
4 tomatoes, blanched, peeled,
    seeded and chopped
2 teaspoons dried basil
1 teaspoon salt
½ teaspoon black pepper
8 fl. oz. [1 cup] Light Vegetable Stock
1 tablespoon flour dissolved in 1
    tablespoon water
2 fl. oz. double cream [¼ cup heavy
    cream]
parsley sprigs (to garnish)

First make the bouchées. Put the flour and salt into a medium-sized mixing bowl. Cut off about 1 tablespoon of the butter. With your fingertips, rub it into the flour. Mix the lemon juice with the water. Make a well in the flour and pour in two-thirds of the liquid. Stir with a table knife until a dough begins to form and add the rest of the liquid if the dough is too dry.

Lightly dust a marble slab, plastic work top or a board with flour. Put the dough on it and knead it for 2 minutes.

Roll out the dough to a square about ½-inch thick. Place the remaining butter between two sheets of greaseproof or waxed paper and flatten it slightly with a rolling pin.

Place the butter in the centre of the dough. Fold the dough up over the butter to enclose it and make a parcel. Wrap the dough in greaseproof or waxed paper and put it in the refrigerator to chill for 15 minutes.

Lightly flour your work surface. Remove the dough from the refrigerator, unwrap it and place it on the work surface with the join facing towards you.

With a strong firm pressure, roll the dough, just to the edge, about 4 times to flatten it.

The dough should be a rectangular shape about ½-inch thick. Fold the dough as carefully as possible into three, bringing the ends to the middle, like a parcel. With your fingertips, press the edges at both ends to seal. Turn the dough around so that one edge faces you. Roll it out again and fold it in three. Wrap it in greaseproof or waxed paper and refrigerate for 15 minutes.

Repeat this process, giving four more 'turns' with a 15 minute rest in the refrigerator after each two turns. If the dough looks streaky, give it an extra turn.

To make the bouchées, on a lightly floured work surface, roll out the dough to a ½-inch thick square. With a pastry brush, evenly paint the dough with the beaten egg-and-salt mixture. Cut out bouchée rounds with a 2½-inch round fluted cutter. Cut them as close to each other as possible so that no dough is wasted.

Sprinkle cold water on a baking sheet to dampen it. Arrange the dough rounds on it. With a 1½-inch round fluted or plain cutter make shallow cuts (not all the way through to the baking sheet) for the lid in the centre of each bouchée.

Place the baking sheet with the bouchées in the refrigerator to chill for 15 minutes.

Preheat the oven to hot 425°F (Gas Mark 7, 220°C).

Transfer the baking sheet to the top part of the oven and bake for 15 to 20 minutes, or until the bouchées are golden brown. Remove the baking sheet from the oven. Transfer the bouchées to a wire rack to cool. With the point of a small sharp knife, lift away the centre lid and, with a teaspoon, scoop out any soft centre. Set the bouchées aside.

Preheat the grill [broiler] to high.

Place the cashews in the grill [broiler] pan and place them under the grill [broiler]. Toast them for 5 minutes or until they are brown. Remove from the heat and set aside.

In a large frying-pan, heat the oil over moderate heat. When the oil is hot, add the onions, garlic and mushrooms. Fry them, stirring occasionally, for 3 minutes. Stir in the tomatoes, basil, salt, pepper and stock.

Increase the heat to high and bring the mixture to the boil. Reduce the heat to low and simmer for 15 minutes.

Stir in the flour and continue cooking, stirring constantly, for 3 to 4 minutes or until the mixture has thickened.

Add the cashews and cream and stir to mix. Cook for a further 5 minutes. Remove the pan from the heat.

Spoon the filling into the bouchée cases and replace the lids. Garnish with the parsley and serve.

Mushroom and Petits Pois Bouchées

These light bouchées are filled with a creamy mixture of mushrooms, petits pois and almonds. To make the bouchée cases, follow the instructions given in the recipe for Vegetable Bouchées.

Preparation and cooking time: 4 hours

12 BOUCHEES

1 oz. [2 tablespoons] butter or margarine
2 tablespoons flour
8 fl. oz. single cream [1 cup light cream]
4 oz. mushrooms, wiped clean and sliced
½ teaspoon salt
¼ teaspoon white pepper
½ teaspoon grated nutmeg
2 tablespoons finely chopped slivered almonds
4 oz. canned petits pois, drained
12 warm bouchée cases

In a medium-sized saucepan, melt the butter or margarine over moderate heat. Remove the pan from the heat and, with a wooden spoon, stir in the flour to make a smooth paste. Gradually add the cream, stirring constantly. Return the pan to low heat and cook the sauce, stirring con-stantly, for 2 to 3 minutes, or until it is thick and smooth.

Add the mushrooms and cook, stirring frequently, for 3 to 4 minutes. Stir in the salt, pepper, nutmeg and almonds and stir well to mix. Add the petits pois and cook, stirring occasionally, for 8 minutes.

Remove the pan from the heat and spoon the filling into the bouchée cases. Replace the lids on a slant and serve.

Curd Cheese and Tomato Quiche

This is a versatile Curd Cheese Quiche in that almost any vegetable or fruit may be substituted for the tomatoes. Try cooked and chopped spinach, peeled and sliced oranges or sliced cucumber. If you use cucumber, sprinkle the top with chives instead of paprika.

Preparation and cooking time: 1¾ hours

6 SERVINGS

PASTRY
6 oz. wholemeal flour [1½ cups wholewheat flour]
2 oz. [½ cup] flour
¼ teaspoon salt
4 oz. [½ cup] plus 1 teaspoon butter or margarine
3 to 4 tablespoons water
FILLING
8 oz. [1 cup] curd cheese
3 eggs, lightly beaten
1 tablespoon flour
4 tablespoons milk or single [light] cream
¼ teaspoon salt
⅛ teaspoon white pepper
3 tomatoes, sliced
1 teaspoon paprika

In a large mixing bowl, combine the flours and salt together. Add 4 ounces [½ cup] of the butter or margarine and cut it into small pieces with a table knife. With your fingertips, rub the fat into the flour until the mixture resembles coarse breadcrumbs.

Make a well in the centre of the flour mixture and pour in 3 tablespoons of the water. With the knife, mix together the water and flour mixture. Then with your hands, knead the dough until it is smooth, adding more water if the dough is too dry.

Form the dough into a ball and wrap it in greaseproof or waxed paper. Place it in the refrigerator to chill for 30 minutes.

Preheat the oven to fairly hot 375°F (Gas Mark 5, 190°C). Lightly grease an 8-inch flan or quiche tin with the teaspoon of butter or margarine. Set aside.

On a lightly floured surface, roll out the dough to a circle about 12-inches in diameter. Lift the dough on your rolling pin and lay it over the flan or quiche tin. Gently ease the dough into the tin. With a sharp knife, cut off any dough hanging over the sides. Crimp the edges.

With a kitchen fork, prick the bottom of the pastry case several times. Line the pastry case with aluminium foil and add enough dried beans or rice to make a ½-inch layer.

Place the pastry case in the centre of the oven and bake for 10 minutes. Then remove the beans or rice and foil and continue baking for 10 minutes, or until the pastry is golden brown.

Remove the pastry case from the oven and set it aside to cool.

In a medium-sized mixing bowl, beat together the curd cheese, eggs, flour, milk or cream, salt and pepper with a wire whisk or rotary beater. When the ingredients are thoroughly combined, spoon the mixture into the pastry case. Arrange the tomato slices on top and sprinkle them with the paprika.

Place the tin in the oven and bake for 20 minutes or until a knife inserted into the centre of the filling comes out clean.

Remove the tin from the oven and allow the quiche to cool slightly before serving.

Cream Cheese Pastry

This melt-in-the-mouth pastry is as easy to make as ordinary shortcrust.
Preparation and cooking time: 50 minutes
8 OUNCES [2 CUPS]

8 oz. [2 cups] flour
2 oz. cream cheese
2 oz. [¼ cup] vegetable fat
1 teaspoon lemon juice
2 tablespoons water

Put the flour into a large mixing bowl. Add the cream cheese and vegetable fat and cut them into small pieces with a table knife. With your fingertips, rub the fat into the flour until the mixture resembles coarse breadcrumbs.

Add the lemon juice and water and, with the knife, mix them into the flour mixture. With your hands, mix and knead the dough until it is smooth. Add more water if the dough is too dry.

Form the dough into a ball and wrap it in greaseproof or waxed paper. Place the dough in the refrigerator to chill for 30 minutes before using.

Spinach and Cheese Pie

A variation of a classic Greek recipe, Spinach and Cheese Pie has a superb flavour. If you cannot obtain Feta cheese, Wensleydale or any other crumbly white cheese may be used instead.
Preparation and cooking time: 2¼ hours
6 SERVINGS

2 lb. spinach, trimmed, washed, drained and chopped
2 pints [5 cups] water
1½ teaspoons salt
2 fl. oz. [¼ cup] olive oil
2 large onions, finely chopped
2 garlic cloves, crushed
2 teaspoons dried tarragon
¼ teaspoon cayenne pepper
8 oz. Feta cheese, finely crumbled
2 tablespoons single [light] cream
4 eggs
4 oz. [1 cup] Cream Cheese Pastry dough
1 egg, lightly beaten

Preheat the oven to warm 325°F (Gas Mark 3, 170°C).

Put the spinach into a large saucepan. Pour in the water and add 1 teaspoon of salt. Place the pan over moderately high heat and bring the water to the boil. Reduce the heat to moderate and cook the spinach for 7 to 12 minutes, or until it is just tender. Remove the pan from the heat and drain the spinach in a colander, pressing down on the spinach with a wooden spoon to extract all excess liquid. Set the spinach aside.

In a large frying-pan, heat the oil over moderate heat. When the oil is hot, add the onions and garlic. Fry them, stirring occasionally, for 5 to 7 minutes, or until the onions are soft and translucent but not brown. Add the spinach, tarragon, the remaining salt and the cayenne. Continue cooking, stirring occasionally, for 5 minutes, or until the liquid in the pan has evaporated.

Remove the pan from the heat and transfer the spinach mixture to a large mixing bowl. Allow it to cool to room temperature. Stir in the cheese, cream and eggs and mix well to blend. Pour the mixture into a baking dish. Set aside.

On a lightly floured surface, roll out the dough to a circle about ¼-inch thick. Lift the dough on your rolling pin and lay it over the baking dish. Press the dough on to the rim of the dish to seal. Trim off any dough hanging over the edge and use the trimmings to make decorative leaves. Place these on top of the pie. With a pastry brush coat the dough with the beaten egg. Make a 2-inch slit in the centre of the dough with a sharp knife.

Place the dish in the oven and bake the pie for 45 to 50 minutes, or until the pastry is golden brown.

Remove the pie from the oven and serve at once.

Mushroom Tart

Serve this tasty light tart with a vegetable casserole or a lush green salad. It is delicious hot or cold.
Preparation and cooking time: 1¼ hours
4–6 SERVINGS

4 oz. [1 cup] Cream Cheese Pastry dough
1 lb. mushrooms, wiped clean and sliced
2 tablespoons lemon juice
2 oz. [¼ cup] butter or margarine
2 medium-sized onions, sliced
12 fl. oz. double cream [1½ cups heavy cream]
½ teaspoon salt
½ teaspoon white pepper
¼ teaspoon ground cloves
1 tablespoon cornflour [cornstarch] dissolved in 1 tablespoon water
1 oz. [¼ cup] Cheddar cheese, grated

Preheat the oven to fairly hot 375°F (Gas Mark 5, 190°C).

On a lightly floured surface, roll out the dough to a circle about ¼-inch thick. Lift the dough on your rolling pin and lay it over an 8-inch flan tin. Gently ease the dough into the tin and trim off any dough hanging over the sides. Crimp the edges.

With a kitchen fork, prick the bottom of the pastry case several times. Line the pastry case with aluminium foil and add enough dried beans or rice to make a ½-inch layer.

Place the pastry case in the centre of the oven and bake for 10 minutes. Then remove the beans or rice and foil and continue baking for 10 minutes, or until the pastry is golden brown.

Remove the pastry case from the oven and set it aside to cool.

To make the filling, put the mushrooms in a large shallow dish and sprinkle them with the lemon juice. Set aside.

In a large frying-pan, melt the butter or margarine over moderate heat. When the foam subsides, add the onions. Fry them, stirring occasionally, for 5 to 7 minutes, or until they are soft and translucent but not brown. Add the mushrooms with the lemon juice to the pan and continue cooking, stirring frequently, for 3 minutes. Remove the pan from the heat and set aside.

In a large saucepan, scald the cream over low heat (bring to just under boiling point). Stir in the salt, pepper, cloves and cornflour [cornstarch]. Continue cooking, stirring constantly, for 4 to 5 minutes or until the sauce is thick. Add the mushroom mixture to the sauce, stirring well to blend. Remove the pan from the heat.

Preheat the grill [broiler] to high.

Pour the mushroom mixture into the pastry case and sprinkle over the grated cheese.

Place the dish under the grill [broiler] and grill [broil] for 4 to 5 minutes or until the cheese is melted and brown.

Remove the dish from the heat and serve.

Shortcrust Pastry

This basic pastry may be used for any of the following savoury quiches and flans. The yield indicates the amount of flour used to make the dough, so if 4 ounces [1 cup] of shortcrust pastry dough is called for, use 4 ounces [1 cup] flour.

Preparation and cooking time: 45 minutes

4 OUNCES [1 CUP]

4 oz. wholemeal flour [1 cup whole-wheat flour], bran sifted out
⅛ teaspoon salt
2 oz. [¼ cup] butter, margarine or vegetable fat
2 to 3 tablespoons water

In a medium-sized mixing bowl, combine the flour and salt. Add the butter, margarine or vegetable fat and cut them into small pieces with a table knife. With your fingertips, rub the fat into the flour until the mixture resembles coarse breadcrumbs.

Add 2 tablespoons of the water and mix it into the flour mixture. Knead the dough until it is smooth, adding more water if the dough is too dry.

Form the dough into a ball and wrap it in greaseproof or waxed paper. Place it in the refrigerator to chill for 30 minutes before using.

Mixed Cheese Pie

This interesting pie of alternate layers of shortcrust pastry and Cheddar and Emmenthal cheeses would be delicious served with piquant Pepper Sauce or Brown Sauce. Suitable accompaniments would be Aniseed Carrots or courgettes [zucchini].

Preparation and cooking time: 1½ hours

4–6 SERVINGS

12 oz. [3 cups] Shortcrust Pastry dough
8 oz. Cheddar cheese, thinly sliced
8 oz. Emmenthal cheese, thinly sliced
1 egg, lightly beaten with 1 table-spoon single [light] cream

Preheat the oven to very hot 425°F (Gas Mark 7, 210°C).

Divide the dough in half. On a lightly floured surface, roll out one piece to a

circle about ⅛-inch thick. Lift the dough on your rolling pin and lay it over a deep 8-inch pie dish. Carefully ease the dough into the dish and trim off any dough hanging over the side.

Arrange the Cheddar cheese slices in the pastry case.

Divide the remaining dough into two unequal portions. Roll out the smaller piece to a circle the same diameter as the pie dish. Place it in the dish on top of the cheese and arrange the Emmenthal cheese slices on top.

Roll out the remaining piece of dough to a circle about 2 inches wider than the pie dish. Lay the dough over the dish and turn under the overhanging dough. Crimp the edges.

With a sharp knife, cut a 2-inch slit in the centre of the pie, cutting all the way through. Using a pastry brush, coat the top layer of dough with the egg and cream glaze.

Put the dish in the oven and bake the pie for 15 minutes. Then reduce the oven temperature to warm 325°F (Gas Mark 3, 170°C) and continue baking for 45 minutes.

Remove the pie from the oven and serve.

Sweetcorn and Asparagus Flan

An attractive flan with a latticed topping, Sweetcorn and Asparagus Flan is nutritious (eggs for protein and asparagus for Vitamins B1 and C) and has a delicate flavour. Serve with a sauce, such as Béchamel.

Preparation and cooking time: 1¼ hours

4 SERVINGS

4 oz. [1 cup] Shortcrust Pastry dough
10 oz. canned cream-style sweetcorn
5 oz. frozen asparagus tips, cooked, drained and halved
2 oz. canned pimiento, drained and chopped
2 eggs, lightly beaten
½ teaspoon salt
¼ teaspoon white pepper

Preheat the oven to fairly hot 375°F (Gas Mark 5, 190°C).

Break off about one-quarter of the dough and set it aside. On a lightly floured surface, roll out the remaining dough to a circle about ¼-inch thick. Lift the dough on your rolling pin and lay it

over an 8-inch flan tin. Gently ease the dough into the tin and trim off any dough hanging over the sides. Crimp the edges. Set the pastry case aside.

In a large mixing bowl, carefully fold the sweetcorn, asparagus tips and pimiento together. Stir in the eggs, salt and pepper. Pour the filling into the pastry case and spread it out evenly.

On a lightly floured surface, roll out the remaining dough to a rectangle about ¼-inch thick. Cut the dough into thin strips, long enough to stretch across the pastry case. Arrange the strips over the filling, in a lattice pattern.

Put the flan into the oven and bake for 35 minutes or until the pastry strips are brown and crisp.

Remove from the oven and serve at once.

Cheese and Onion Tart

Light yet sustaining, Cheese and Onion Tart is a classic French dish. Petits Pois Garnis or Peas with Fennel would complement it very well.

Preparation and cooking time: 1 hour

4 SERVINGS

4 oz. [1 cup] Shortcrust Pastry dough
3 medium-sized onions, finely chopped
6 oz. [1½ cups] Cheddar cheese, grated
2 fl. oz. single cream [¼ cup light cream]
½ teaspoon salt
¼ teaspoon black pepper
½ teaspoon grated nutmeg

Preheat the oven to fairly hot 400°F (Gas Mark 6, 200°C).

On a lightly floured surface, roll out the dough to a circle about ¼-inch thick. Lift the dough on your rolling pin and lay it over a 9-inch pie dish. Gently ease the dough into the dish and trim off any dough hanging over the sides. Crimp the edges.

Spread the onions evenly over the bottom of the pastry case.

In a medium-sized mixing bowl, combine the cheese with the cream, beating with a fork until they are blended. Stir in the salt, pepper and nutmeg.

Pour the cheese and cream mixture over the onions in the pastry case.

Put the tart in the oven and bake for 10 minutes. Reduce the oven temperature to moderate 350°F (Gas Mark 4, 180°C) and continue baking for a further 15 minutes, or until the filling is set.

Remove the tart from the oven and serve at once.

Pasta, Curry and Rice Dishes

Italian cannelloni stuffed with spinach and cream cheese, Spanish paella, Indian aviyal – just three of the marvellous international pasta, rice and curry dishes in this section for you to try.

Wholemeal semolina, pasta and unpolished brown rice are suggested as a basis for these recipes. Once you accept that spaghetti and rice don't have to be white, bleached and anaemic looking to taste 'right', you will be rewarded by a richer, nuttier flavour and texture. Wholemeal pasta is usually only available from health food stores, or supermarkets with a health food section. Unpolished brown rice can be bought almost anywhere.

Rice is important for its high starch content, and it is one of the most easily digested foods. However, it contains very little protein or fat and therefore should only be eaten with other foods such as eggs, cheese or vegetables, or as part of a main dish.

Pasta

Spaghetti with Italian Tomato Sauce

A delicious yet simple way to serve pasta, Spaghetti with Italian Tomato Sauce needs only a tossed green salad and some crusty bread to make a complete light meal.
Preparation and cooking time: 1 hour

4 SERVINGS

4 fl. oz. [½ cup] olive oil
2 large onions, thinly sliced
2 garlic cloves, crushed
3 fl. oz. [⅜ cup] Dark Vegetable Stock
1½ teaspoons salt
½ teaspoon black pepper
1 tablespoon chopped fresh parsley
1 tablespoon chopped fresh basil, or
  1½ teaspoons dried basil
2 lb. fresh tomatoes, blanched,
  peeled, seeded and chopped, or
  2 lb. canned peeled tomatoes,
  drained and chopped
3 pints [7½ cups] water
1 lb. wholemeal spaghetti
1 oz. [¼ cup] Romano cheese, grated

In a large, deep frying-pan, or medium-sized saucepan, heat the oil over moderate heat. When the oil is hot, add the onions and garlic. Fry them, stirring occasionally, for 5 to 7 minutes, or until the onions are soft and translucent but not brown. Add the vegetable stock and increase the heat to high. Bring to the boil. Reduce the heat to moderate and stir in ½ teaspoon of the salt, the pepper, parsley and basil.

Add the tomatoes to the pan and stir well to mix. Bring to the boil again. Reduce the heat to low, cover the pan and simmer the sauce, stirring occasionally, for 30 to 35 minutes, or until it is thick.

Meanwhile, in a large saucepan, bring the water and remaining salt to the boil over high heat. Add the spaghetti, a little at a time, winding the strands around the pan so that they will not break. Reduce the heat to moderate and cook the spaghetti for 10 to 12 minutes, depending on whether you like your pasta *al dente* (just tender) or slightly soft. Remove the pan from the heat and drain the spaghetti in a colander.

Transfer the spaghetti to a large, deep serving dish or bowl. Remove the tomato sauce from the heat and pour it over the spaghetti, tossing the pasta and sauce together with two large spoons so that all the spaghetti strands are well coated.

Sprinkle on the grated cheese and serve.

Potato Gnocchi

A deliciously filling pasta course, Potato Gnocchi may also be served, with a light salad, as a light supper meal on its own.
Preparation and cooking time: 2 hours

4-6 SERVINGS

2 lb. potatoes, scrubbed, cooked,
  peeled and mashed
2 eggs
3 teaspoons salt
⅛ teaspoon black pepper
⅛ teaspoon grated nutmeg
6 oz. [1½ cups] flour

½ teaspoon baking powder
4 pints [5 pints] water
12 fl. oz. [1½ cups] hot Tomato Sauce II
2 oz. [½ cup] Parmesan cheese, grated

Put the potatoes into a large mixing bowl. Add the eggs, 1 teaspoon of salt, the pepper and nutmeg and, using a fork or wooden spoon, beat the ingredients together. Gradually sift the flour and baking powder into the mixture, beating constantly, and beat until the dough is smooth and well blended.

Turn the dough out on to a lightly floured board or marble slab and knead it for 5 to 8 minutes, or until it is shiny and pliable.

Form the dough into finger-shaped mounds, about 1- to 2-inches long, then shape them into rough crescents. Dust them lightly with flour and place them in the refrigerator to chill for 15 minutes.

Remove the gnocchi from the refrigerator and set aside.

Pour the water into a large saucepan and add the remaining salt. Place the pan over high heat and bring the water to the boil. Drop a few of the gnocchi into the boiling water and cook them for about 5 minutes, or until they rise to the surface. With a slotted spoon, remove the gnocchi from the pan and drain them on kitchen paper towels. Keep them warm while you cook the remaining gnocchi in the same way.

Arrange the gnocchi in a large, shallow serving dish and pour over the hot tomato sauce. Sprinkle the grated cheese over the top and serve.

Macaroni and Sweetcorn Casserole

This pasta dish is baked in the oven and is an attractive and delicious main dish.
Preparation and cooking time: 1 hour
                                    4 SERVINGS

1½ oz. [3 tablespoons] plus 1 teaspoon
    butter or margarine
 2 pints [5 cups] water
1½ teaspoons salt
 1 lb. wholemeal macaroni
 3 tablespoons flour
15 fl. oz. [1⅞ cups] milk
 4 oz. [1 cup] Cheddar cheese, grated
 7 oz. canned sweetcorn, drained
 ½ teaspoon ground mace
 2 large eggs, lightly beaten

Preheat the oven to fairly hot 375°F (Gas Mark 5, 190°C). Lightly grease a medium-sized baking dish with the teaspoon of butter or margarine. Set aside.

In a large saucepan, bring the water to the boil over high heat. Add 1 teaspoon of the salt and the macaroni. Reduce the heat to moderately high and cook the macaroni for 10 to 12 minutes, depending on whether you like your pasta *al dente* (just tender) or slightly soft.

Meanwhile, in a large saucepan, melt the remaining butter or margarine over moderate heat. Remove the pan from the heat and, with a wooden spoon, stir in the flour to make a smooth paste. Gradually add the milk, stirring constantly. Return the pan to the heat and cook the sauce, stirring constantly, for 3 to 4 minutes, or until it is thick and smooth.

Reduce the heat to low and stir in the cheese. When the cheese is completely incorporated, stir in the sweetcorn, mace, remaining salt and the eggs. Blend well. Remove the pan from the heat.

When the macaroni is cooked, drain it in a colander. Add the macaroni to the sauce in the saucepan and mix the two together thoroughly.

Turn the mixture into the baking dish and place it in the oven. Bake for 30 minutes.

Remove the dish from the oven and serve immediately.

Noodle Savoury

A filling meal in itself, accompanied by a salad, Noodle Savoury is easy to make.
Preparation and cooking time: 45 minutes
                                    6 SERVINGS

3 fl. oz. [⅜ cup] olive oil
2 medium-sized onions, thinly sliced
2 garlic cloves, crushed
1 large green pepper, white pith
    removed, seeded and thinly sliced
6 oz. mushrooms, wiped clean and
    sliced
1½ teaspoons salt
 ½ teaspoon black pepper
1½ teaspoons dried oregano
 4 fl. oz. [½ cup] Dark Vegetable Stock
 2 oz. tomato purée
 4 pints [5 pints] water
1½ lb. ribbon noodles
 1 oz. [¼ cup] Parmesan cheese, grated

In a large saucepan, heat the olive oil over moderate heat. When the oil is hot, add the onions, garlic and green pepper. Fry them, stirring occasionally, for 5 to 7 minutes, or until the onions are soft and translucent but not brown. Add the mushrooms to the pan and cook, stirring frequently, for 3 minutes.

Stir in ½ teaspoon of the salt, the black pepper and oregano and pour in the vegetable stock. Increase the heat to moderately high and bring the liquid to the boil. Stir in the tomato purée. Reduce the heat to low and simmer for 15 minutes.

Meanwhile, in a large saucepan, bring the water and remaining salt to the boil over high heat. Add the noodles to the pan, reduce the heat to moderate and cook them for 10 to 12 minutes, depending on whether you like your pasta *al dente* (just tender) or slightly soft. Remove the pan from the heat and drain the noodles in a colander.

Arrange the noodles in a large, deep serving dish or bowl. Remove the sauce from the heat and pour it over the noodles. Sprinkle the grated cheese on top and serve.

Spaghetti alla Genovese
SPAGHETTI WITH BASIL AND GARLIC SAUCE

An exotically different pasta dish, Spaghetti alla Genovese is the speciality of the city of Genoa. The sauce may be used to garnish almost any kind of pasta.
Preparation and cooking time: 25 minutes
                                    4 SERVINGS

3 pints [7½ cups] water
1½ teaspoons salt
 1 lb. wholemeal spaghetti
 4 medium-sized bunches of fresh
    basil, washed and chopped
 3 garlic cloves, crushed
 ½ teaspoon black pepper
 1 tablespoon pine nuts
 2 oz. [½ cup] Parmesan or Romano
    cheese, grated
 8 fl. oz [1 cup] olive oil

In a large saucepan, bring the water and 1 teaspoon of the salt to the boil over high heat. Add the spaghetti, a little at a time, winding the strands around the pan so that they will not break. Reduce the heat to moderate and cook the spaghetti for 10 to 12 minutes, depending on whether you like your pasta *al dente* (just tender) or slightly soft.

Meanwhile, put the basil, garlic, remaining salt, the pepper and pine nuts into a large mortar or medium-sized mixing bowl. With a pestle or the back of a wooden spoon, pound the mixture to a paste. Gradually pound in the grated cheese. When the mixture is smooth and the ingredients are blended, gradually stir in the olive oil, beating until the mixture has a sauce-like consistency. Alternatively, you can make the sauce in a blender by combining the sauce ingredients together at high speed. When the sauce is made, set it aside.

Remove the saucepan from the heat and drain the spaghetti in a colander. Transfer the spaghetti to a large, deep serving dish or bowl. Add the sauce and, using two large spoons, toss the spaghetti and sauce together until all the spaghetti strands are well coated.

Serve at once.

Noodles with Beans in Tomato Sauce

A hearty and sustaining meal in itself, Noodles with Beans in Tomato Sauce makes an excellent winter supper dish.
Preparation and cooking time: 2 hours
                                    6 SERVINGS

12 oz. dried white haricot beans,
    soaked overnight and drained
 5 pints [6 pints] water
2½ teaspoons salt
 1 oz. [2 tablespoons] butter or
    margarine
 1 large onion, finely chopped
 3 garlic cloves, crushed
 2 lb. canned peeled tomatoes,
    drained and chopped
 5 fl. oz. [⅝ cup] Tomato Sauce II
 1 small green chilli, seeds removed
    and chopped
 1 teaspoon dried basil
 2 tablespoons chopped fresh parsley
 ½ teaspoon black pepper
 1 lb. ribbon noodles
 3 tablespoons grated Parmesan
    cheese

Put the beans into a large saucepan and pour in half of the water and 1 teaspoon of the salt. Place the pan over moderate heat and bring the water to the boil. Reduce the heat to moderately low and simmer the beans for 45 minutes, or until they are just tender. Remove the pan from the heat and drain the beans in a colander. Set aside.

In a large saucepan, melt the butter or margarine over moderate heat. When the foam subsides, add the onion and garlic. Fry them, stirring occasionally, for 5 to 7 minutes, or until the onion is soft and translucent but not brown. Add the tomatoes, tomato sauce, chilli, basil, parsley, ½ teaspoon of the salt and the pepper and mix well. Bring to the boil. Reduce the heat to low and stir in the beans. Cover the pan and simmer for 30 minutes.

Meanwhile, in a large saucepan, bring the remaining water and salt to the boil over high heat. Add the noodles and reduce the heat to moderate. Cook them for 6 to 8 minutes, depending on whether you like your pasta *al dente* (just tender) or slightly soft. Remove the pan from the heat and drain the noodles thoroughly in a colander.

Arrange the noodles in a large, deep serving dish or bowl. Pour over the beans and tomato sauce mixture and, using two large spoons, toss well.

Sprinkle the grated cheese on top and serve at once.

Noodles Baked with Spinach

An attractive dish to serve for lunch or supper, this is a filling meal in itself.
Preparation and cooking time: 1 hour
4-6 SERVINGS

2 pints [5 cups] water
1½ teaspoons salt
12 oz. noodles
4 oz. [½ cup] butter or margarine
2 medium-sized onions, finely chopped
3 lb. spinach, cooked, drained and finely chopped
¼ teaspoon black pepper
2 eggs, lightly beaten
3 oz. [¾ cup] Parmesan cheese, grated
15 fl. oz. [1⅞ cups] thick Béchamel Sauce
3 oz. [1 cup] dry breadcrumbs

Preheat the oven to fairly hot 375°F (Gas Mark 5, 190°C).

In a large saucepan, bring the water and 1 teaspoon of the salt to the boil over high heat. Add the noodles and reduce the heat to moderate. Cook them for 12 to 15 minutes, depending on whether you like your pasta *al dente* (just tender) or slightly soft.

Meanwhile in a large frying-pan, melt half of the butter or margarine over moderate heat. When the foam subsides, add the onions. Fry them for 8 to 10 minutes, or until they are light brown.

With a wooden spoon, stir in the spinach, the remaining salt and the pepper

and continue cooking, stirring constantly, for 5 minutes. Stir in the eggs and cook for a further 2 minutes, or until the eggs are just beginning to set. Remove the pan from the heat.

When the noodles are cooked, drain them in a colander. Arrange half of the noodles on the bottom of a medium-sized ovenproof casserole. Sprinkle them with half of the cheese and cover with half of the spinach mixture. Cover with the remaining noodles, cheese and the spinach mixture. Pour the béchamel sauce over the mixture.

In a small frying-pan, melt the remaining butter or margarine over low heat. Stir in the breadcrumbs and remove the pan from the heat. Cover the top of the béchamel sauce in the casserole with the breadcrumb mixture.

Place the casserole in the oven and bake for 20 minutes, or until the top is crisp and brown.

Remove the casserole from the oven and serve immediately.

Macaroni and Cheese

A delicious and slightly spicy version of the popular Macaroni and Cheese, this is a very filling dish. Serve it with a light salad, such as a Caesar Salad.
Preparation and cooking time: 1 hour
4 SERVINGS

1 teaspoon butter or margarine
3 pints [7½ cups] water
1½ teaspoons salt
1 lb. wholemeal macaroni
8 oz. [2 cups] Cheddar cheese, grated
1 tablespoon Worcestershire sauce
½ teaspoon white pepper
⅛ teaspoon cayenne pepper
15 fl. oz. [1⅞ cups] hot Béchamel Sauce

Preheat the oven to moderate 350°F (Gas Mark 4, 180°C). Grease a medium-sized casserole with the butter or margarine. Set aside.

In a large saucepan, bring the water and 1 teaspoon of the salt to the boil over high heat. Add the macaroni to the pan and reduce the heat to moderate. Cook for 10 to 12 minutes, depending on whether you like your pasta *al dente* (just tender) or slightly soft. Remove the pan from the heat and drain the macaroni in a colander.

Arrange half of the macaroni in the bottom of the casserole. Cover the macaroni with half of the grated Cheddar, then top with the remaining macaroni. Mix the Worcestershire sauce, the remaining salt, the white pepper and the cayenne into the béchamel sauce and pour the mixture into the casserole. Sprinkle the remaining grated cheese on top.

Put the casserole into the oven and bake for 20 to 25 minutes, or until the cheese has melted and the top is golden brown.

Remove the casserole from the oven and serve at once.

Stuffed Cannelloni

One of the more impressive of the pastas, this particular cannelloni is stuffed with a delicious combination of tomatoes, mushrooms and T.V.P. mince.
Preparation and cooking time: 1¾ hours
6-8 SERVINGS

2 pints [5 cups] water
1 teaspoon salt
8 oz. cannelloni
1 tablespoon olive oil
10 fl. oz. [1¼ cups] Tomato Sauce II
4 oz. [1 cup] Parmesan cheese, grated
STUFFING
4 oz. [1 cup] T.V.P. mince
8 fl. oz. [1 cup] water
2 oz. [¼ cup] butter or margarine
2 medium-sized onions, finely chopped
2 garlic cloves, crushed
8 oz. mushrooms, wiped clean and chopped
2 oz. [1 cup] fresh brown breadcrumbs
3 oz. tomato purée
1 egg, lightly beaten
1 teaspoon dried basil
1 teaspoon salt
½ teaspoon black pepper
6 oz. mozzarella cheese, cut into small strips

In a large saucepan, bring the water and salt to the boil over high heat. Add the cannelloni and reduce the heat to moderate. Cook the cannelloni for 12 to 15 minutes, depending on whether you like your pasta *al dente* (just tender) or slightly soft. Remove the pan from the heat and drain the cannelloni in a colander. Toss the cannelloni with the olive oil, then set it aside while you make the stuffing.

Preheat the oven to moderate 350°F (Gas Mark 4, 180°C).

Put the T.V.P. mince into a medium-sized saucepan and stir in the water. Place the pan over moderate heat, cover and hydrate the T.V.P. for 5 minutes. Remove the pan from the heat and set the T.V.P. aside.

In a large frying-pan, melt the butter or margarine over moderate heat. When the foam subsides, add the onions and garlic to the pan. Fry them, stirring occasionally, for 5 to 7 minutes, or until the onions are soft and translucent but not brown. Add the mushrooms, breadcrumbs, tomato purée and T.V.P. mince and, stirring constantly, cook the mixture for 3 minutes. Remove the pan from the heat and transfer the mixture to a large mixing bowl.

Add the egg, basil, salt and pepper to the mixture, stirring well. Mix in the mozzarella cheese.

With a spoon, or with your fingers, carefully fill the cannelloni with the stuffing.

Place the stuffed cannelloni in a large casserole or roasting tin. Pour the tomato sauce around the pasta and sprinkle half of the Parmesan cheese on top. Place the casserole or tin in the oven and bake for 30 minutes, or until the cheese is melted and brown.

Remove the casserole or tin from the oven and serve at once, accompanied by the remaining Parmesan cheese.

Curries

Aviyal
VEGETABLE CURRY

An Indian dish of mixed vegetables cooked with coconut and spices, Aviyal (ah-VEE-yahl) should be served with boiled rice. You may use a combination of any vegetables—carrots, beans, aubergines [eggplants], turnips, cauliflower, green peppers, potatoes, spring onions [scallions] and okra.
Preparation and cooking time: 45 minutes
4 SERVINGS

- 4 tablespoons vegetable oil
- 1 teaspoon mustard seeds
- 2-inch piece fresh root ginger, peeled and minced
- 2 garlic cloves, peeled and cut into quarters lengthways
- 1 onion, minced
- 1 green chilli, minced
- 1½ teaspoons turmeric
- 1 tablespoon ground coriander
- 1½ lb. mixed vegetables, sliced
- 1 teaspoon salt
- 8 oz. [1 cup] fresh coconut puréed in an electric blender with 6 fl. oz. [¾ cup] water, or 1-inch slice creamed coconut
- 2 tablespoons chopped coriander leaves (optional)

In a large saucepan, heat the oil over moderately high heat. Add the mustard seeds, ginger and garlic and fry them for 30 seconds. Add the onion and green chilli, reduce the heat to moderately low and, stirring occasionally, fry gently for 10 minutes, or until the onion is golden.

Add the turmeric and ground coriander and cook for 1 minute. Add the vegetables and stir to mix well with the fried spices. Add the salt and the coconut purée or creamed coconut and stir to mix. If the mixture is too dry, add 1 or 2 spoonfuls of water.

Cover the pan and simmer for 30 minutes, or until the vegetables are tender when pierced with the point of a sharp knife.

Turn the Aviyal into a warmed serving dish. Sprinkle with the chopped coriander leaves and serve.

Eggs in Curried Coconut Sauce

A delicious and easy-to-make snack supper or lunch, Eggs in Curried Coconut Sauce need only be accompanied by boiled rice and a green salad to make an excellent meal.
Preparation and cooking time: 50 minutes
4 SERVINGS

- 2 fl. oz. [¼ cup] vegetable oil
- 2 medium-sized onions, finely chopped
- 2 garlic cloves, crushed
- 1 green chilli, seeds removed and finely chopped
- 2-inch piece fresh root ginger, peeled and finely chopped
- ½ teaspoon ground cumin
- ½ teaspoon ground coriander
- ½ teaspoon turmeric
- ¼ teaspoon hot chilli powder
- 12 fl. oz. [1½ cups] Tomato Sauce II
- 2-inch piece creamed coconut
- 1 tablespoon chopped fresh coriander leaves
- 8 hard-boiled eggs, sliced

In a large saucepan, heat the oil over moderate heat. When the oil is hot, add the onions, garlic, chilli and ginger. Fry them, stirring occasionally, for 5 to 7 minutes, or until the onions are soft and translucent but not brown.

In a small bowl, combine the cumin, coriander, turmeric and chilli powder together and mix well. Stir the spice mix-

ture into the onion mixture and cook for a further 5 minutes, stirring constantly. Pour in the tomato sauce and increase the heat to high. Bring to the boil. Reduce the heat to low and simmer the sauce, stirring occasionally, for 15 minutes.

Add the creamed coconut and stir until it dissolves and the liquid thickens. Cook the sauce for a further 3 minutes. Remove the pan from the heat and stir in the coriander leaves.

Arrange the egg slices on a large, shallow serving dish. Pour over the sauce and serve.

Dried Fruit Curry

Dried fruit commends itself particularly to curry flavouring and results in a spicy and fragrant mixture of tastes. This dish may be served either hot or cold. Accompany this dish with plain boiled rice.
Preparation and cooking time: 50 minutes
6 SERVINGS

- 4 oz. [½ cup] butter or margarine
- 4 oz. [⅔ cup] dried apricots, soaked overnight, drained and chopped
- 4 oz. [⅔ cup] dried prunes, soaked overnight, drained, stoned and chopped
- 4 oz. [⅔ cup] dried apple slices, soaked overnight, drained and chopped
- 3 oz. [½ cup] seedless raisins, soaked in cold water for 30 minutes and drained
- 3 oz. [½ cup] slivered almonds
- 1 medium-sized cucumber, thinly sliced
- 2 oz. canned pineapple chunks, drained and finely chopped
- 1 teaspoon ground cloves
- ½ teaspoon ground ginger
- 1 teaspoon ground cardamom
- ½ teaspoon ground cumin
- ½ teaspoon dry mustard
- ¼ teaspoon hot chilli powder
- 1 tablespoon finely chopped lemon rind
- 10 fl. oz. [1¼ cups] Light Vegetable Stock
- 1-inch slice creamed coconut

In a large flameproof casserole, melt the butter or margarine over moderate heat. When the foam subsides, add the apricots, prunes, apples, raisins, almonds, cucumber and pineapple. Cook, stirring frequently, for 5 minutes.

In a small bowl, combine the cloves, ginger, cardamom, cumin, mustard, chilli powder and lemon rind and mix well to blend. Add the spice mixture to the fruit mixture and mix well. Pour in the vegetable stock and increase the heat to high. Bring to the boil. Reduce the heat to low, partly cover the casserole and simmer, stirring occasionally, for 15 minutes.

Stir in the coconut, mixing until it dissolves and the liquid thickens. Continue to cook for 5 minutes.

Remove the casserole from the heat and pour the curry into a heated serving dish. Serve at once with rice.

Curried Cauliflower

This is an excellent way of spicing up a rather delicately flavoured vegetable. Serve Curried Cauliflower with saffron- or turmeric-coloured rice for a marvellous meal.
Preparation and cooking time: 1 hour
4-6 SERVINGS

2 oz. [¼ cup] butter or margarine
2 medium-sized onions, chopped
1 garlic clove, crushed
1 green chilli, seeds removed and chopped
1 apple, peeled, cored and chopped
2 large tomatoes, blanched, peeled, seeded and chopped
1 teaspoon garam masala
½ teaspoon ground cumin
½ teaspoon ground coriander
½ teaspoon turmeric
¼ teaspoon hot chilli powder
8 fl. oz. [1 cup] water
8 fl. oz. [1 cup] tomato juice
1 tablespoon flour
1 tablespoon fruit chutney
2 tablespoons seedless raisins
1 tablespoon slivered almonds
1 large cauliflower, cooked, broken into flowerets and kept warm

In a large saucepan, melt the butter or margarine over moderate heat. When the foam subsides, add the onions, garlic and chilli. Fry them, stirring occasionally, for 5 to 7 minutes, or until the onions are soft and translucent but not brown. Add the apple and tomatoes and cook for 3 minutes.

In a small bowl, combine the garam masala, cumin, coriander, turmeric and chilli powder and mix well. Add the spice mixture to the onion and tomato mixture and mix well to coat the vegetables. Pour in the water and tomato juice and increase the heat to high. Bring to the boil. Remove the pan from the heat and stir in the flour, mixing until it has dissolved and the liquid has thickened.

Return the pan to low heat, cover and simmer the sauce for 15 minutes. Stir in the chutney, raisins and almonds and simmer for a further 5 minutes.

Arrange the cooked cauliflower in a large, warmed serving dish. Remove the pan from the heat and pour over the curry sauce. Serve at once.

Channa Dhal

CURRIED CHICK-PEAS

Simple and inexpensive to make, Channa Dhal (Chun-nah dahl) is often served as part of an Indian meal. It also makes a delicious—and exotic—accompaniment to any spicy dish. Remember to begin the preparation the day before as the chick-peas should soak in water overnight.
Preparation and cooking time: 2 hours
6 SERVINGS

12 oz. chick-peas, washed thoroughly, soaked in cold water overnight and drained
2½ pints [6¼ cups] water
1 teaspoon salt
3 tablespoons clarified butter or margarine or melted butter or margarine
1 teaspoon cumin seeds
1 medium-sized onion, finely chopped
1-inch piece fresh root ginger, peeled and finely chopped
1 teaspoon turmeric
½ teaspoon ground cumin
1 teaspoon ground coriander
1 teaspoon garam masala
¼ to ½ teaspoon chilli powder
1 tablespoon chopped fresh coriander leaves

Put the chick-peas in a medium-sized saucepan. Pour over the water and add the salt. Place the pan over moderately high heat and bring the water to the boil. Reduce the heat to low, half-cover the pan and cook gently for 1 hour.

In a large saucepan, heat the clarified or melted butter or margarine over moderate heat. Add the cumin seeds and cook for 1 minute. Add the onion and cook, stirring occasionally, for 5 minutes. Stir in the ginger and continue cooking for 4 minutes, or until the onion becomes golden brown.

In a small mixing bowl combine the turmeric, ground cumin, coriander, garam masala and chilli powder with 2 tablespoons of water to make a paste. Add the paste to the onion mixture in the pan and fry for 3 to 4 minutes, stirring constantly, or until the mixture is well blended.

Add the chick-peas and the cooking liquid to the pan. Increase the heat to high and, stirring constantly, bring the mixture to the boil. Cover the pan, reduce the heat to low and simmer for 30 minutes, or until the chick-peas are tender but still whole.

Taste the mixture and add more salt if necessary. Pour the Channa Dhal into a warmed serving dish, sprinkle the top with the chopped coriander leaves and serve.

Vegetable Pulao

Indian food is spicy and exotic and, on the whole, surprisingly simple to prepare. This complicated looking Vegetable Pulao is no exception and makes a wonderfully impressive dinner party meal. Serve with plain yogurt, pappadums and a selection of chutneys for a very special meal.
Preparation and cooking time: 1¼ hours
4 SERVINGS

8 oz. [1⅓ cups] long-grain brown rice, washed, soaked in cold water for 30 minutes and drained
1 pint [2½ cups] plus 2 tablespoons Light Vegetable Stock or water
1 teaspoon salt
3 fl. oz [⅜ cup] vegetable oil
3 medium-sized onions, thinly sliced
4 large carrots, scraped and sliced
1 large green pepper, white pith removed, seeded and sliced
6 oz. frozen petits pois, thawed
1 teaspoon ground cumin
1 teaspoon ground coriander
½ teaspoon turmeric
½ teaspoon garam masala
¼ teaspoon hot chilli powder
¼ teaspoon saffron threads dissolved in 1 teaspoon hot water

Put the rice into a large saucepan. Pour over all but 2 tablespoons of the stock or water and add the salt. Place the pan over high heat and bring the stock or water to the boil. Cover the pan, reduce the heat to very low and simmer for 20 to 25 minutes, or until the rice is tender and all the liquid has been absorbed. Remove the pan from the heat and set aside.

Preheat the oven to moderate 350°F (Gas Mark 4, 180°C).

In a large frying-pan, heat the oil over moderate heat. When the oil is hot, add the onions, carrots, green pepper and petit pois. Cook them, stirring occasionally, for 5 to 7 minutes, or until the onions are soft and translucent but not brown.

In a small bowl, combine the cumin, coriander, turmeric, garam masala and chilli powder with the 2 tablespoons of stock or water, mixing until a smooth paste is formed.

Add the paste to the frying-pan, stirring to coat the vegetables well. Cook the mixture, stirring frequently, for 3 minutes. Remove the pan from the heat.

Arrange one-half of the rice on the bottom of a fairly large, heavy casserole. Cover with the vegetable mixture. Spread half of the remaining rice over the top of the vegetable mixture. Stir the saffron into the remaining rice, mixing well.

Spread the saffron rice on top of the casserole mixture.

Cover the casserole and place it in the oven. Bake for 20 minutes.

Remove the casserole from the oven and serve at once.

Mixed Vegetable Curry

A marvellously tasty and exotic meal, Mixed Vegetable Curry makes a colourful centrepiece to a dinner party, or may be served as the main dish in an Indian meal. Serve accompanied by boiled rice and a selection of chutneys.

Preparation and cooking time: 1½ hours
6 SERVINGS

1½ tablespoons flour
1 teaspoon salt
½ teaspoon black pepper
4 teaspoons turmeric
½ teaspoon hot chilli powder
1 small cauliflower, trimmed, washed and broken into flowerets
2 medium-sized carrots, scraped and sliced
1 small turnip, peeled and sliced
3 small courgettes [zucchini], trimmed, washed and cut into ¼-inch slices
4 fl. oz. [½ cup] vegetable oil
2 large onions, thinly sliced
2 medium-sized tart apples, peeled, cored and sliced
1 green chilli, seeds removed and chopped
2-inch piece fresh root ginger, peeled and chopped
14 oz. canned peeled tomatoes
1 teaspoon ground coriander
1 teaspoon ground cumin
1 teaspoon garam masala
½ teaspoon ground fenugreek
4 tablespoons yogurt
2 tablespoons chopped fresh coriander leaves

In a shallow plate, combine the flour, salt, pepper, 3 teaspoons of the turmeric and ¼ teaspoon of the chilli powder together, mixing to blend well. Roll the cauliflower flowerets, carrots, turnip and courgette [zucchini] slices in the seasoned flour, shaking off any excess. Set aside.

In a very large saucepan, heat the oil over moderate heat. When the oil is hot, add the vegetables to the pan. Cook them, stirring occasionally, for 10 minutes, or until they are lightly browned. With a slotted spoon, transfer the vegetables to a large mixing bowl and keep warm.

Add the onions, apples, chilli and ginger to the pan. Cook them, stirring occasionally, for 5 to 7 minutes, or until the onions are soft and translucent but not

brown. Stir in the tomatoes with their can juice, the coriander, cumin, garam masala, fenugreek, and the remaining turmeric and chilli powder. Stir well to blend and bring the mixture to the boil.

Reduce the heat to low. Return the vegetables to the pan, cover and simmer, stirring occasionally, for 30 minutes or until the vegetables are tender.

Stir in the yogurt, then the coriander leaves. Simmer for a further 2 minutes. Remove the pan from the heat and arrange the vegetable mixture in a warmed, deep serving dish. Serve at once.

Mixed Fruit Curry

A delicious combination of apricots, pears, bananas, melon, mangoes and pineapple, this unusual curry is served cold.

Preparation and cooking time: 4 hours
4 SERVINGS

4 fresh apricots, peeled, stoned and chopped
4 fresh pears, peeled, cored and chopped
3 medium-sized bananas, sliced
½ small honeydew melon, peeled, seeded and chopped
4 oz. canned mangoes, drained and chopped
2 oz. canned pineapple chunks, drained and chopped
4 tablespoons clear honey mixed with 10 fl. oz. [1¼ cups] boiling water
½ teaspoon ground cumin
½ teaspoon ground coriander
½ teaspoon turmeric
½ teaspoon ground cloves
¼ teaspoon ground fenugreek
⅛ teaspoon hot chilli powder
1 teaspoon lemon juice
5 fl. oz. [⅝ cup] yogurt
1-inch slice creamed coconut

Put the apricots, pears, bananas, melon, mangoes and pineapple into a large saucepan. Pour on the honey and water mixture. Place the pan over low heat, cover and poach the fruit gently for 10 minutes. Remove the pan from the heat and set aside.

In a small bowl, combine the cumin, coriander, turmeric, cloves, fenugreek and chilli powder and mix well to blend. Stir the spices into the fruit mixture. Return the pan to low heat and cook, stirring frequently, for a further 5 minutes. Add the lemon juice and yogurt and simmer the mixture gently, stirring occasionally, for 20 minutes.

Stir in the creamed coconut, mixing until it dissolves and the liquid thickens. Simmer for a further 3 minutes. Remove the pan from the heat and allow the mix-

ture to cool. Transfer the curry to a serving dish and place it in the refrigerator to chill for at least 3 hours. Just before serving, stir the mixture once or twice.

Vegetable Biryani

A North Indian dish, Vegetable Biryani is a fragrant combination of aubergine [eggplant], red pepper, butter [dried lima] beans, tomatoes, spices, nuts and turmeric-coloured rice. Serve it with a Cucumber and Yogurt Salad.

Preparation and cooking time: 2 hours
6 SERVINGS

12 oz. [2 cups] long-grain brown rice, washed, soaked in cold water for 30 minutes and drained
1½ pints [3¾ cups] water
3 teaspoons salt
4½ teaspoons turmeric
1 large aubergine [eggplant]
3 oz. [⅜ cup] plus 1 tablespoon butter or margarine
1 teaspoon poppy seeds
1½ teaspoons mustard seeds
¼ teaspoon cayenne pepper
1 teaspoon garam masala
½ teaspoon ground coriander
1 large red pepper, white pith removed, seeded and sliced
4 oz. canned butter [dried lima] beans, drained
3 tomatoes, blanched, peeled, seeded and chopped
2 oz. [⅓ cup] slivered almonds
2 oz. [⅓ cup] seedless raisins

Put the rice into a very large saucepan. Pour in the water and add 1 teaspoon of the salt and 4 teaspoons of the turmeric. Place the pan over high heat and bring the water to the boil. Cover the pan, reduce the heat to very low and simmer for 20 to 25 minutes, or until the rice is tender and all the liquid has been absorbed.

Meanwhile, peel the aubergine [eggplant] and cut it into small cubes. Place the cubes in a colander, sprinkle on the remaining salt and leave the aubergine [eggplant] to dégorge for 30 minutes. Dry the cubes thoroughly with kitchen paper towels and set aside.

When the rice is cooked, remove the pan from the heat and set aside.

Preheat the oven to moderate 350°F (Gas Mark 4, 180°C).

In a large, deep frying-pan, or saucepan, melt 3 ounces [⅜ cup] of the butter or margarine over moderate heat. When the foam subsides, add the poppy seeds and mustard seeds. Cover the pan and cook the seeds for 2 minutes. Uncover the pan and add the cayenne, remaining turmeric, the garam masala and coriander, stirring to blend them into the melted butter or margarine.

Add the aubergine [eggplant] cubes, red pepper, butter [lima] beans and tomatoes and cook, stirring frequently, for 10 minutes. Remove the pan from the heat and set aside.

Arrange one-third of the rice on the bottom of a deep, heavy casserole. Spread one-half of the spiced vegetables on top and cover with another third of the rice. Add the remaining vegetables to the dish and top with the remaining rice. Cover the casserole and place it in the oven. Bake for 30 minutes.

About 5 minutes before the end of the cooking time, in a small saucepan, melt the remaining butter or margarine over moderate heat. When the foam subsides, add the slivered almonds and raisins. Cook, stirring frequently, for 3 minutes, or until the almonds are toasted. Remove the pan from the heat.

Remove the casserole from the oven and uncover it. Sprinkle over the almonds and raisins and serve at once, straight from the casserole.

Tomato Curry

A fragrant and mild dish, Tomato Curry may be served as a vegetable accompaniment, or as part of a summer buffet.
Preparation and cooking time: 40 minutes
4 SERVINGS

4 oz. [⅔ cup] long-grain brown rice, washed, soaked in cold water for 30 minutes and drained
10 fl. oz. [1¼ cups] Light Vegetable Stock
1½ teaspoons salt
1 oz. [2 tablespoons] butter or margarine
1 small onion, finely chopped
1 garlic clove, crushed
1 medium-sized tart apple, peeled, cored and chopped
1 teaspoon cider vinegar
2 teaspoons curry powder
1 lb. tomatoes, blanched, peeled, seeded and chopped, or 14 oz. canned peeled tomatoes, drained

Put the rice into a large saucepan. Pour over the vegetable stock and add 1 teaspoon of the salt. Place the pan over high heat and bring the stock to the boil. Cover the pan, reduce the heat to very low and simmer for 20 to 25 minutes, or until the rice is tender and all the liquid has been absorbed.

Meanwhile, in a medium-sized frying-pan, melt the butter or margarine over moderate heat. When the foam subsides,

add the onion and garlic. Fry them, stirring occasionally, for 5 to 7 minutes, or until the onion is soft and translucent but not brown. Add the apple and vinegar and cook, stirring occasionally, for 4 minutes. Stir in the curry powder, the remaining salt and the tomatoes and cook, stirring frequently, for 5 minutes. Remove the pan from the heat.

When the rice is cooked, transfer it to a warmed serving dish. Pour the tomato mixture over the rice and toss well to blend. Serve at once.

Rice

Hawaiian Rice

A subtle blend of sweet and sour, Hawaiian Rice makes a colourful centrepiece for an informal dinner buffet. Or serve it with a salad for a delightful spring lunch.
Preparation and cooking time: 1 hour
4 SERVINGS

4 oz. [⅔ cup] long-grain brown rice, washed, soaked in cold water for 30 minutes and drained
10 fl. oz. [1¼ cups] water
1½ teaspoons salt
2 fl. oz. [¼ cup] vegetable oil
1 medium-sized onion, finely chopped
1 garlic clove, crushed
4 oz. cabbage, coarse outer leaves removed, washed and shredded
2-inch piece fresh root ginger, peeled and finely chopped
½ small red pepper, white pith removed, seeded and chopped
1½ tablespoons soy sauce
4 oz. canned pineapple chunks, drained, with the juice reserved
1 teaspoon cornflour [cornstarch]
2 oz. [⅓ cup] blanched almonds, toasted

Put the rice in a medium-sized saucepan. Pour in the water and add 1 teaspoon of the salt. Place the pan over high heat and bring the water to the boil. Cover the pan, reduce the heat to very low and simmer for 20 to 25 minutes, or until the rice is tender and all the liquid has been absorbed. Remove the pan from the heat and set aside.

In a large saucepan, heat half of the oil over moderate heat. When the oil is hot, add the onion and garlic. Fry them, stirring constantly, for 2 minutes. Add the cabbage, ginger and red pepper and, stirring constantly, cook the mixture for 3 minutes. Stir in the remaining salt and ½ tablespoon of the soy sauce and cook for a further 1 minute. Remove the pan from the heat and set aside.

In a large frying-pan, heat the remaining oil over moderate heat. When the oil is hot, add the rice and pineapple and cook, stirring constantly, for 2 minutes. Stir in the remaining soy sauce. Cook the mixture for a further 2 minutes, stirring constantly. Remove the pan from the heat and add the rice mixture to the ginger and red pepper mixture, stirring to blend well.

In a small bowl, dissolve the cornflour [cornstarch] in the reserved pineapple juice, stirring well until the mixture is smooth. Stir the cornflour [cornstarch] mixture into the vegetable and rice mixture and return the pan to moderate heat. Cook, stirring constantly, for 3 minutes.

Remove the pan from the heat and stir in the toasted almonds. Turn the rice mixture into a heated serving dish and serve.

Rice Balls in Tomato Sauce

A deliciously different dish, Rice Balls in Tomato Sauce makes a wonderful supper or luncheon dish and needs no accompaniment other than a salad.
Preparation and cooking time: 45 minutes
4 SERVINGS

1 oz. [2 tablespoons] butter or margarine
1 large onion, finely chopped
1 lb. fresh tomatoes, blanched, peeled, seeded and chopped, or 1 lb. canned peeled tomatoes, drained and chopped
1 teaspoon dried basil
½ teaspoon dried thyme
1 teaspoon salt
½ teaspoon black pepper
3 fl. oz. [⅜ cup] dry white wine
10 fl. oz. [1¼ cups] Light Vegetable Stock
1 lb. cooked long-grain brown rice
1 egg, lightly beaten
1 tablespoon flour
4 oz. Emmenthal or Mozzarella cheese, cut into small cubes
1 tablespoon chopped fresh parsley

In a medium-sized saucepan, melt the butter or margarine over moderate heat. When the foam subsides, add the onion. Fry it, stirring occasionally, for 5 to 7 minutes, or until it is soft and translucent but not brown. Add the tomatoes, basil, thyme, salt and pepper and cook for a further 3 minutes. Stir in the wine and stock and increase the heat to high. Bring the liquid to the boil. Reduce the heat to low, cover the pan and simmer the sauce for 15 minutes.

Meanwhile, in a large mixing bowl, combine the rice with the egg and flour and mix until they are well blended. The mixture should be quite stiff.

Take a tablespoonful of the rice mixture and form it into a ball. Make a hollow in the ball with your thumb and insert a cube of cheese. Close up the hollow, completely enclosing the cheese, and set aside. Continue making rice balls in the same way until all of the rice mixture and cheese have been used.

Add the rice balls to the sauce and simmer for a further 10 minutes.

Remove the pan from the heat and turn the rice balls and sauce into a warmed serving dish. Sprinkle over the parsley and serve.

Pain Mimosa
RICE MOULD

This adaptation of a classic French dish is very pretty and would look lovely on a buffet table. Serve it with a well-chilled Sylvaner or Chablis.
Preparation and cooking time: 5 hours
4-6 SERVINGS

9 oz. [1½ cups] long-grain rice, washed, soaked in cold water for 30 minutes and drained
1¼ pints [3 cups] water
1½ teaspoons salt
1 oz. [2 tablespoons] plus 1 teaspoon butter or margarine
2 large onions, finely chopped
1 garlic clove, crushed
1 green pepper, white pith removed, seeded and chopped
1½ teaspoons mild curry powder
6 hard-boiled eggs
3 tablespoons olive oil
1½ tablespoons vinegar
1 tablespoon finely chopped fresh coriander leaves
2 tomatoes, quartered
watercress sprigs (to garnish)

Put the rice in a medium-sized saucepan. Pour in the water and add 1 teaspoon of the salt. Place the pan over high heat and bring the water to the boil. Cover the pan, reduce the heat to very low and simmer for 20 to 25 minutes, or until the rice is tender and all the liquid has been absorbed. Remove the pan from the heat.

In a large frying-pan, melt 1 ounce [2 tablespoons] of the butter or margarine over moderate heat. When the foam subsides, add the onions, garlic and green pepper. Cook, stirring occasionally, for 5 minutes. Stir in the rice and 1 teaspoon of curry powder. Cook, stirring frequently, for 5 minutes, or until the rice becomes brown. Remove the pan from the heat and transfer the rice mixture to a large mixing bowl. Allow the rice mixture to

cool to room temperature, then place the bowl in the refrigerator and chill for 30 minutes.

Finely chop four of the hard-boiled eggs. Stir the chopped eggs into the chilled rice mixture.

In a small mixing bowl, beat the oil, vinegar, remaining salt and curry powder and the coriander together with a fork. Add the mixture to the rice and toss well to blend.

Lightly grease a 2-pint [5-cup] mould with the remaining teaspoon of butter or margarine. Spoon the rice mixture into the mould and place it in the refrigerator. Chill for 3 hours.

To unmould the Pain, place a serving dish, inverted, over the mould. Reverse the two—the Pain should slide out easily.

Arrange the tomato quarters decoratively around the Pain. Slice the remaining eggs and place them around the Pain. Garnish with the watercress and serve.

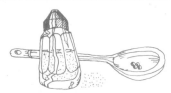

Riso Arancia
RICE WITH CARROTS, NUTS AND ORANGE RIND

A fresh-tasting dish of Middle Eastern origin, Riso Arancia (ree-soh ah-rahn-see-yah) *is a colourful main dish of vegetables and rice flavoured with turmeric, orange rind, nuts and honey.*
Preparation and cooking time: 45 minutes
6-8 SERVINGS

4 oz. [½ cup] butter or margarine
4 medium-sized carrots, scraped and cut into 1-inch strips
1 medium-sized onion, thinly sliced
2 tablespoons grated orange rind
4 oz. canned green beans, drained
3 oz. [¾ cup] slivered almonds
2 oz. [½ cup] chopped pistachio nuts
8 fl. oz [1 cup] clear honey
1 teaspoon turmeric
1½ teaspoons salt
12 oz. [2 cups] long-grain brown rice, washed, soaked in cold water for 30 minutes and drained
1½ pints [3¾ cups] water

In a medium-sized saucepan, melt the butter or margarine over moderate heat. When the foam subsides, add the carrots and onion. Cook, stirring occasionally, for 5 to 7 minutes, or until the onion is soft and translucent but not brown.

Stir in the orange rind, green beans, almonds, pistachios, honey, turmeric and ½ teaspoon of the salt. Reduce the heat to

low and simmer the mixture, stirring occasionally, for 30 minutes.

Meanwhile put the rice in a large saucepan. Pour in the water and add the remaining salt. Place the pan over high heat and bring the water to the boil. Reduce the heat to low, cover the pan and simmer for 20 to 25 minutes, or until the rice is tender and all the liquid has been absorbed.

Arrange the rice in a large, warmed serving dish. Spoon over the vegetable and honey mixture and serve.

Vegetable Paella

A colourful and exotic vegetable version of the Spanish national dish, Vegetable Paella is really delicious.
Preparation and cooking time: 1 hour
4-6 SERVINGS

4 fl. oz. [½ cup] olive oil
2 large onions, thinly sliced
2 garlic cloves, crushed
1 large red pepper, white pith removed, seeded and sliced
12 oz. [2 cups] long-grain brown rice, washed, soaked in cold water for 30 minutes and drained
1 pint [2½ cups] Light Vegetable Stock
4 large tomatoes, blanched, peeled, seeded and chopped
4 oz. frozen and thawed green beans, or 4 oz. canned green beans, drained
3 oz. frozen and thawed petit pois, or 3 oz. canned petit pois, drained
2 celery stalks, chopped
18 black olives, halved and stoned
1 teaspoon salt
1 teaspoon black pepper
¼ teaspoon crushed saffron threads dissolved in 2 teaspoons hot water
2 oz. [½ cup] slivered almonds

In a very large saucepan, heat the oil over moderate heat. When the oil is hot, add the onions, garlic and red pepper. Cook, stirring occasionally, for 5 to 7 minutes, or until the onions are soft and translucent but not brown. Stir in the rice, coating it well with the oil, and continue cooking, stirring occasionally, for 5 minutes. Pour in the stock and increase the heat to high. Bring the liquid to the boil. Reduce the heat to low and stir in the tomatoes, green beans, petits pois, celery, olives, salt, pepper and saffron. Cover the pan and simmer the mixture for 30 to 35 minutes, or until the rice is tender.

Remove the pan from the heat and turn the paella into a warmed serving dish. Sprinkle the almonds on top and serve.

Greek Pilaff

Rice dishes are very popular in the Middle and Near East and while Greece is geographically situated within Europe, its cuisine owes much to the nearer parts of Asia Minor. This tasty pilaff is no exception and its exotic blend of fruits and vegetables recalls some of the great Persian rice dishes. Marinated Pepper Salad would complement this dish very well. Remember that the apricots and prunes will need to be soaked overnight.

Preparation and cooking time: 1¼ hours

6-8 SERVINGS

12 oz. [2 cups] long-grain brown rice, washed, soaked in cold water for 30 minutes and drained
1½ pints [3¾ cups] water
1½ teaspoons salt
2 oz. [¼ cup] butter or margarine
2 medium-sized onions, thinly sliced
1 garlic clove, crushed
1 large red pepper, white pith removed, seeded and sliced
½ small lettuce, outer leaves removed, washed and shredded
6 oz. frozen and thawed petits pois, or 5 oz. canned petits pois, drained
½ teaspoon freshly ground black pepper
2 oz. [⅓ cup] dried apricots, soaked overnight, drained and chopped
2 oz. [⅓ cup] dried prunes, soaked overnight, drained and chopped
2 oz. [⅓ cup] seedless raisins, soaked in cold water for 15 minutes and drained
2 oz. [⅓ cup] blanched almonds
2 tablespoons finely grated orange rind
½ teaspoon grated nutmeg
4 fl. oz. [½ cup] boiling Light Vegetable Stock

Put the rice into a very large saucepan. Pour in the water and add 1 teaspoon of the salt. Place the pan over high heat and bring the water to the boil. Cover the pan, reduce the heat to very low and simmer for 20 to 25 minutes, or until the rice is tender and all of the liquid has been absorbed. Remove the pan from the heat and set aside.

Preheat the oven to moderate 350°F (Gas Mark 4, 180°C).

Meanwhile, in a large frying-pan, melt half of the butter or margarine over moderate heat. When the foam subsides, add the onions, garlic and red pepper. Cook them, stirring occasionally, for 5 to 7 minutes, or until the onions are soft and translucent but not brown. Add the lettuce, petits pois, remaining salt and the black pepper and continue cooking, stir-ring frequently, for 3 minutes. Remove the pan from the heat and set aside.

In a medium-sized frying-pan, melt the remaining butter or margarine over moderate heat. When the foam subsides, add the apricots, prunes, raisins, almonds, orange rind and nutmeg. Cook, stirring frequently, for 5 minutes. Remove the pan from the heat and set aside.

Arrange one-third of the rice on the bottom of a large, heavy earthenware casserole. Cover it with the red pepper and lettuce mixture. Top with another one-third of the rice, then spread over the dried fruit mixture. Top with the remaining rice. Pour in the stock. Cover the casserole and place it in the oven. Bake for 30 minutes.

Remove the casserole from the oven and serve.

Rice Valenciana

A fragrant, colourful dish, Rice Valenciana makes a wonderful summer buffet. Serve it with a salad and a well-chilled Spanish Chablis for an enjoyable meal.

Preparation and cooking time: 40 minutes

4-6 SERVINGS

8 oz. [1⅓ cups] long-grain brown rice, washed, soaked in cold water for 30 minutes and drained
1 pint [2½ cups] Light Vegetable Stock
1½ teaspoons salt
2 oz. [¼ cup] butter or margarine
3 medium-sized onions, thinly sliced
2 garlic cloves, crushed
1 large green pepper, white pith removed, seeded and sliced
1 large red pepper, white pith removed, seeded and sliced
3 large tomatoes, blanched, peeled and sliced
3 large bananas, thinly sliced
1 oz. [¼ cup] shredded almonds
2 oz. [⅓ cup] seedless raisins
1 tablespoon grated orange rind
½ teaspoon white pepper
1½ teaspoons turmeric
2 hard-boiled eggs, sliced
6 parsley sprigs

Put the rice into a very large saucepan. Pour in the stock and add 1 teaspoon of the salt. Place the pan over high heat and bring the stock to the boil. Cover the pan, reduce the heat to very low and simmer for 20 to 25 minutes, or until the rice is tender and all the liquid has been absorbed.

Meanwhile, in a large frying-pan, melt the butter or margarine over moderate heat. When the foam subsides, add the onions, garlic and green and red peppers. Cook them, stirring occasionally, for 5 to 7 minutes, or until the onions are soft and translucent but not brown. Add the tomatoes, bananas, almonds, raisins, orange rind, the remaining salt, the pepper and turmeric and stir well to blend. Cook the mixture, stirring occasionally, for 3 minutes. Remove the pan from the heat.

When the rice is cooked, stir in the tomato and pepper mixture. Continue to simmer gently, uncovered, for 2 to 3 minutes.

Remove the pan from the heat and turn the rice mixture into a warmed serving dish. Garnish with the egg slices and parsley sprigs and serve.

Pilaff of Fruit and Nuts

A fresh and different-tasting rice dish, Pilaff of Fruit and Nuts makes a beautiful summer lunch or supper. Serve it with a well-chilled light Sylvaner wine.

Preparation and cooking time: 40 minutes

4-6 SERVINGS

2 fl. oz. [¼ cup] corn oil
4 oz. [⅔ cup] dried apricots, soaked overnight, drained and chopped
2 oz. [⅓ cup] dried prunes, soaked overnight, drained and chopped
3 oz. [½ cup] seedless raisins, soaked in cold water for 30 minutes and drained
2 carrots, scraped and thinly sliced
5 fl. oz. [⅝ cup] orange juice
2 large bananas, thinly sliced
3 oz. [½ cup] walnuts, chopped
2 tablespoons pine kernels
1 tablespoon clear honey
8 oz. [1⅓ cups] long-grain brown rice, washed, soaked in cold water for 30 minutes and drained
15 fl. oz. [1⅞ cups] water
1 small onion, sliced and pushed out into rings

In a large saucepan, heat the oil over moderate heat. When the oil is hot, add the apricots, prunes, raisins, carrots and orange juice. Cook, stirring occasionally, for 5 minutes. Reduce the heat to low and add the bananas, walnuts, pine kernels and honey and stir well to blend.

Add the rice to the pan and pour in the water. Increase the heat to high and bring the liquid to the boil. Cover the pan, reduce the heat to low and simmer, stir-ring occasionally, for 20 to 25 minutes or until the rice is tender and all the water has been absorbed.

Remove the pan from the heat and transfer the mixture to a warmed serving dish. Arrange the onion rings on top and serve.

Right Savoury Brazil Ring Bake (page 60) is a tempting nutty main dish. Try it with a green salad. *Left* Melt-in-the-mouth Mushroom and Petits Pois Bouchées (page 69) make exquisite hors d'oeuvre. *Top* Flaky pastry with a creamy filling makes Curd Cheese and Tomato Quiche (page 69) a delicious dish.

Always popular for family lunches or suppers, Wholemeal Pizza (page 68) is so easy to prepare. Try serving it with a simple tomato salad and a bowl of cubed mozzarella cheese and olives for an informal supper party – with lots of Chianti wine, of course!

Bottom Topped with a creamy sauce, Noodles baked with Spinach (page 74) is succulent layers of noodles, cheese, spinach and eggs. *Left* Stuffed Cannelloni (page 74), with spinach and cheese, is an impressive meal-in-itself. *Top* Spaghetti with Italian Tomato Sauce (page 72) makes an excellent simple family meal.

Top An elegant moulded rice dish, Pain Mimosa (page 79) makes a lovely centrepiece for a summer buffet table. *Centre* Delicately flavoured Riso Arancia (page 79) is a colourful Middle Eastern dish combining rice, vegetables, nuts, honey and turmeric. *Bottom* Rice, apricots, prunes, raisins, carrots, orange juice, bananas and walnuts are just some of the delicious ingredients in Pilaff of Fruit and Nuts (page 80).

Top An aromatic mixed vegetable curry, Aviyal (page 75) is flavoured with coconut and spices. It is simple to prepare and you may use any combination of your favourite vegetables. It is delicious served on a bed of fluffy rice. *Bottom* Channa Dhal (page 76) is an inexpensive and exotic accompaniment to almost any spicy vegetable dish.

Top Light-as-air Spinach Soufflé (page 98) is so easy to prepare. It makes a perfect first course for a dinner party, or serve it alone, for a simple family lunch or supper. Elegant Cold Gruyère cheese Soufflettes (page 100) are a perfect dinner party hors d'oeuvre as they may be prepared well in advance.

Top Vegetable Crêpes (page 106) are wafer-thin crêpes rolled around a mouth-watering mixture of red pepper, cabbage, apple and onion. *Bottom* A sumptuous hors d'oeuvre for a formal dinner party, fluffy Omelette Soufflée Princesse (page 104) is filled with an exquisite combination of asparagus, cream and truffles.

A cheese and sour cream soufflé, Alivenci (page 100) is an adaption of an old Romanian recipe. It may be served as a first course for a dinner party or as a light family lunch. It also makes a delicious dessert sprinkled lightly with sugar and accompanied by a hot fruit sauce.

Top Layers of fluffy pancake, thick apricot jam and whipped cream make Stacked Pancakes (page 109) a really spectacular dessert. *Bottom* A sophisticated dinner party dessert, classic Crêpes Suzettes (page 108) are thin crêpes, dipped in orange butter, folded and flamed with orange liqueur and brandy.

This glorious array of cakes and biscuits [cookies] includes, *clockwise from top*, sophisticated Black Pepper Cookies (page 114), moist Almond Parkin (page 111), succulent Blackberry Kiss Cakes (page 114), Almond Petits Fours (page 114) in a variety of shapes, topped with cherries, almonds and angelica, chewy Cherry Biscuits (page 114), Orange Almond Ring Cake (page 111) and *Centre* Bergward Torte (page 115).

Top Filled with the goodness of walnuts, brown sugar, glacé cherries, raisins, angelica, and sherry, sumptuous Christmas Cake (page 113) is a handsome fruit cake. *Bottom* An unusual American Jewish cake, Carrot Cake (page 113) is made with eggs, carrots and ground almonds. It has the delightfully moist consistency of cheesecake.

A heavenly moulded dessert, Bombe Coppelia (page 119) is coffee ice-cream filled with praline and rum. It is a magnificent dessert to serve for a dinner party and, although it does take a little time to prepare, the compliments you will receive from your guests will make it well worth the effort.

Top Children will love Coriander Fruit Crumble (page 121), a summery dessert made with fresh blackberries, apples, brown sugar and cinnamon. Serve it hot or cold with whipped cream. *Bottom* Luscious Apricot Bourdaloue Tart (page 123) is flaky pastry filled with apricots and a creamy, orange-flavoured custard.

This page left Light, creamy Apricot Fool (page 118), topped with fresh orange slices, is a perfect summer dessert. *Top* Rum-flavoured Jamaican Trifle (page 116) is luscious layers of biscuits [cookies], fresh pineapple and cream. *Bottom* Ricotta Cheese Pudding with Chocolate Sauce (page 117) is an unusual dessert.

This page left Golden meringue covering a tangy lemon and cream filling has made Lemon Meringue Pie (page 122) a popular dessert for generations. *Right* A light melt-in-the-mouth water ice, Fruit Sorbet (page 120) is so easy to prepare and you may make it with any combination of ripe fruit.

Top Warming Mulled Claret (page 124) will brighten up a winter party. *Centre* Crudités avec Aïoli (page 126) is crisp vegetables arranged decoratively around a creamy garlic dip. *Bottom left* A refreshing summer drink, Citrus Ponets (page 126) is made with wine, vodka and fresh fruit juices. *Bottom right* These savoury biscuits [crackers] are topped with a colourful selection of spreads (page 127).

Soufflés, Omelets, Crêpes and Pancakes

A well-known French cook once said "Soufflés are *so* simple . . . it is impossible to have a disaster!" If you follow the directions carefully in each of these soufflé recipes, you will find she was right!

Omelets are always marvellous – sweet or savoury, they make a welcome offering for any meal, be it breakfast, brunch, lunch or dinner. Those included run the gamut from a simple ricotta cheese omelet to an elaborate soufflé omelet with an asparagus and truffle filling.

Light, versatile crêpes – just eggs, milk and a little flour – can be made long before you need them. Stack and store them (alternating the crêpes with pieces of greaseproof or waxed paper) in the refrigerator until you are ready to fill, heat and serve them.

Crêpes can be sophisticated desserts, for example the Crêpes Suzette which is flamed with brandy, or they can make delicious savoury first courses or main dishes filled with cabbage, raisins and apples or mushrooms. They can be rolled around any tasty leftover, heated, and then covered with a hot creamy sauce.

Pancakes are a little heavier and more substantial than crêpes and are also extremely versatile. But served simply, smothered in butter and maple syrup, they are one of the best ways to please your family and friends.

Soufflés

Tomato and Pasta Soufflé

A filling Italian-style soufflé, this is well complemented by a Mixed Salad.
Preparation and cooking time: 1¾ hours
4 SERVINGS

1 pint [2½ cups] water
1½ teaspoons salt
4 oz. small wholemeal pasta (noodles or macaroni)
1 oz. [2 tablespoons] plus 1 teaspoon butter or margarine
2 tablespoons dry breadcrumbs
2 tablespoons flour
10 fl. oz. [1¼ cups] milk
5 oz. tomato purée
2 oz. [½ cup] Parmesan cheese, grated
¼ teaspoon black pepper
3 egg yolks
4 egg whites

In a large saucepan, bring the water with 1 teaspoon of the salt to the boil over high heat. Reduce the heat to moderate and add the pasta. Cook the pasta for 10 to 12 minutes, or until it is just tender. Remove the pan from the heat and drain the pasta in a colander. Set aside.

Preheat the oven to fairly hot 375°F (Gas Mark 5, 190°C). Grease a 2-pint [5-cup] soufflé dish with 1 teaspoon of the butter or margarine. Sprinkle in the breadcrumbs and press them on to the bottom and sides of the dish with your fingertips. Set aside.

In a large saucepan, melt the remaining butter or margarine over moderate heat. Remove the pan from the heat and, with a wooden spoon, stir in the flour to make a smooth paste. Gradually add the milk, stirring constantly. Stir in the tomato purée. Return the pan to low heat and cook the sauce, stirring constantly, for 2 to 3 minutes, or until it is smooth and thick.

Remove the pan from the heat. Stir in the cheese, a little at a time. Stir in the remaining salt, the pepper and the pasta and mix well to blend. Add the egg yolks, one at a time, beating well between each addition.

In a medium-sized mixing bowl, beat the egg whites with a wire whisk or rotary beater until they form stiff peaks. With a metal spoon, carefully fold the egg whites into the pasta mixture.

Spoon the mixture into the prepared soufflé dish. Place the dish in the oven and bake the soufflé for 35 to 40 minutes, or until it is puffed up and lightly browned.

Remove the soufflé from the oven and serve at once.

Mushroom Soufflé

A simply delicious soufflé, this, like all other soufflés, is remarkably easy to prepare. If you prefer, leave the mushrooms in slices instead of puréeing them.
Preparation and cooking time: 1¼ hours
4 SERVINGS

1 oz. [2 tablespoons] plus 1 teaspoon butter or margarine
2 tablespoons dry breadcrumbs
8 oz. mushrooms, wiped clean and sliced
15 fl. oz. [1⅞ cups] Béchamel Sauce
3 egg yolks
3 oz. [¾ cup] Cheddar cheese, grated
½ teaspoon grated nutmeg
½ teaspoon salt
¼ teaspoon white pepper
4 egg whites

Preheat the oven to fairly hot 375°F (Gas Mark 5, 190°C). Grease a 2-pint [5-cup] soufflé dish with 1 teaspoon of the butter or margarine. Sprinkle in the breadcrumbs and press them on to the bottom and sides of the dish with your fingertips. Set aside.

In a medium-sized saucepan, melt the remaining butter or margarine over moderate heat. When the foam subsides, add the mushrooms. Cook them, stirring oc-

97

casionally, for 5 minutes. Remove the pan from the heat and drain the mushrooms in a fine strainer. Purée the mushrooms in a food mill or in a blender and transfer the purée to a large mixing bowl.

Add the béchamel sauce and blend well. Add the egg yolks, one at a time, beating well between each addition. Beat in the cheese, nutmeg, salt and pepper.

In a medium-sized mixing bowl, beat the egg whites with a wire whisk or rotary beater until they form stiff peaks. With a metal spoon, carefully fold the egg whites into the mushroom mixture.

Spoon the mixture into the prepared soufflé dish. Place the dish in the oven and bake the soufflé for 20 to 25 minutes, or until it is puffed up and lightly browned.

Remove the soufflé from the oven and serve at once.

Spinach Soufflé

This green Spinach Soufflé would go well with Honey-glazed Carrots or Tomatoes with Herbs.

Preparation and cooking time: $1\frac{1}{4}$ hours

4 SERVINGS

1 tablespoon plus 1 teaspoon butter or margarine
2 tablespoons dry breadcrumbs
1 tablespoon flour
5 fl. oz. [$\frac{5}{8}$ cup] milk
3 oz. cooked and puréed spinach
3 egg yolks
2 oz. [$\frac{1}{2}$ cup] Cheddar cheese, grated
$\frac{1}{2}$ teaspoon salt
$\frac{1}{4}$ teaspoon white pepper
$\frac{1}{4}$ teaspoon grated nutmeg
5 egg whites

Preheat the oven to fairly hot 375°F (Gas Mark 5, 190°C). Grease a 2-pint [5-cup] soufflé dish with the teaspoon of butter or margarine. Sprinkle in the breadcrumbs and press them on to the bottom and sides of the dish with your fingertips. Set aside.

In a medium-sized saucepan, melt the remaining butter or margarine over moderate heat. Remove the pan from the heat and, with a wooden spoon, stir in the flour to make a smooth paste. Gradually add the milk, stirring constantly. Return the pan to low heat and cook, stirring constantly, for 2 to 3 minutes, or until the sauce is thick and smooth. Stir in the puréed spinach and remove the pan from the heat. Add the egg yolks, one at a time, beating well between each addition. Gradually beat in the grated cheese, and then stir in the salt, pepper and nutmeg.

In a medium-sized bowl, beat the egg whites with a wire whisk or rotary beater until they form stiff peaks. With a metal spoon, carefully fold the egg whites into the spinach mixture.

Spoon the mixture into the prepared soufflé dish. Place the dish in the oven and bake the soufflé for 20 to 25 minutes, or until it is puffed up and lightly browned.

Remove the soufflé from the oven and serve immediately.

Aubergine [Eggplant] Soufflé

These delicately flavoured individual Aubergine [Eggplant] *Soufflés would make an elegant first course for a dinner party, or, if served with a salad, a light luncheon.*

Preparation and cooking time: $2\frac{1}{4}$ hours

4 SERVINGS

2 small aubergines [eggplants]
$1\frac{1}{2}$ teaspoons salt
1 oz. [2 tablespoons] butter or margarine
$1\frac{1}{4}$ pints [3 cups] boiling water
2 teaspoons vinegar
$1\frac{1}{2}$ oz. [$\frac{3}{4}$ cup] fresh breadcrumbs
2 egg yolks, lightly beaten
1 tablespoon melted butter or margarine
2 oz. [$\frac{1}{2}$ cup] Cheddar cheese, grated
$\frac{1}{4}$ teaspoon black pepper
$\frac{1}{2}$ teaspoon dried basil
3 egg whites
2 tablespoons fine dry breadcrumbs

Cut the aubergines [eggplants] in half, lengthways, and scoop out the flesh. Place the flesh in a colander and sprinkle over 1 teaspoon of the salt. Leave the aubergine [eggplant] flesh to dégorge for 30 minutes. Dry the flesh with kitchen paper towels.

Preheat the oven to fairly hot 375°F (Gas Mark 5 190°C). Grease four small individual soufflé or ramekin dishes with half of the butter or margarine. Set aside.

Put the aubergine [eggplant] flesh into a medium-sized saucepan. Pour over the water and add the vinegar. Place the pan over low heat and simmer for 15 minutes, or until the flesh is tender. Drain the flesh and place it in a large mixing bowl. Reserve the cooking liquid.

With a fork, mash the flesh to a purée. Add the breadcrumbs, egg yolks, melted butter or margarine, grated cheese, remaining salt and the pepper and basil. Mix well to blend. If the mixture is too stiff, add a spoonful of the reserved cooking liquid.

In a medium-sized mixing bowl, beat the egg whites with a wire whisk or rotary beater until they form stiff peaks. With a metal spoon, carefully fold the egg whites into the aubergine [eggplant] mixture.

Spoon the mixture into the prepared soufflé or ramekin dishes. Sprinkle the dry breadcrumbs on top. Cut the remaining butter or margarine into small pieces and dot them on top of the breadcrumbs.

Place the soufflé or ramekin dishes in a large roasting tin and pour in enough boiling water to come halfway up the sides of the dishes. Place the tin in the oven and bake the soufflés for 20 minutes, or until they are puffed up and lightly golden.

Remove the tin from the oven and serve the soufflés at once, in the dishes.

Carrot Soufflettes

These individual Carrot Soufflettes are light as a feather. Serve them with a green vegetable or salad and crusty Bran Bread for a delicious and healthy supper.

Preparation and cooking time: $1\frac{1}{2}$ hours

4 SERVINGS

8 oz. carrots, scraped and quartered
1 pint [$2\frac{1}{2}$ cups] water
1 teaspoon salt
1 tablespoon butter or margarine
2 tablespoons dry breadcrumbs
$\frac{1}{2}$ teaspoon black pepper
3 egg yolks
5 egg whites

Put the carrots into a large saucepan. Pour over the water and add $\frac{1}{2}$ teaspoon of the salt. Place the pan over moderately high heat and bring the water to the boil. Reduce the heat to moderate and cook the carrots for 10 minutes, or until they are just tender. Remove the pan from the heat and drain the carrots in a colander. With a wooden spoon, rub the carrots through a strainer into a large mixing bowl. Alternatively, purée the carrots in a food mill or in a blender. Set aside.

Preheat the oven to fairly hot 375°F (Gas Mark 5, 190°C). Grease four small individual soufflé or ramekin dishes with the butter or margarine. Sprinkle in the breadcrumbs and press them on to the bottoms and sides of the dishes with your fingertips. Set aside.

Stir the remaining salt and the pepper into the carrot purée. Add the egg yolks, one at a time, beating well between each addition.

In a medium-sized mixing bowl, beat the egg whites with a wire whisk or rotary beater until they form stiff peaks. With a metal spoon, carefully fold the egg whites into the carrot mixture.

Spoon the mixture into the prepared soufflé dishes. Place the dishes in the oven and bake the soufflettes for 20 minutes, or until they are puffed up and lightly browned.

Remove the soufflettes from the oven and serve at once.

Layered Pea and Cauliflower Soufflé

This unusual soufflé has alternating layers of a rich egg yolk sauce and cauliflower flowerets and petits pois. To make it successfully, the egg whites must be beaten until they are very stiff. You should be able to turn the mixing bowl upside-down without the whites falling out.

Preparation and cooking time: 2 hours

4 SERVINGS

½ small cauliflower, trimmed, washed and broken into small flowerets
1½ pints [3¾ cups] water
1½ teaspoons salt
1 bay leaf
4 oz. frozen petits pois
1 oz. [2 tablespoons] plus 1 teaspoon butter or margarine
2 tablespoons flour
15 fl. oz. [1⅞ cups] milk
½ teaspoon white pepper
1 teaspoon chopped fresh mint
3 egg yolks
5 egg whites

Put the cauliflower into a medium-sized saucepan. Pour over the water and add 1 teaspoon of the salt and the bay leaf. Place the pan over moderately high heat and bring the water to the boil. Reduce the heat to moderate and cook the cauliflower for 10 to 12 minutes, or until it is just tender. Remove the pan from the heat and drain the cauliflower in a colander. Set the flowerets aside in a large mixing bowl.

Cook the petits pois according to the instructions on the package. Add them to the cauliflower and set aside.

Preheat the oven to fairly hot 375°F (Gas Mark 5, 190°C). Grease a 2-pint [5-cup] soufflé dish with 1 teaspoon of the butter or margarine. Set aside.

In a medium-sized saucepan, melt the remaining butter or margarine over moderate heat. Remove the pan from the heat and, with a wooden spoon, stir in the flour to make a smooth paste. Gradually add the milk, stirring constantly. Return the pan to low heat and cook the sauce, stirring constantly, for 2 to 3 minutes, or until it is thick and smooth. Remove the pan from the heat and set it aside to cool slightly.

Stir the remaining salt, the pepper and mint into the sauce and mix well. Add the egg yolks, one at a time, beating well between each addition.

In a medium-sized mixing bowl, beat the egg whites with a wire whisk or rotary beater until they form stiff peaks. With a metal spoon, carefully fold the egg whites into the egg yolk mixture.

Spoon about one-third of the egg mixture into the prepared soufflé dish. Add about one-half of the cooked vegetables. Top with another one-third of the egg mixture, then add the remaining vegetables. Cover with the remaining egg mixture. Place the soufflé dish in the oven and bake the soufflé for 25 to 30 minutes, or until it is puffed up and lightly browned.

Remove the soufflé from the oven and serve at once.

Potato Soufflé

This soufflé may not sound very interesting, but in fact it is rich and spicy as it is made with potatoes, onion, Béchamel Sauce, cream and paprika. Asparagus au Naturel would be a good accompaniment.

Preparation and cooking time: 1¼ hours

4 SERVINGS

1 oz. [2 tablespoons] plus 1 teaspoon butter or margarine
1 medium-sized onion, finely chopped
8 oz. potatoes, cooked and mashed
1½ teaspoons paprika
2 tablespoons dry breadcrumbs
12 fl. oz. [1½ cups] Béchamel Sauce
1 tablespoon single [light] cream
½ teaspoon salt
½ teaspoon white pepper
3 egg yolks
5 egg whites

In a small frying-pan, melt 1 ounce [2 tablespoons] of the butter or margarine over moderate heat. When the foam subsides, add the onion. Fry it, stirring occasionally, for 5 to 7 minutes, or until it is soft and translucent but not brown. Remove the pan from the heat.

Put the mashed potatoes into a large mixing bowl and stir in the onion with its cooking juices and the paprika. Set aside.

Preheat the oven to fairly hot 375°F (Gas Mark 5, 190°C). Grease a 2-pint [5-cup] soufflé dish with the remaining butter or margarine. Sprinkle in the breadcrumbs and press them on to the bottom and sides of the dish with your fingertips. Set aside.

In a medium-sized mixing bowl, combine the béchamel sauce with the cream, salt and pepper and stir well to blend. Add the béchamel sauce mixture to the potato mixture, stirring well. Add the egg yolks, one at a time, beating well between each addition.

In a medium-sized mixing bowl, beat the egg whites with a wire whisk or rotary beater until they form stiff peaks. With a metal spoon, carefully fold the egg whites into the potato mixture.

Spoon the mixture into the prepared soufflé dish. Place the dish in the oven and bake the soufflé for 20 to 25 minutes, or until it is puffed up and lightly browned.

Remove the soufflé from the oven and serve at once.

Leek Soufflé

The national emblem of Wales makes a superb soufflé. Be sure to wash the leeks very thoroughly under cold running water.

Preparation and cooking time: 1¾ hours

4 SERVINGS

4 large leeks, white part only, trimmed and washed
2 pints [5 cups] water
1½ teaspoons salt
1 tablespoon plus 1 teaspoon butter or margarine
2 tablespoons dry breadcrumbs
2 tablespoons flour
12 fl. oz. [1½ cups] milk
3 egg yolks
½ teaspoon white pepper
½ teaspoon ground mace
4 egg whites

Put the leeks into a large saucepan. Pour over the water and add 1 teaspoon of the salt. Place the pan over moderately high heat and bring the water to the boil. Reduce the heat to moderate and cook the leeks for 12 to 15 minutes, or until they are just tender. Remove the pan from the heat and drain the leeks in a colander. Allow the leeks to cool a little, then cut them into ¼-inch thick slices. Set aside.

Preheat the oven to fairly hot 375°F (Gas Mark 5, 190°C). Grease a 2-pint [5-cup] soufflé dish with 1 teaspoon of the butter or margarine. Sprinkle in the breadcrumbs and press them on to the bottom and sides of the dish with your fingertips. Set aside.

In a medium-sized saucepan, melt the remaining butter or margarine over moderate heat. Remove the pan from the heat and, with a wooden spoon, stir in the flour to make a smooth paste. Gradually add the milk, stirring constantly. Return the pan to low heat and cook the sauce, stirring constantly, for 2 to 3 minutes, or until it is thick and smooth. Remove the pan from the heat.

Add the egg yolks, one at a time, beating well between each addition. Stir in the remaining salt, the pepper and mace. Add the leek slices to the mixture and stir well to blend.

In a medium-sized mixing bowl, beat the egg whites with a wire whisk or rotary beater until they form stiff peaks. With a metal spoon, carefully fold the egg whites into the leek mixture.

Spoon the mixture into the prepared soufflé dish. Place the dish in the oven and bake the soufflé for 20 to 25 minutes, or until it is puffed up and lightly browned.

Remove the soufflé from the oven and serve at once.

Corn Soufflé

This cheesy Corn Soufflé takes very little time to prepare and it makes a filling main dish. Serve it with a Cabbage and Pepper Salad or a Summer Garden Salad for an attractive and nourishing meal.

Preparation and cooking time: 1 hour

4 SERVINGS

1 teaspoon butter or margarine
2 tablespoons dry breadcrumbs
15 fl. oz. [1⅞ cups] hot Béchamel Sauce
10 oz. canned sweetcorn, heated and drained
½ teaspoon salt
¼ teaspoon white pepper
3 egg yolks
3 oz. [¾ cup] Cheddar cheese, grated
4 egg whites

Preheat the oven to fairly hot 375°F (Gas Mark 5, 190°C). Grease a 2-pint [5-cup] soufflé dish with the butter or margarine. Sprinkle in the breadcrumbs and press them on to the bottom and sides of the dish with your fingertips. Set aside.

In a large mixing bowl, combine the hot béchamel sauce with the sweetcorn, salt and pepper and mix well to blend. Add the egg yolks, one at a time, beating well between each addition. Gradually add the cheese and beat until the mixture is well blended.

In a medium-sized mixing bowl, beat the egg whites with a wire whisk or rotary beater until they form stiff peaks. With a metal spoon, carefully fold the egg whites into the corn mixture.

Spoon the mixture into the prepared soufflé dish. Place the dish in the oven and bake the soufflé for 25 to 30 minutes, or until it is puffed up and lightly browned.

Remove the soufflé from the oven and serve at once.

Cold Gruyère Soufflettes

These individual cold Gruyère cheese Soufflettes would make a tasty main dish served with a Tomato Salad and crusty bread.

Preparation and cooking time: 3 hours

6 SERVINGS

1 tablespoon butter or margarine
3 tablespoons fine dry breadcrumbs
12 fl. oz. [1½ cups] Béchamel Sauce
⅛ teaspoon salt
½ teaspoon white pepper

¼ teaspoon grated nutmeg
3 egg yolks
2 teaspoons agar-agar dissolved in 3 tablespoons boiling Light Vegetable Stock
4 oz. [1 cup] Gruyère cheese, grated
4 egg whites
2 tablespoons snipped chives

Grease six individual soufflé or ramekin dishes with the butter or margarine. Sprinkle in the breadcrumbs and press them on to the bottom and sides of the dishes with your fingertips. Set aside.

In a large mixing bowl, combine the béchamel sauce with the salt, pepper and nutmeg. Add the egg yolks, one at a time, beating well between each addition. Beat in the dissolved agar-agar and then the grated cheese.

Place the bowl in the refrigerator and chill the cheese mixture for 30 minutes, or until it is very thick, but not yet on the point of setting.

In a medium-sized mixing bowl, beat the egg whites with a wire whisk or rotary beater until they form stiff peaks. With a metal spoon, carefully fold the egg whites into the cheese mixture.

Spoon the mixture into the soufflé dishes. Place the dishes in the refrigerator and chill the soufflettes for 1½ to 2 hours, or until they are completely set.

Just before serving, garnish each soufflette with a teaspoon of the chives.

Alivenci

CHEESE AND SOUR CREAM SOUFFLE

Adapted from an old Romanian recipe, Alivenci (ah-lee-VEEN-che) can be served with a salad as an unusual lunch or light supper dish. Sprinkled lightly with icing [confectioners'] sugar and accompanied by a hot fruit sauce it is a delicious dessert.

Preparation and cooking time: 1¼ hours

4 SERVINGS

1 teaspoon butter or margarine
2 tablespoons dry breadcrumbs
8 oz. cream cheese
3 fl. oz. [⅜ cup] sour cream
3 egg yolks
3 fl. oz. [⅜ cup] milk
½ teaspoon salt
2 teaspoons flour
3 egg whites

Preheat the oven to moderate 350°F (Gas Mark 4, 180°C). Lightly grease a 2-pint [5-cup] soufflé dish with the butter or margarine. Sprinkle in the breadcrumbs and press them on to the bottom and sides of the dish with your fingertips. Set aside.

In a large mixing bowl, beat the cream

cheese with a wooden spoon until it is soft. Gradually beat in the sour cream and continue beating until the mixture is smooth. Add the egg yolks, one at a time, beating well between each addition.

When the egg yolks have been incorporated, beat in the milk, salt and flour.

In a medium-sized mixing bowl, beat the egg whites with a wire whisk or rotary beater until they form stiff peaks. With a metal spoon, carefully fold the egg whites into the cream cheese mixture.

Spoon the mixture into the prepared soufflé dish. Place the dish in the oven and bake the soufflé for 30 to 35 minutes, or until it is puffed up and lightly browned.

Remove the soufflé from the oven and serve at once.

Soufflé Grand Marnier

SOUFFLE WITH ORANGE LIQUEUR

A classic French dessert, Soufflé Grand Marnier is worth every moment you spend in making it. Serve it for an extra special dinner party—your efforts will be rewarded with much praise.

Preparation and cooking time: 1½ hours

4 SERVINGS

1 oz. [2 tablespoons] plus 2 teaspoons butter or margarine
8 fl. oz [1 cup] milk
2 tablespoons sugar
2 tablespoons flour
1 tablespoon finely grated orange rind
2 fl. oz. [¼ cup] Grand Marnier
¼ teaspoon ground cinnamon
3 egg yolks
5 egg whites

Preheat the oven to fairly hot 400°F (Gas Mark 6, 200°C). Lightly grease a 2-pint [5-cup] soufflé dish with 1 teaspoon of the butter or margarine. Grease a folded sheet of greaseproof or waxed paper with the remaining teaspoon of butter or margarine and tie it securely around the soufflé dish, so that it extends 2 inches above the rim. Set aside.

In a small saucepan, scald the milk and sugar over moderate heat (bring to just under boiling point), stirring to dissolve the sugar. Remove the pan from the heat.

In a medium-sized saucepan, melt the remaining butter or margarine over moderate heat. Remove the pan from the heat and, with a wooden spoon, stir in the flour to make a smooth paste. Gradually add the milk and sugar mixture, stirring constantly. Return the pan to the heat and cook the sauce, stirring constantly, for 2 to 3 minutes, or until it is thick and smooth. Stir in the grated orange rind, the Grand Marnier and the cinnamon.

Remove the pan from the heat and add the egg yolks, one at a time, beating well between each addition.

In a medium-sized mixing bowl, beat the egg whites with a wire whisk or rotary beater until they form stiff peaks. With a metal spoon, carefully fold the egg whites into the liqueur mixture.

Spoon the mixture into the prepared soufflé dish. Place the dish in the oven and bake the soufflé for 30 to 35 minutes, or until it is puffed up and lightly browned.

Remove the soufflé from the oven. Remove the paper collar and serve at once.

Apricot Soufflé

Serve this delicious soufflé with brandy-flavoured whipped cream and plain chocolate biscuits [cookies] for a very impressive dessert.

Preparation and cooking time: 1¾ hours
4 SERVINGS

2 teaspoons butter or margarine
2 tablespoons castor [fine] sugar
6 oz. dried apricots, soaked over-night and drained
2 oz. [⅓ cup] soft brown sugar
1 tablespoon brandy
1 tablespoon lemon juice
3 egg yolks
5 egg whites
1 tablespoon icing [confectioners'] sugar, sifted

Preheat the oven to fairly hot 375°F (Gas Mark 5, 190°C). Grease a 2-pint [5-cup] soufflé dish with half of the butter or margarine. Sprinkle in the castor sugar and press it on to the bottom and sides of the dish with your fingertips. Grease a folded sheet of greaseproof or waxed paper with the remaining butter or margarine and tie it securely around the soufflé dish so that it extends 2 inches above the rim. Set aside.

Put the apricots into a medium-sized saucepan and pour over enough water just to cover them. Place the pan over high heat and bring the water to the boil. Reduce the heat to moderate and cook the apricots for 15 minutes or until they are very soft. Remove the pan from the heat and drain the apricots in a colander. With a wooden spoon, rub the apricots through a strainer into a large mixing bowl or purée them in a food mill or blender and transfer them to the bowl.

Stir the brown sugar, brandy and lemon juice into the apricot purée and mix well to blend. Set the purée aside and

allow it to cool slightly. When the purée is cool, add the egg yolks, one at a time, beating well between each addition.

In a medium-sized mixing bowl, beat the egg whites with a wire whisk or rotary beater until they form stiff peaks. With a metal spoon, carefully fold the egg whites into the apricot mixture.

Spoon the mixture into the prepared soufflé dish. Place the dish in the oven and bake the soufflé for 35 to 40 minutes, or until it is puffed up and lightly browned.

Remove the soufflé from the oven. Remove the paper collar. Sprinkle the soufflé with the icing [confectioners'] sugar and serve at once.

Chocolate Soufflé

Light and delicate, this hot Chocolate Soufflé is an elegant dessert to serve for a luncheon or dinner party.

Preparation and cooking time: 1¼ hours
4 SERVINGS

3½ oz. dark [semi-sweet] cooking chocolate, broken into small pieces
2 tablespoons water
15 fl. oz. [1⅞ cups] milk
3 tablespoons vanilla sugar or 1 teaspoon vanilla essence and 3 tablespoons sugar
3 tablespoons arrowroot
1 tablespoon butter or margarine, cut into small pieces
2 teaspoons butter or margarine, softened
3 egg yolks
5 egg whites
1 tablespoon icing [confectioners'] sugar, sifted

Put the chocolate and water in a heavy, medium-sized saucepan. Melt the chocolate over low heat, stirring occasionally.

Put the milk in another heavy, medium-sized saucepan and scald it over low heat (bring to just under boiling point). Spoon out about 3 tablespoons of the milk, put it in a cup and place to one side. Add the vanilla sugar or vanilla essence and sugar to the milk in the saucepan and stir well with a wooden spoon. When the sugar has dissolved, add the melted chocolate and stir well. Remove the pan from the heat.

Add the arrowroot to the reserved 3 tablespoons of milk in the cup and mix to a smooth paste. Add the dissolved arrowroot to the milk and chocolate mixture in the pan and stir well. Replace the saucepan on moderate heat and bring to the boil. As soon as boiling point is reached, remove the pan from the heat.

Dot the surface of the mixture with the pieces of butter or margarine, cover the pan and leave to cool to room temperature.

While the chocolate mixture is cooling, prepare the soufflé dish. Grease a 2-pint [5-cup] soufflé dish with half of the softened butter or margarine. Grease a folded sheet of greaseproof or waxed paper with the remaining softened butter or margarine and tie it around the outside of the dish, projecting 2-inches above the rim.

Preheat the oven to fairly hot 375°F (Gas Mark 5, 190°C).

When the chocolate mixture has cooled, add the egg yolks, one at a time, beating well between each addition.

In a medium-sized mixing bowl, beat the egg whites with a wire whisk or rotary beater until they form stiff peaks. With a metal spoon, carefully fold the egg whites into the chocolate mixture.

Spoon the mixture into the prepared soufflé dish and place it in the oven. Bake the soufflé for 30 minutes, or until it is puffed up and lightly browned.

After 25 minutes, remove the soufflé from the oven and quickly dust the top with the icing [confectioners'] sugar. Slide the soufflé back into the oven and bake for a further 5 minutes.

Remove the soufflé from the oven and remove the paper collar.

Serve immediately.

Cold Orange and Sherry Soufflé

This cold soufflé has a superb flavour and texture. It takes quite a long time to prepare; however, unlike hot soufflés, it doesn't have to be served as soon as it is ready.

Preparation and cooking time: 4 hours
4 SERVINGS

2 teaspoons butter or margarine
4 oz. [½ cup] plus 2 tablespoons sugar
6 fl. oz. [¾ cup] fresh orange juice
1 teaspoon agar-agar
3 egg yolks
4 fl. oz. [½ cup] medium-dry or sweet sherry
8 fl. oz. double cream [1 cup heavy cream]
4 egg whites
3 tablespoons finely chopped walnuts

Grease a 2-pint [5-cup] soufflé dish with 1 teaspoon of the butter or margarine. Sprinkle in 2 tablespoons of the sugar and press it on to the bottom and sides of the dish with your fingertips. Grease a folded sheet of greaseproof or waxed paper with the remaining butter or margarine and carefully tie it around the rim of the soufflé dish so that it extends about 2-inches above the rim. Set aside.

In a medium-sized saucepan, bring the orange juice to the boil over moderate heat. With a wire whisk or rotary beater, beat in the agar-agar. Continue whisking for 3 minutes. Remove the pan from the heat and allow the orange juice mixture to cool slightly.

Add the egg yolks, one at a time, beating well between each addition. Gradually stir in the remaining sugar and the sherry.

Pour the orange juice and sherry mixture into a large mixing bowl and place it in the refrigerator. Chill for 45 minutes, or until the mixture is on the point of setting.

In a medium-sized mixing bowl, beat the cream with a wire whisk or rotary beater until it is very thick. With a metal spoon, fold almost all of the cream into the orange juice and sherry mixture. Reserve the rest of the cream for the decoration.

In another medium-sized mixing bowl, beat the egg whites with a wire whisk or rotary beater until they form stiff peaks. With a metal spoon, carefully fold the egg whites into the orange juice and cream mixture.

Spoon the mixture into the prepared soufflé dish. Place the dish in the refrigerator and chill the soufflé for 1½ to 2 hours, or until it is completely set.

Just before serving, remove the paper collar. Pipe the reserved cream around the top and sprinkle it with the walnuts.

Omelets

Pasta Omelet

A novel combination of pasta, eggs and cheese, Pasta Omelet makes a wonderful snack supper. Serve, cut into wedges, with a salad and well-chilled white Frascati wine.
Preparation and cooking time: 45 minutes
4 SERVINGS

1 pint [2½ cups] plus 1 tablespoon water
1½ teaspoons salt
6 oz. small wholemeal pasta
6 eggs
½ teaspoon black pepper
½ teaspoon garlic powder
2 oz. mozzarella cheese, cut into small cubes
2 fl. oz. [¼ cup] olive oil

In a large saucepan, bring 1 pint [2½ cups] of the water and 1 teaspoon of the salt to

the boil over high heat. Reduce the heat to moderate and add the pasta. Cook for 12 to 15 minutes, depending on whether you prefer your pasta *al dente* (just tender) or slightly soft. Remove the pan from the heat and drain the pasta in a colander. Set the pasta aside and keep it warm.

In a large mixing bowl, combine the eggs, the remaining water, the remaining salt, the pepper and garlic powder together with a fork or wire whisk, beating just until the mixture is blended. Stir in the cheese cubes. Set aside.

Preheat the grill [broiler] to high.

In a large omelet pan, heat the oil over moderate heat. When the oil is hot, pour in the egg mixture. Cook for 4 minutes, lifting the set edges of the omelet to allow the liquid egg mixture to cook, or until the eggs are half set. Gently fold in the pasta and cook for a further 2 minutes, or until the eggs are nearly set. Remove the pan from the heat and place the omelet under the grill [broiler]. Grill [broil] for 2 minutes, or until the top is brown.

Serve at once.

Crumblet

A solid and very tasty omelet, Crumblet is a mixture of cream-style sweetcorn, breadcrumbs and eggs. Serve with Caramelized Tomatoes for a filling lunch or supper.
Preparation and cooking time: 25 minutes
2-3 SERVINGS

7 oz. canned cream-style sweetcorn
4 oz. [2 cups] fresh brown breadcrumbs
4 eggs
½ teaspoon salt
¼ teaspoon black pepper
⅛ teaspoon cayenne pepper
1 oz. [2 tablespoons] butter or margarine

In a large mixing bowl, combine all of the ingredients except the butter or margarine together, beating with a fork until they are well blended.

Preheat the grill [broiler] to high.

In a large omelet pan, melt the butter or margarine over moderate heat. Add the sweetcorn and egg mixture and cook for 6 to 8 minutes, lifting the set edges of the omelet to allow the liquid egg mixture to cook. When the underside of the omelet is golden brown, remove the pan from the heat and place it under the grill [broiler]. Grill [broil] the top of the omelet for 2 minutes, or until it turns golden brown.

Remove the pan from the heat and slide the crumblet on to a warmed serving dish. Serve at once.

Omelette Savoyarde
OMELET WITH POTATOES AND CHEESE

Another regional classic from France, Omelette Savoyard (ah-muh-let sa-voh-yahr) makes a sturdy and filling lunch or supper dish. Serve it with Tomato Salad and crusty Wholewheat Bread.
Preparation and cooking time: 25 minutes
2 SERVINGS

2 oz. [¼ cup] butter or margarine
2 medium-sized potatoes, cooked and sliced
6 eggs
1 tablespoon water
2 oz. [½ cup] Gruyère cheese, grated
½ teaspoon salt
¼ teaspoon white pepper

In a large omelet pan, melt the butter or margarine over moderate heat. When the foam subsides, add the potato slices. Cook them, turning occasionally, for 5 minutes, or until they are lightly browned.

In a medium-sized mixing bowl combine the eggs, water, cheese, salt and pepper together, beating until all the ingredients are well blended.

Pour the egg mixture over the potato slices and cook for 5 minutes, lifting the set edges of the omelet to allow the liquid egg mixture to be cooked.

When the eggs have set, fold the omelet in half and remove the pan from the heat. Slide the omelet on to a warmed serving dish and cut it into two portions. Serve immediately.

Hungarian-Style Omelet

A delicious and filling lunch or supper dish, Hungarian-Style Omelet, with spinach, sour cream and paprika filling, may be served with crusty bread.
Preparation and cooking time: 1½ hours
4 SERVINGS

1½ lb. spinach, trimmed, washed, drained and chopped
2½ teaspoons salt
5½ oz. [⅝ cup plus 1 tablespoon] butter or margarine
1 teaspoon black pepper
1 large onion, thinly sliced
1 garlic clove, crushed
5 fl. oz. [⅝ cup] sour cream
1 teaspoon paprika
12 eggs
4 tablespoons water

Put the spinach into a large saucepan. Pour over enough water just to cover and add 1 teaspoon of the salt. Place the pan over high heat and bring the water to the boil. Cover the pan, reduce the heat to moderately low and cook the spinach for

7 to 12 minutes, or until it is just tender. Remove the pan from the heat and drain the spinach in a colander, pressing down on the spinach with the back of a wooden spoon to extract all excess liquid. Transfer the spinach to a mixing bowl.

Stir in 1 tablespoon of the butter or margarine, ½ teaspoon of the salt and ½ teaspoon of the pepper, mixing well until the butter or margarine has melted and the spinach is well coated. Set aside.

In a medium-sized frying-pan, melt 1 ounce [2 tablespoons] of the butter or margarine over moderate heat. When the foam subsides, add the onion and garlic. Fry them, stirring occasionally, for 5 to 7 minutes, or until the onion is soft and translucent but not brown. Stir in the spinach and cook the mixture, stirring constantly, for 3 minutes.

Remove the pan from the heat and stir in the sour cream, then the paprika. Return the pan to low heat and gently simmer the mixture, stirring frequently, for 5 minutes or until the cream is hot but not boiling. Remove the pan from the heat. Keep the spinach filling warm while you make the omelets.

In a small mixing bowl, lightly beat three of the eggs with 1 tablespoon of the water, ¼ teaspoon of the salt and ⅛ teaspoon of the pepper.

In an omelet pan, melt 1 ounce [2 tablespoons] of the remaining butter or margarine over moderate heat. When the foam subsides, pour the beaten eggs into the pan. Cook for 5 to 6 minutes, lifting the set edges of the omelet so that the liquid eggs can be cooked. When the eggs are set, spoon about one-quarter of the spinach filling on to the centre.

Fold the omelet in half and slide it on to a warmed serving dish. Keep it warm while you cook the remaining three omelets in the same way, using the rest of the butter or margarine.

Serve hot.

Cheddar Cheese and Apple Omelet

Delicious and fresh-tasting, Cheddar Cheese and Apple Omelet makes an excellent light supper dish.
Preparation and cooking time: 1 hour
4 SERVINGS

6 oz. [¾ cup] butter or margarine
2 medium-sized tart apples, cored and chopped
½ teaspoon grated nutmeg
12 eggs
4 tablespoons water
1 teaspoon salt
½ teaspoon black pepper
4 oz. [1 cup] Cheddar cheese, grated

In a small saucepan, melt one-third of the butter or margarine over moderate heat. When the foam subsides, add the apples and nutmeg. Cook, stirring frequently, for 2 to 3 minutes, or until the apples are just beginning to soften. Remove the pan from the heat and set it aside.

In a small mixing bowl, lightly beat three of the eggs with 1 tablespoon of the water, ¼ teaspoon of the salt and ⅛ teaspoon of the pepper.

In an omelet pan, melt 1 ounce [2 tablespoons] of the remaining butter or margarine over moderate heat. When the foam subsides, pour the beaten eggs into the pan. Cook for 5 to 6 minutes, lifting the set edges of the omelet so that the liquid eggs can be cooked. When the eggs are on the point of setting, spoon about one-quarter of the apple mixture on to the centre of the omelet. Sprinkle about one-quarter of the cheese on top and cook the omelet for a further 2 minutes or until it is set and the cheese begins to melt.

Fold the omelet in half and slide it on to a warmed serving dish. Keep it warm while you make the remaining three omelets in the same way, using the rest of the butter or margarine.

Serve hot.

Omelette Arlésienne
OMELET WITH AUBERGINE [EGGPLANT] AND TOMATOES

A wonderfully colourful dish, Omelette Arlésienne (ah-muh-let ar-lay-zee-ehn) makes an excellent spring or summer supper dish.
Preparation and cooking time: 2¼ hours
4 SERVINGS

1 large aubergine [eggplant]
3½ teaspoons salt
2 fl. oz. [¼ cup] olive oil
2 medium-sized onions, finely chopped
2 garlic cloves, crushed
1 lb. tomatoes, blanched, peeled, seeded and chopped, or 14 oz. canned peeled tomatoes, drained
2 tablespoons chopped fresh basil or 2 teaspoons dried basil
1½ teaspoons black pepper
12 eggs
4 tablespoons water
4 oz. [½ cup] butter or margarine

Peel the aubergine [eggplant] and cut it into small cubes. Place the cubes in a colander, sprinkle over 1 teaspoon of the salt and leave the aubergine [eggplant] to dégorge for 30 minutes. Dry the aubergine [eggplant] cubes with kitchen paper towels.

In a medium-sized saucepan, heat the oil over moderate heat. When the oil is hot, add the onions, garlic and aubergine [eggplant] cubes. Cook them, stirring occasionally, for 10 minutes, or until the aubergine [eggplant] cubes are tender. Reduce the heat to low and add the tomatoes, basil, ½ teaspoon of the salt and ½ teaspoon of the pepper. Stir well to blend. Simmer the mixture, stirring occasionally, for 20 minutes. Remove the pan from the heat and keep the filling warm while you make the omelets.

In a small mixing bowl, lightly beat three of the eggs with 1 tablespoon of the water, ½ teaspoon of the salt and ¼ teaspoon of the pepper.

In an omelet pan, melt 1 ounce [2 tablespoons] of the butter or margarine over moderate heat. When the foam subsides, pour the beaten egg mixture into the pan. Cook for 5 to 6 minutes, lifting the set edges of the omelet to allow the liquid eggs to be cooked. When the omelet is set, spoon about one-quarter of the aubergine [eggplant] filling on to the centre.

Fold the omelet in half and slide it on to a warmed serving dish. Keep it warm while you make the remaining three omelets in the same way, using the rest of the butter or margarine.

Serve hot.

Frittata con Ricotta
RICOTTA OMELET

Frittata is the Italian word for omelet and Frittata con Ricotta (free-tah-tah kohn ree-koh-tah) is, therefore, a modest cheese omelet. But the cheese is special because it is made from the whey of other rich Italian cheeses and has no fat content. Ricotta has a taste all its own—and blends beautifully with eggs. If ricotta is unavailable in your area, curd cheese or cottage cheese may be substituted, although the taste will not be quite the same.
Preparation and cooking time: 1 hour
3 SERVINGS

2 tablespoons olive oil
1 medium-sized onion, finely chopped
1 garlic clove, crushed
8 oz. ricotta cheese
2 oz. [½ cup] Parmesan cheese, grated
2 teaspoons salt
1 teaspoon white pepper
9 eggs
3 tablespoons water
3 oz. [⅜ cup] butter or margarine

In a small frying-pan, heat the olive oil over moderate heat. When the oil is hot, add the onion and garlic. Fry them, stir-

103

ring occasionally, for 5 to 7 minutes, or until the onion is soft and translucent but not brown. Remove the pan from the heat and set aside.

In a medium-sized mixing bowl, beat the ricotta and the Parmesan cheese together. Stir in the onion mixture, $\frac{1}{2}$ teaspoon of the salt and $\frac{1}{4}$ teaspoon of the pepper. Set the cheese filling aside while you make the omelets.

In a small mixing bowl, lightly beat three of the eggs with 1 tablespoon of the water, $\frac{1}{2}$ teaspoon of the salt and $\frac{1}{4}$ teaspoon of the pepper.

In an omelet pan, melt 1 ounce [2 tablespoons] of the butter or margarine over moderate heat. When the foam subsides, pour the egg mixture into the pan. Cook for 3 to 4 minutes, lifting the set edges of the omelet to allow the liquid eggs to cook.

When the eggs are half set, gently spoon over about one-third of the ricotta mixture. Cook the omelet for a further 2 to 3 minutes or until the eggs have set.

Fold the omelet in half and slide it on to a warmed serving dish. Keep it warm while you cook the remaining omelets in the same way, using the rest of the butter or margarine.

Serve hot.

Spanish Omelet

Spanish Omelet is more solid than the classic French version and looks a little like an egg pizza. It may be served cut into wedges, with a tomato or mushroom sauce. It is delicious—and spicy. The vegetable filling below is merely our suggestion —any vegetable can be used, with an eye to interesting combinations of colour and texture.

Preparation and cooking time: 1$\frac{1}{4}$ hours

4 SERVINGS

3 fl. oz. [$\frac{3}{8}$ cup] olive oil
2 medium-sized onions, thinly sliced
2 garlic cloves, crushed
1 medium-sized green pepper, white pith removed, seeded and sliced
1 medium-sized sweet potato, peeled and cut into small cubes
4 large tomatoes, quartered
1 teaspoon dried thyme
1 teaspoon salt
$\frac{1}{2}$ teaspoon black pepper
$\frac{1}{4}$ teaspoon cayenne pepper
2 oz. [$\frac{1}{4}$ cup] butter or margarine
12 eggs, lightly beaten

In a large frying-pan, heat the oil over moderate heat. When the oil is hot, add the onions, garlic, green pepper and sweet potato. Cook, stirring occasionally, for 10

104

minutes. Add the tomatoes and carefully stir in the thyme, salt, pepper and cayenne. Cook the mixture for a further 3 minutes. Remove the pan from the heat.

In a large omelet pan, melt half of the butter or margarine over moderate heat. When the foam subsides, add half of the vegetable mixture. Reduce the heat to low and pour in half of the lightly beaten eggs. Stir to mix. Cook the omelet for 6 to 8 minutes, shaking the pan occasionally to prevent the omelet from sticking, or until the eggs are on the point of setting. Turn the omelet over and cook for a further 2 to 3 minutes, or until the omelet is quite solid.

Slide the omelet out of the pan on to a warmed serving dish. Keep it warm while you cook the second omelet in the same way, using the rest of the butter or margarine.

Serve hot.

Omelette Soufflé Princesse

SOUFFLE OMELET WITH ASPARAGUS, CREAM AND TRUFFLES

A classic and elegant French omelet, Omelette Soufflée Princesse (ah-muh-let soo-flay pran-cess) may be served as the first course for a formal dinner party. The omelet is first cooked on top of the stove and then browned quickly in the oven. Leave the oven door open so that the handle of the pan sticks out.

Preparation and cooking time: 1$\frac{1}{2}$ hours

4 SERVINGS

1$\frac{1}{2}$ pints [3$\frac{3}{4}$ cups] water
1$\frac{1}{2}$ teaspoons salt
10 oz. asparagus, trimmed, washed, and tied in small bunches
4 fl. oz. double cream [$\frac{1}{2}$ cup heavy cream]
$\frac{1}{2}$ teaspoon dried tarragon
1 truffle, chopped
12 eggs, separated
4 tablespoons water
$\frac{1}{2}$ teaspoon white pepper
4 oz. [$\frac{1}{2}$ cup] butter or margarine

In a large, deep saucepan, bring the water and 1 teaspoon of the salt to the boil over high heat. Reduce the heat to moderate and place the asparagus in the water, tips just above the water line. Cook for 12 minutes, or until the asparagus is just tender.

Remove the pan from the heat and drain the asparagus in a colander. Untie the bunches. Set most of the asparagus aside in a large mixing bowl. Reserve 4 to 8 stalks for the garnish. Keep warm.

In a medium-sized saucepan, gently heat the cream over low heat until it is hot. Stir in the tarragon and remove the

pan from the heat. Gently fold the cream into the asparagus in the mixing bowl. Set aside and keep warm.

Preheat the oven to hot 425°F (Gas Mark 7, 220°C).

In a large mixing bowl, lightly beat the truffle with the egg yolks, water, remaining salt and pepper.

In a medium-sized mixing bowl, beat the egg whites with a wire whisk or rotary beater until they form stiff peaks. With a metal spoon, carefully fold the egg whites into the egg yolk mixture.

In an omelet pan, melt 1 ounce [2 tablespoons] of the butter or margarine over moderate heat. When the foam subsides, pour about one-quarter of the egg mixture into the pan. Cook for 5 to 6 minutes, or until the bottom of the omelet is lightly browned. Transfer the pan to the oven and bake, leaving the oven door open, for about 3 minutes, or until the top of the omelet is firm and lightly browned.

Spoon about one-quarter of the asparagus and cream mixture on to the centre of the omelet. Fold it carefully in half and slide it on to a warmed serving dish. Keep it warm while you cook the remaining three omelets in the same way, using the rest of the butter or margarine.

When all the omelets are cooked, garnish them with the reserved asparagus. Serve hot.

Eggah with Courgettes [Zucchini]

This substantial family dish of eggs and courgettes [zucchini] is delicious served on its own or with a green salad.

Preparation and cooking time: 1 hour 10 minutes

4 SERVINGS

1 lb. small courgettes [zucchini], trimmed, washed and thinly sliced
$\frac{1}{4}$ teaspoon grated nutmeg
10 fl. oz. [1$\frac{1}{4}$ cups] milk
2 tablespoons olive oil
1 small onion, halved and very thinly sliced
1 large garlic clove, crushed
8 eggs
$\frac{1}{2}$ teaspoon salt
$\frac{1}{4}$ teaspoon black pepper
1 tablespoon snipped chives
2 oz. [1 cup] fresh breadcrumbs
1 oz. [2 tablespoons] butter or margarine

Lay the sliced courgettes [zucchini] in a large shallow dish. Sprinkle the nutmeg on top. Pour on the milk and leave the courgettes [zucchini] to soak for 30 minutes. Drain off the milk, retaining 2 tablespoons, and discard the rest.

In a large frying-pan, heat the oil over moderate heat. When the oil is hot, add the courgette [zucchini] slices, onion and garlic. Fry, stirring occasionally, for 5 to 7 minutes or until the onion is soft and translucent but not brown. Remove the pan from the heat. Transfer the courgettes [zucchini], onion and garlic to a plate and set aside. Wipe out the frying-pan with kitchen paper towels and set it aside.

In a large mixing bowl, beat the eggs, reserved 2 tablespoons of milk, the salt, pepper and chives together with a fork or wire whisk. Stir in the cooked courgette [zucchini] slices, onion, garlic and breadcrumbs.

In the clean frying-pan, melt the butter or margarine over moderate heat. When the foam subsides, reduce the heat to low. Pour in the egg and courgette [zucchini] mixture and cook slowly for 15 minutes, or until the underside of the eggah is golden brown.

Preheat the grill [broiler] to high.

Remove the pan from the heat and place it under the grill [broiler]. Cook for 5 minutes, or until the eggah is golden brown on top.

Serve hot, cut into thick wedges.

Vegetable Eggah

An eggah is an Arab-style omelet which is firm and thick like an egg cake. To serve, cut the eggah into thick wedges as you would a pie.
Preparation and cooking time: 40 minutes
4 SERVINGS

3 oz. [⅜ cup] butter or margarine
2 medium-sized potatoes, cooked and sliced
1 small turnip, peeled and sliced
3 oz. mushrooms, wiped clean and sliced
6 oz. green peas, cooked
2 medium-sized beetroots [beets], cooked and sliced
1 teaspoon salt
1 teaspoon black pepper
1 tablespoon chopped fresh parsley
5 eggs, lightly beaten
3 tablespoons grated Cheddar cheese

In a large frying-pan, melt the butter or

margarine over moderate heat. When the foam subsides, add the potatoes and turnip to the pan. Cook, stirring occasionally, for 10 minutes, or until the vegetables are lightly browned.

Add the mushrooms, peas and beetroots [beets] and continue cooking, stirring occasionally, for 5 minutes.

Reduce the heat to low and stir in the salt, pepper, parsley and eggs. Sprinkle the cheese on top of the mixture, cover the pan and cook for 10 to 12 minutes or until the eggs have set.

Remove the pan from the heat, slide the eggah on to a warmed serving dish and serve immediately.

Pipérade

One of the classics of French regional cuisine, Pipérade (pee-pair-rahd) is a gay profusion of vegetables mixed with scrambled eggs and it is quite delicious. Pipérade may be served as part of a supper menu or it may be served on toast for a tasty snack.
Preparation and cooking time: 40 minutes
3 SERVINGS

2 fl. oz. [¼ cup] olive oil
1 medium-sized onion, thinly sliced
2 garlic cloves, crushed
1 medium-sized green pepper, white pith removed, seeded and sliced
1 medium-sized red pepper, white pith removed, seeded and sliced
4 large tomatoes, blanched, peeled, seeded and chopped
½ teaspoon dried thyme
½ teaspoon dried oregano
½ teaspoon salt
½ teaspoon black pepper
4 large eggs, lightly beaten

In a large, deep frying-pan, heat the oil over moderate heat. When the oil is hot, add the onion, garlic and green and red peppers. Cook, stirring occasionally, for 5 to 7 minutes, or until the onion is soft and translucent but not brown. Reduce the heat to low and add the tomatoes, thyme, oregano, salt and pepper. Cook, stirring frequently, for a further 10 minutes.

Pour in the eggs and continue cooking, stirring constantly, for 5 to 6 minutes or until the eggs are cooked and set.

Transfer the Pipérade to a warmed serving dish and serve.

Orange Raisin Omelet

A sweet soufflé omelet, Orange Raisin Omelet is easy to prepare and makes a delicious and rich dessert.
Preparation and cooking time: 45 minutes

1 teaspoon butter or margarine
2 oz. [⅓ cup] seedless raisins
3 tablespoons orange marmalade
1 tablespoon orange juice
2 eggs, separated
2 teaspoons flour dissolved in 3 tablespoons clear honey

Preheat the grill [broiler] to high.

Grease a 10-inch omelet pan with the teaspoon of butter or margarine.

In a small, heavy saucepan, warm the raisins, marmalade and orange juice over low heat for 5 minutes or until the mixture is hot but not boiling. Remove the pan from the heat, cover and set it aside.

In a medium-sized mixing bowl, beat the egg yolks and flour and honey mixture together with a fork until they are blended. Set aside.

In a medium-sized mixing bowl, beat the egg whites with a wire whisk or rotary beater until they form stiff peaks. With a metal spoon, carefully fold the egg whites into the egg yolk mixture.

Place the omelet pan over moderate heat. When the pan is hot, pour in the egg mixture. Cook for 4 minutes, or until the underside is lightly browned.

Remove the pan from the heat and place it under the grill [broiler]. Grill [broil] the omelet for 2 minutes, or until the top is lightly browned.

Spread over the orange and raisin mixture and fold the omelet in half. Slide it on to a warmed serving dish and serve immediately.

Omelette Soufflée Surprise
SOUFFLE OMELET WITH STRAWBERRIES, KIRSCH AND SPONGE CAKE SLICES

A wonderfully impressive dessert, Omelette Soufflée Surprise (ah-muh-let soo-flay sur-preez) is, like the majority of soufflé omelets, cooked in the oven rather than on top of the stove. As its name suggests, it is light and airy with a rich sweet filling—a marvellous summer dessert when fresh strawberries are available.
Preparation and cooking time: 1¾ hours
4 SERVINGS

8 oz. fresh strawberries, washed and hulled, or 8 oz. frozen strawberries, thawed
2 fl. oz. [¼ cup] kirsch
1 teaspoon butter or margarine
2½ tablespoons icing [confectioners'] sugar
2 oz. [¼ cup] sugar
4 egg yolks
6 egg whites
1 small 6-inch sponge cake, cut into ¼-inch thick slices

Arrange the strawberries in a medium-sized, shallow dish and pour over the kirsch. Leave the strawberries to marinate at room temperature for 1 hour, basting occasionally. Drain the strawberries, reserving the marinating liquid. Set the strawberries aside.

Preheat the oven to fairly hot 375°F (Gas Mark 5, 190°C). Lightly grease a fairly shallow baking dish with the teaspoon of butter or margarine. Sprinkle ½ tablespoon of icing [confectioners'] sugar on the bottom and sides of the dish. Set aside.

In a large mixing bowl, beat the sugar and egg yolks together with a wire whisk or rotary beater until the mixture is pale and thick and will make a ribbon trail on itself when the whisk is lifted.

In a medium-sized mixing bowl, beat the egg whites with a wire whisk or rotary beater until they form stiff peaks. With a metal spoon, carefully fold the egg whites into the egg yolk mixture.

Arrange the strawberries on the bottom of the baking dish. Cover with the sponge cake slices, then pour in the kirsch marinade. Pour the egg mixture on top and place the baking dish in the centre of the oven. Bake the omelet for 12 to 15 minutes, or until it is lightly browned.

Remove the dish from the oven, sprinkle with the remaining icing [confectioners'] sugar and serve immediately, straight from the dish.

Crêpes and Pancakes

Crêpe Batter (Savoury)

Savoury crêpes may be filled with diced cheese or savoury butters as well as any vegetable combination you choose. The number of crêpes made depends on the size of your pan, but the following recipe will serve four to six people.
Preparation and cooking time: 3 hours
8 OUNCES [2 CUPS]

8 oz. [2 cups] flour
½ teaspoon salt
4 eggs
4 tablespoons melted butter or
    margarine
7½ fl. oz. [⅞ cup plus 1 tablespoon] milk
7½ fl. oz. [⅞ cup plus 1 tablespoon] water
2 tablespoons vegetable oil

Sift the flour and salt into a medium-sized mixing bowl. Make a well in the centre of the flour and add the eggs and the melted butter or margarine. With a wooden spoon, fold the eggs and butter slowly into the flour. Gradually add the milk and water, beating well until the mixture forms a smooth batter. Strain

the batter, if necessary, to get rid of any lumps. Cover the bowl and set it aside in a cool place for 2 hours.

To make the batter in a blender, put the milk, water, eggs and salt into the blender jar. Add the flour and butter or margarine. Cover and blend at high speed for 1 minute. If the batter is not properly blended, blend for a further 10 or 15 seconds. Cover and set aside in a cool place for 2 hours.

With a pastry brush, lightly grease a medium-sized, heavy frying-pan with a little of the oil. Place the pan over moderate heat and warm the oil until it is very hot. The first crêpe will be a test one, so adjust the amount of batter if necessary when making the rest of the crêpes. Remove the pan from the heat and pour about 4 tablespoons of the batter into the centre of the pan.

Quickly tilt the pan in all directions to spread out the batter, discarding any batter that doesn't stick to the pan. Adjust the amount for your next crêpe accordingly. Return the pan to the heat and cook the crêpe for just over 1 minute. Shake the pan to loosen the crêpe. To see if the crêpe is cooked, lift one edge of it with a spatula. The crêpe should be a light golden colour underneath. If it is not, cook for a further 10 seconds.

With a palette knife or spatula, turn the crêpe over by lifting it up and over. Brown the reverse side for 30 seconds. This second side will be less evenly browned and is the side on which fillings should be spread. Slide the crêpe on to an ovenproof plate and keep it warm while you are making the rest of the crêpes in the same way.

Vegetable Crêpes

Just to prove how universal the crêpe really is, here is our adaptation of a popular Russian recipe. Serve Vegetable Crêpes with sour cream and rye bread for an authentic touch.
Preparation and cooking time: 1½ hours
4 SERVINGS

8 oz. [2 cups] Savoury Crêpe Batter
2 fl. oz. [¼ cup] vegetable oil
2 medium-sized onions, finely
    chopped
1 small red pepper, white pith
    removed, seeded and chopped
½ small green cabbage, coarse outer
    leaves removed, washed and
    shredded
1 small tart apple, peeled, cored and
    chopped
1 teaspoon salt
½ teaspoon black pepper
1 teaspoon dried dill leaves

Fry the crêpes according to the instructions in the basic recipe and keep them warm.

In a medium-sized frying-pan, heat the oil over moderate heat. When the oil is hot, add the onions and red pepper. Fry them, stirring occasionally, for 5 minutes. Add the cabbage, apple, salt, pepper and dill to the pan and, stirring frequently, cook the mixture for a further 5 minutes. Remove the pan from the heat.

Spread the crêpes out on a flat surface. Place 1 or 2 tablespoons of the filling on the centre of each one and roll it up, completely enclosing the filling.

Arrange the crêpes on a warmed shallow serving dish and serve.

Spinach and Cream Cheese Crêpes

A delicious and filling lunch or supper dish, Spinach and Cream Cheese Crêpes may be served with Tomato or Mushroom Salad and crusty bread.
Preparation and cooking time: 2 hours
4 SERVINGS

2 lb. spinach, trimmed, washed,
    drained and chopped
2 pints [5 cups] water
1½ teaspoons salt
8 oz. [2 cups] Savoury Crêpe Batter
1½ oz. [3 tablespoons] plus 1 teaspoon
    butter or margarine
1 large onion, finely chopped
1 garlic clove, crushed
½ teaspoon grated nutmeg
½ teaspoon white pepper
2 oz. cream cheese
2 oz. [½ cup] Parmesan cheese, grated

Put the spinach into a large saucepan. Pour in the water and add 1 teaspoon of the salt. Place the pan over moderately high heat and bring the water to the boil. Reduce the heat to moderate and cook the spinach for 7 to 12 minutes, or until it is just tender. Remove the pan from the heat and drain the spinach in a colander, pressing down with the back of a wooden spoon to extract all excess liquid. Set the spinach aside.

Fry the crêpes according to the instructions in the basic recipe and keep them warm.

Preheat the grill [broiler] to high. Grease a shallow, flameproof baking dish with the teaspoon of butter or margarine. Set aside.

In a medium-sized saucepan, melt the remaining butter or margarine over moderate heat. When the foam subsides, add the onion and garlic. Fry them, stirring occasionally, for 5 to 7 minutes, or until the onion is soft and translucent but not brown. Stir in the spinach, nutmeg, remaining salt and the pepper and mix well. Reduce the heat to low and add the cream cheese, stirring to mix. Cook the mixture, stirring constantly, for 3 minutes. Remove the pan from the heat.

Spread the crêpes out on a flat surface and spoon about one-eighth of the spinach and cream cheese mixture on to the centre of each one. Roll up the crêpes and place them in the baking dish. Sprinkle the grated cheese over the top and place the dish under the grill [broiler].

Grill [broil] the crêpes for 3 to 4 minutes, or until the cheese melts and browns. Remove the dish from the heat and serve immediately.

Crêpes Stuffed with Cabbage

Savoury crêpes rolled around a mixture of cabbage, apple, raisins, onion and vinegar and coated with Béchamel Sauce and cheese, this is a very filling dish and really needs no accompaniment.

Preparation and cooking time: 1 hour

6 SERVINGS

10 oz. [2½ cups] Savoury Crêpe Batter
2 oz. [¼ cup] plus 1 teaspoon butter or margarine
1 medium-sized onion, finely chopped
1 garlic clove, crushed
1 lb. green cabbage, cooked and shredded
1 large tart apple, peeled, cored, and chopped
4 oz. [⅔ cup] sultanas or seedless raisins
1 tablespoon cider vinegar
½ teaspoon salt
¼ teaspoon black pepper
10 fl. oz. [1¼ cups] hot Béchamel Sauce
2 tablespoons grated Cheddar cheese

Fry the crêpes according to the instructions in the basic recipe and keep them warm.

In a large saucepan, melt 2 ounces [¼ cup] of the butter or margarine over moderate heat. When the foam subsides, add the onion and garlic. Fry them, stirring occasionally, for 5 to 7 minutes, or

until the onion is soft and translucent but not brown. Add the cabbage, apple, raisins, vinegar, salt and pepper and cook, stirring frequently, for 5 minutes. Remove the pan from the heat and set aside.

Preheat the grill [broiler] to high. Grease a large, shallow baking dish with the teaspoon of butter or margarine.

Spread the crêpes out on a flat surface. Spoon about 3 tablespoons of the cabbage filling on to the centre of each crêpe and roll it up. Arrange the rolled crêpes in the baking dish and pour over the hot béchamel sauce. Sprinkle the grated cheese on top. Place the dish under the grill [broiler] and grill [broil] for 3 to 4 minutes, or until the cheese has melted and the top is brown.

Remove the dish from the heat and serve at once.

Creamed Sweetcorn Crêpes

A tasty snack, Creamed Sweetcorn Crêpes may be rolled or folded into quarters and served with butter and maple syrup for an unusual breakfast or light lunch.

Preparation and cooking time: 2 hours

4 SERVINGS

2 tablespoons flour
½ teaspoon baking powder
½ teaspoon sugar
¼ teaspoon salt
7 oz. canned cream-style sweetcorn
2 fl. oz. [¼ cup] sour cream
1 egg, separated
1 tablespoon vegetable oil

Sift the flour, baking powder, sugar and salt into a large mixing bowl. Make a well in the centre and pour in the sweetcorn, sour cream and the egg yolk. With a fork or wooden spoon, blend the liquid into the flour mixture, beating briskly until the mixture is well blended.

In a medium-sized mixing bowl, beat the egg white with a wire whisk or rotary beater until it forms stiff peaks. With a metal spoon, carefully fold it into the batter mixture. Set the batter aside to rest at room temperature for 1 hour.

With a pastry brush, lightly coat a small frying-pan with a little of the vegetable oil. Drop about 4 to 5 tablespoons of the batter into the frying-pan. Quickly tilt the pan to spread out the batter. Cook for 2 to 3 minutes, or until the underside of the crêpe is brown. With tongs or two spoons, quickly flip the crêpe up and over. Cook for a further 2 minutes, or until the other side is brown. Slide the crêpe out of the pan and keep it warm while you cook the remaining crêpes in the same way.

Serve hot.

Crêpe Batter (Sweet)

Sweet crêpes may be filled with fruit, jam, sweetened cream, or spices. The number of crêpes made depends on the size of your pan, but the following recipe will serve four to six people.

Preparation and cooking time: 3 hours

5 OUNCES [1¼ cups]

5 oz. [1¼ cups] flour
1 tablespoon sugar
3 egg yolks
5 tablespoons melted butter or margarine
4 fl. oz. [½ cup] milk
4 fl. oz. [½ cup] cold water
3 tablespoons cherry-flavoured liqueur
2 tablespoons vegetable oil

Sift the flour and sugar into a medium-sized mixing bowl. Make a well in the centre of the flour mixture and add the egg yolks and the melted butter or margarine. With a wooden spoon, fold the eggs and butter or margarine slowly into the flour. Gradually add the milk and water, beating well until the mixture forms a smooth batter. Stir in the cherry-flavoured liqueur and beat well. Strain the batter, if necessary, to get rid of any lumps. Cover the bowl and set it aside in a cool place for 2 hours.

To make the batter in a blender, put the milk, water, cherry-flavoured liqueur and eggs into the blender jar. Add the flour, salt, sugar and butter or margarine. Cover and blend at high speed for 1 minute. If the batter is not properly blended, blend for a further 10 or 15 seconds. Cover and set aside in a cool place for 2 hours

With a pastry brush, grease a medium-sized, heavy frying-pan with a little of the oil. Place the pan over moderate heat and warm the oil until it is very hot. The first crêpe will be a test one, so adjust the amount of batter if necessary when making the rest of the crêpes. Remove the pan from the heat and pour about 4 tablespoons of the batter into the centre of the pan.

Quickly tilt the pan in all directions to spread out the batter, discarding any batter that doesn't stick to the pan. Adjust the amount for your next crêpe accordingly. Return the pan to the heat and cook the crêpe for just over 1 minute. Shake the pan to loosen the crêpe. To see if the crêpe is cooked, lift one edge of it with a spatula. The crêpe should be a light golden colour underneath. If it is not, cook for a further 10 seconds.

With a palette knife or spatula, turn the crêpe over by lifting it up and over. Brown the reverse side for 30 seconds.

107

This second side will be less evenly browned and is the side on which fillings should be spread. Slide the crêpe on to an ovenproof plate and keep it warm while you are making the rest of the crêpes in the same way.

Raspberry Crêpes

One of the great delights of Austrian cuisine, hot Raspberry Crêpes served with sour cream make a marvellously rich and fattening dessert.

Preparation and cooking time: 50 minutes

4-6 SERVINGS

8 oz. [2 cups] Sweet Crêpe Batter
8 oz. raspberry jam
2 oz. [⅓ cup] walnuts, very finely
  chopped
2 tablespoons brandy
10 fl. oz. [1¼ cups] sour cream

Fry the crêpes according to the instructions in the basic recipe and keep them warm.

In a small saucepan, heat the jam, walnuts and brandy over low heat for 5 minutes, stirring frequently. Remove the pan from the heat.

Spread the crêpes out on a flat surface. Spoon 2 or 3 tablespoons of the jam mixture on to the centre of each crêpe and roll it up.

Arrange the crêpes in a large, shallow serving dish and serve, accompanied by the sour cream.

Crêpes aux Amandes
ALMOND CREPES

An attractive dessert, Crêpes aux Amandes (krep oh-zah-mahn) are simple enough to serve as a dessert for a family lunch or supper, yet elegant enough for a formal dinner party.

Preparation and cooking time: 50 minutes

4-6 SERVINGS

5 oz. [1¼ cups] Sweet Crêpe Batter
7 oz. [1¼ cups] ground almonds
3 oz. [⅜ cup] plus 1 tablespoon butter
  or margarine, melted
3 fl. oz. [⅜ cup] honey
2 oz. [¾ cup] blanched whole almonds
2 oz. [⅓ cup] raisins

Fry the crêpes according to the instruc-

tions in the basic recipe and keep them warm.

In a small heavy saucepan, combine the ground almonds, melted butter and the honey. Place the pan over moderate heat and cook for 2 minutes, stirring occasionally. Remove the pan from the heat.

Lay the crêpes out on a flat surface and spoon about 2 tablespoons of the almond-and-honey mixture on to the centre of each one. Decorate the top of each crêpe with about 6 blanched almonds and 1 teaspoon of raisins.

Serve immediately.

Crêpes Suzettes
CREPES FLAMED WITH ORANGE LIQUEUR

An impressive dessert to serve for a dinner party, Crêpes Suzettes (krep soo-zet) are not difficult to prepare although you may need to practice folding and flaming the crêpes before the party. The crêpes may be made well in advance but should be covered with greaseproof or waxed paper to prevent them from drying out.

Preparation and cooking time: 1½ hours

4-6 SERVINGS

5 oz. [1¼ cups] Sweet Crêpe Batter
4 sugar lumps
2 medium-sized oranges, washed
  and dried
4 tablespoons castor [fine] sugar
6 oz. [¾ cup] unsalted butter, softened
3 fl. oz. [⅜ cup] orange juice
5 tablespoons orange-flavoured
  liqueur
3 tablespoons brandy

Fry the crêpes according to the instructions in the basic recipe and keep them warm.

Rub the sugar lumps over the rind of the oranges so that they absorb the oil. Put the sugar lumps in a medium-sized mixing bowl and mash them with the back of a wooden spoon.

With a small sharp knife, or a vegetable peeler, peel the oranges. Discard any white pith on the inside of the rind. Chop the orange rind very finely and add it to the bowl with the mashed sugar lumps. Add half of the castor sugar and the softened butter. With the back of a wooden spoon, cream the butter, sugar and orange rind together until the mixture is light and fluffy.

Stir in the orange juice, a little at a time. Add 3 tablespoons of the orange-flavoured liqueur and beat until the orange butter mixture is creamy.

In a small frying-pan, melt the orange butter over very low heat. Holding the outer edges of a crêpe with your finger-

tips, dip it into the heated butter mixture until it is well soaked. Carefully fold the crêpe in half, then fold it again into quarters. Transfer it to a shallow serving dish. Repeat the process with the remaining crêpes until they are all coated and in the serving dish.

Sprinkle the remaining sugar over the top of the crêpes and pour in any remaining melted orange butter.

In a small saucepan, warm the remaining orange-flavoured liqueur and the brandy over very low heat. Do not let the liqueur come to the boil. Pour the liqueur over the crêpes. Ignite it and shake the dish gently. When the flame dies down, serve.

Andean Potato Pancakes

The potato was known to the South American Indians long before it was grown in Europe. It was, in fact, one of the staples of the Indian civilization that stretched from Ecuador to Bolivia. This is a modern version of a potato pancake, eaten since time immemorial.

Preparation and cooking time: 1½ hours

4 SERVINGS

2 lb. potatoes, cooked and mashed
4 oz. [½ cup] butter or margarine
1 small egg, lightly beaten
¼ teaspoon garlic powder
½ teaspoon salt
1 teaspoon black pepper
½ teaspoon crushed saffron threads,
  dissolved in 1 tablespoon hot water
SAUCE
2 tablespoons olive oil
2 medium-sized onions, finely
  chopped
1 garlic clove, crushed
1 green chilli, seeds removed and
  finely chopped
4 tomatoes, blanched, peeled,
  seeded and chopped, or 10 oz.
  canned peeled tomatoes, drained
  and chopped

In a large mixing bowl, beat the potatoes, one-quarter of the butter or margarine, the egg, garlic powder, salt, pepper and saffron together until all the ingredients are well blended. Divide the mixture into six pieces and form each piece into a round patty, about ¼-inch thick. Place the patties in the refrigerator to chill for 30 minutes.

To make the sauce, in a medium-sized saucepan, heat the oil over moderate heat. When the oil is hot, add the onions, garlic and chilli. Cook, stirring occasionally, for 5 to 7 minutes, or until the onions are soft and translucent but not brown. Reduce the heat to low, add the tomatoes to the pan and continue to cook, stirring occasionally, for 15 minutes more. Remove the pan from the heat, cover and keep the sauce warm.

Remove the patties from the refrigerator. In a medium-sized frying-pan, melt half of the remaining butter or margarine over moderate heat. When the foam subsides, add the patties, one or two at a time, and cook them for 4 to 5 minutes on each side, or until they are a rich brown all over. With a slotted spoon, remove the patties from the pan and keep them warm while you fry the remaining patties in the same way, using the rest of the butter or margarine.

Arrange the Potato Pancakes in a warmed, shallow serving dish. Pour over the sauce and serve.

Stacked Pancakes

Delicious to look at and equally delicious to eat, Stacked Pancakes make an ideal dessert for a dinner party.
Preparation and cooking time: 2 hours
4 SERVINGS

6 oz. [1 cup] corn meal
2 oz. [½ cup] flour
1 teaspoon bicarbonate of soda [baking soda]
½ teaspoon salt
16 fl. oz. [2 cups] sour cream
2 tablespoons vegetable oil
FILLING
1 lb. thick apricot jam
2 tablespoons brandy
2 tablespoons finely chopped almonds
10 fl. oz. double cream [1¼ cups heavy cream], stiffly whipped
4 fl. oz. [½ cup] whipping cream, stiffly whipped

Sift the corn meal, flour, bicarbonate of soda [baking soda] and salt into a large mixing bowl. Make a well in the centre and pour in the sour cream. Gradually incorporate the flour mixture into the cream, beating with a wooden spoon or a fork until the mixture forms a smooth and fairly thick batter. Set the batter aside to rest at room temperature for 1 hour.

In a medium-sized saucepan, heat the apricot jam over low heat for 3 minutes. Stir in the brandy and 1 tablespoon of the chopped almonds and mix well to blend. Remove the pan from the heat, cover and keep warm while you make the pancakes.

With a pastry brush, lightly grease a large, heavy griddle or frying-pan with a little of the vegetable oil. Place the griddle or pan over moderate heat. When it is hot, drop tablespoonfuls of the batter

on to the pan. You should be able to cook three or four pancakes at a time, depending on the size of your pan. Fry the pancakes for 3 minutes, or until the tops bubble slightly. Turn them over quickly and fry for 2 more minutes, or until the other side is brown. Remove the pancakes from the griddle or pan and keep them warm while you cook the remaining pancakes in the same way.

Place four pancakes on a very large flat serving dish, well apart. Spread a little of the jam mixture over each pancake and spoon over a little of the double [heavy] cream. Top with a second batch of pancakes and cover with the jam mixture and double [heavy] cream. Repeat the layers until there are four stacks of pancakes, each four pancakes high. Finish with a pancake layer.

Fold the remaining almonds into the whipping cream. Decorate the tops of the stacked pancakes with the cream mixture and serve at once.

Traditional Scottish Pancakes

Serve these delicious pancakes with butter and honey for a great snacktime treat.
Preparation and cooking time: 2 hours
30 PANCAKES

8 oz. [2 cups] flour
2 teaspoons baking powder
1 oz. [2½ tablespoons] light brown sugar
¼ teaspoon salt
2 eggs
9 fl. oz. [1⅛ cups] milk
2 tablespoons vegetable oil

Sift the flour, baking powder, sugar and salt into a large mixing bowl. Make a well in the centre and pour in the eggs and milk. Gradually incorporate the dry ingredients into the wet ingredients, beating with a wooden spoon until the mixture forms a smooth batter. Set the batter aside to rest at room temperature for 1 hour.

With a pastry brush, lightly grease a heavy griddle or frying-pan with a little of the vegetable oil. Place the griddle or pan over moderate heat. When it is hot, drop tablespoonfuls of the batter on to the griddle or pan. You should be able to cook three or four pancakes at a time.

Fry the pancakes for 3 minutes, or until the tops bubble slightly. Turn them over quickly and fry for 2 more minutes, or until the other side is brown. Remove the pancakes from the griddle or pan and keep them warm while you cook the remaining pancakes in the same way.

Serve hot or cold.

Connecticut Yankees

An American variation of Scottish Pancakes, Connecticut Yankees may be served with butter and maple syrup for a hearty breakfast or brunch.
Preparation and cooking time: 9½ hours
4-6 SERVINGS

½ oz. fresh yeast
½ teaspoon sugar
8 fl. oz. [1 cup] lukewarm milk
6 oz. [1½ cups] buckwheat flour
2 tablespoons flour
½ teaspoon salt
8 fl. oz. [1 cup] lukewarm water
¼ teaspoon bicarbonate of soda [baking soda] dissolved in 3 fl. oz. [⅜ cup] lukewarm water
1 tablespoon black treacle [molasses]
2 tablespoons vegetable oil

Crumble the yeast into a small mixing bowl and mash in the sugar with a kitchen fork. Add 2 tablespoons of the milk and cream the yeast and milk together. Set the bowl aside in a warm, draught-free place for 20 minutes, or until the yeast mixture is puffed up and frothy.

Put the flours and salt into a large mixing bowl. Make a well in the centre and pour in the yeast mixture, remaining milk and the water. Using your fingers or a spatula, gradually incorporate the flour into the liquid, mixing until a smooth batter is formed. Cover the bowl with a warm, damp cloth and set it aside in a warm, draught-free place to rise for 8 hours or overnight.

Stir the batter and stir in the soda mixture and the treacle [molasses]. Set aside for 30 minutes.

With a pastry brush, lightly coat a griddle or heavy frying-pan with a little of the vegetable oil. Place the griddle or pan over moderate heat. When it is hot, drop tablespoonfuls of the batter on to the griddle or pan. You should be able to cook about 3 or 4 pancakes at a time. Fry the pancakes for 3 minutes, or until the tops bubble slightly. Turn them over quickly and fry for 2 more minutes, or until the other side is brown. Remove the pancakes from the griddle or pan and keep them warm while you fry the remaining pancakes in the same way.

Serve hot.

Cakes and Biscuits [Cookies]

Would you believe that anything as beautiful as a Genoese Sponge Cake with Strawberries – a luscious froth of cream and fruit – or as dignified and handsome as an 'olde English' Christmas Cake, could actually be good for you?

Almost everyone is tempted by the combination of eggs, butter, sugar, cream and fruit, especially when they are whipped, moulded and shaped into heavenly cakes or tasty little biscuits [cookies]. And all these ingredients are so nutritious.

Sugar, one of the very best energy foods, is an important ingredient in most cakes and biscuits [cookies]. All fruits and some vegetables have large quantities of natural sugar. Carrots, for example, have a lot of natural sugar, as well as a high Vitamin A and C content, and they, with the addition of ground almonds, make the Jewish-American Carrot Cake a rich, moist delicacy.

Dried fruits are not as high in ascorbic acid (Vitamin C) as fresh fruits. They are, however, quite a good source of small amounts of iron and calcium, and because they are extremely high in calories, they are invaluable for 'nibbles' on picnics, hikes or other strenuous outdoor activities. Nuts, of course, are a known high protein food.

Cakes and biscuits [cookies] are a pleasant way to provide some of the essential protein and energy foods which ensure a healthy balance in your family's diet.

Honey Cake

Made with the goodness of honey, and flavoured with a slight tang of ginger, Honey Cake may be served plain or iced.
Preparation and cooking time: 1¾ hours
ONE 2-POUND CAKE

2 oz. [¼ cup] plus 2 teaspoons butter or margarine
8 fl. oz. [1 cup] clear honey
4 oz. [⅔ cup] light brown sugar
10 fl. oz. [1¼ cups] water
12 oz. self-raising wholemeal flour [3 cups self-rising wholewheat flour]
¼ teaspoon salt
1½ teaspoons ground ginger
2 eggs, lightly beaten

Preheat the oven to moderate 350°F (Gas Mark 4, 180°C). Lightly grease a 7- x 11- x 1½-inch cake tin with 1 teaspoon of the butter or margarine. Line the tin with greaseproof or waxed paper and grease the paper with another teaspoon of the butter or margarine. Set the tin aside.

In a medium-sized saucepan, warm the honey, sugar, remaining butter or margarine and the water over low heat, stirring constantly. As soon as the butter or margarine has melted and the sugar has dissolved, remove the pan from the heat.

Set aside to cool slightly.

Sift the flour, salt and ginger into a large mixing bowl. Make a well in the centre and pour in the eggs and the sugar mixture. Gradually draw the flour mixture into the liquids and continue mixing until the ingredients are well blended.

Pour the mixture into the prepared tin. Place the tin in the oven and bake for 1 hour, or until a skewer inserted into the centre of the cake comes out clean.

Remove the cake from the oven and allow it to cool in the tin before turning it out on to a wire rack to cool completely.

Banana Sponge Sandwich Cake

A heavenly light banana-flavoured sponge, Banana Sponge Sandwich Cake has a rich buttercream and nut filling.
Preparation and cooking time: 1¾ hours
ONE 7-INCH SANDWICH CAKE

4 oz. [½ cup] plus 2 teaspoons butter or margarine
2 tablespoons flour
4 oz. [⅔ cup] light brown sugar
1 large banana, peeled and mashed
2 eggs
4 oz. [1 cup] self-raising flour
2 tablespoons castor [fine] sugar

FILLING

2 oz. [¼ cup] butter or margarine
4 oz. [⅔ cup] light brown sugar
¼ teaspoon vanilla essence
2 oz. [⅓ cup] walnuts or pecans, finely chopped

Preheat the oven to moderate 350°F (Gas Mark 4, 180°C). Lightly grease two 7-inch shallow cake tins with 2 teaspoons of the butter or margarine. Sprinkle a tablespoon of flour into each tin and tip and rotate the tins to distribute the flour evenly. Set the tins aside.

In a large mixing bowl, cream the remaining butter or margarine until it is soft. Beat in the brown sugar and continue beating until the mixture is light and fluffy. Beat in the banana.

Add the eggs, one at a time, beating well between each addition. Sift the flour into the bowl and blend it thoroughly into the banana mixture.

Spoon the mixture into the prepared tins. Place the tins in the oven and bake for 25 to 30 minutes or until the centres of the cakes spring back when lightly pressed with a fingertip.

Remove the tins from the oven and turn the cakes out on to a wire rack. Cool them completely before filling.

To make the filling, in a medium-sized

mixing bowl, cream the butter or margarine with a wooden spoon until it is soft. Beat in the sugar and vanilla essence and continue beating until the mixture is light and fluffy. Thoroughly blend in the nuts.

Place one cake on a decorative serving platter. Spread over the filling. Place the other cake on top. Sprinkle the castor sugar on top and serve.

Genoese Sponge Cake with Strawberries

A perfect circle of sponge filled with strawberries and liqueur-flavoured cream, Genoese Sponge Cake with Strawberries is a superb dessert for a dinner party.
Preparation and cooking time: 1¾ hours
6-8 SERVINGS

1 teaspoon vegetable oil
2 teaspoons flour
CAKE
3 eggs
4 oz. [⅔ cup] light brown sugar
3 oz. [¾ cup] self-raising flour
¼ teaspoon salt
2 oz. [¼ cup] butter or margarine, melted
FILLING
1½ pints ripe strawberries, hulled and sliced
5 fl. oz. [⅝ cup] clear honey
15 fl. oz. double cream [1⅞ cups heavy cream]
2 tablespoons Framboise liqueur (optional)

Preheat the oven to fairly hot 375°F (Gas Mark 5, 190°C). Grease a 9-inch ring mould with the vegetable oil. Sprinkle in the 2 teaspoons of flour and tip and rotate the mould to distribute the flour evenly. Turn the mould over and rap it on the bottom to shake out any excess flour. Set the mould aside.

In a medium-sized heatproof mixing bowl placed over a saucepan of hot water, beat the eggs and sugar together with a wire whisk or rotary beater until the mixture is pale and thick and will form a ribbon trail on itself when the whisk is lifted.

Remove the bowl from the heat and fold in the flour, salt and melted butter or margarine. Pour the batter into the ring mould.

Place the mould in the centre of the oven and bake for 25 minutes.

Remove the mould from the oven and set it aside to cool completely.

In a medium-sized mixing bowl, toss the strawberry slices in the honey until they are well coated. Set the strawberry slices aside.

In another medium-sized mixing bowl,

beat the cream with a wire whisk or rotary beater until it is thick. Add the liqueur, if you are using it, and continue beating until the cream is stiff.

Fold the strawberries and honey into the cream. Set aside.

Run a knife around the edge of the ring mould to loosen the sponge. Place a serving dish, inverted, over the top of the mould. Holding the two firmly together, reverse them. The sponge should slide out easily on to the dish.

Fill the centre with the strawberries and cream mixture and serve immediately.

Almond Parkin

A parkin is a type of gingerbread from the North of England, and Almond Parkin is a particularly rich moist cake. Serve it either plain or spread with butter and honey.
Preparation and cooking time: 1½ hours
ONE 1½-POUND PARKIN

4 oz. [½ cup] plus 2 teaspoons butter or margarine
4 tablespoons clear honey
4 tablespoons black treacle [molasses]
4 oz. [⅔ cup] dark brown sugar
1 egg
4 oz. [1 cup] flour
2 teaspoons baking powder
½ teaspoon almond essence
3 fl. oz. [⅜ cup] milk
4 oz. [1⅓ cups] rolled oats
1 tablespoon flaked almonds

Preheat the oven to warm 325°F (Gas Mark 3, 170°C). Lightly grease an 11- x 7- x 1¼-inch cake tin with 1 teaspoon of the butter or margarine. Line the tin with greaseproof or waxed paper and grease the paper with another teaspoon of the butter or margarine. Set the tin aside.

In a large saucepan, melt the remaining butter or margarine over low heat. When the butter or margarine has melted, stir in the honey, treacle [molasses] and sugar. Cook, stirring constantly, until the sugar has dissolved. Remove the pan from the heat and set it aside to cool.

When the sugar mixture has cooled, beat in the egg with a wooden spoon. Sift the flour and baking powder into the pan and blend the dry ingredients

thoroughly into the sugar and egg mixture. Stir in the almond essence, milk and rolled oats, mixing well.

Spoon the mixture into the prepared tin and sprinkle over the almonds. Place the tin in the centre of the oven and bake for 50 to 55 minutes, or until the Parkin shrinks slightly from the sides of the tin and the centre springs back when it is lightly pressed with a fingertip.

Remove the Parkin from the oven and allow it to cool in the tin before turning it out on to a wire rack. Peel off the paper and leave the Parkin to cool completely before serving.

Orange Almond Ring Cake

A very attractive cake to serve for a special tea party, Orange Almond Ring Cake is an almond-flavoured ring cake. The centre is filled with mandarin oranges and the cake may be decorated with whipped cream. The cake does not keep well, so it should be eaten the day it is baked.
Preparation and cooking time: 2 hours
ONE 8-INCH CAKE

1 teaspoon butter or margarine
1 tablespoon flour
4 eggs
8 oz. [1⅓ cups] light brown sugar
8 oz. [1⅓ cups] ground almonds
½ teaspoon almond essence
8 oz. self-raising wholemeal flour [2 cups self-rising wholewheat flour]
11 oz. canned mandarin oranges, drained
5 fl. oz. double cream [⅝ cup heavy cream], stiffly whipped (optional)

Preheat the oven to moderate 350°F (Gas Mark 4, 180°C). Lightly grease a medium-sized ring mould with the butter or margarine. Sprinkle in the tablespoon of flour and tilt and rotate the mould to distribute the flour evenly. Shake out any excess and set the mould aside.

In a large mixing bowl, beat the eggs, sugar, ground almonds and almond essence together with a wooden spoon until the mixture is thick and smooth.

Sift the flour into the bowl and fold it into the almond mixture. When the flour is thoroughly incorporated, spoon the batter into the mould.

Place the mould in the centre of the oven and bake for 1¼ hours.

Remove the mould from the oven and allow the cake to cool slightly before turning it out on to a wire rack to cool completely.

Transfer the cooled cake to a decorative serving platter. Fill the centre with the mandarin oranges and, if you wish, pipe the cream round the top.

Apple Cake

This Apple Cake is lovely served with coffee. If you like, add ½ teaspoon of ground cinnamon or grated nutmeg for a spicier mixture.

Preparation and cooking time: 1½ hours
ONE 7-INCH CAKE

4 oz. [½ cup] plus 1 teaspoon butter
  or margarine
4 oz. [⅔ cup] light brown sugar
½ teaspoon vanilla essence
1 crisp eating apple, peeled, cored
  and very thinly sliced
8 oz. self-raising wholemeal flour
  [2 cups self-rising wholewheat flour]
2 to 3 tablespoons milk

Preheat the oven to warm 325°F (Gas Mark 3, 170°C). Line a shallow 7- x 11-inch cake tin with greaseproof or waxed paper. Lightly grease the paper with the teaspoon of butter or margarine and set the tin aside.

In a large mixing bowl, cream the remaining butter or margarine with a wooden spoon until it is soft and fluffy. Beat in the sugar and vanilla essence.

Stir in the apple slices. Sift the flour into the bowl and fold it into the butter and apple mixture. Stir in enough milk to give the batter a dropping consistency.

Spoon the batter into the prepared tin and place it in the centre of the oven. Bake for 50 minutes, or until the cake springs back when lightly pressed with a fingertip.

Cool the cake on a wire rack.

Chocolate Victoria

A rich chocolate cake sandwiched with a chocolate butter filling, Chocolate Victoria is a lovely dessert.

Preparation and cooking time: 1½ hours
ONE 7-INCH CAKE

4 oz. [½ cup] plus 2 teaspoons butter
  or margarine
2 tablespoons flour
4 oz. [⅔ cup] light brown sugar
2 eggs
4 oz. [1 cup] self-raising flour
1 oz. [¼ cup] cocoa powder
⅛ teaspoon salt
FILLING
3 oz. [⅜ cup] butter or margarine
3 oz. [½ cup] light brown sugar
2 oz. dark [semi-sweet] cooking
  chocolate, finely grated

Preheat the oven to fairly hot 375°F (Gas Mark 5, 190°C). Lightly grease two 7-inch cake tins with the 2 teaspoons of butter or margarine. Sprinkle in the 2 tablespoons of flour and tip and rotate the tins to distribute the flour evenly. Shake out any excess flour and set the tins aside.

In a large mixing bowl, cream the remaining butter or margarine with a wooden spoon until it is soft and fluffy. Beat in the sugar. Add the eggs, one at a time, beating well between each addition.

Sift the flour, cocoa and salt into the bowl and blend them thoroughly into the egg mixture.

Spoon the batter into the cake tins and place them in the oven. Bake the cakes for 20 to 25 minutes, or until they are done. Test by lightly pressing the centres with a fingertip. If the cakes are ready, they will spring back. Remove the tins from the oven and turn the cakes out on to a wire rack to cool completely.

To make the filling, in a small mixing bowl, cream the butter or margarine with a wooden spoon until it is soft and fluffy. Beat in the sugar. When the sugar has been incorporated, stir in the chocolate.

Place one of the cakes on a decorative serving platter. Spread the filling over it. Place the other cake on top.

Apricot Swiss [Jelly] Roll

A light Swiss [jelly] roll, this is filled with apricot jam, but any other jam may be used instead. Serve the cake with sweetened vanilla-flavoured whipped cream for a special treat, or use the cream as the filling instead of jam.

Preparation and cooking time: 1½ hours
6-8 SERVINGS

1 teaspoon vegetable oil
2 large eggs
3 oz. [½ cup] light brown sugar
3 oz. [¾ cup] flour
1 tablespoon castor sugar
4 oz. apricot jam

Preheat the oven to very hot 475°F (Gas Mark 9-10, 230°C). Line a 12- x 8-inch Swiss [jelly] roll tin with greaseproof or waxed paper. Grease the paper with the vegetable oil and set the tin aside.

In a large mixing bowl, beat the eggs with a wire whisk or rotary beater until they are pale and frothy. Sift the sugar into the bowl and whisk until the mixture is thick and will form a ribbon trail on itself when the whisk is lifted.

Sift the flour into the bowl and, with a

metal spoon, carefully and quickly fold it into the egg and sugar mixture.

Pour the batter into the prepared tin, tilting the tin to spread out the batter evenly. Place the tin in the oven and bake for 8 minutes, or until the cake is lightly browned. Do not overcook the cake or it will not roll up without cracking. It is ready if it springs back when lightly pressed with a fingertip.

Meanwhile, spread out a sheet of greaseproof or waxed paper, the same size as the Swiss [jelly] roll tin, on a flat surface. Sprinkle the paper with the castor sugar. Saturate a clean cloth with cold water and wring it out. Set aside.

Remove the cake from the oven. With a table knife, loosen the edges. Tip the cake carefully on to the sugared paper and rub the paper on top with the wet cloth. The paper should now peel off easily.

Trim the cake into a neat rectangle and roll it up, with the sugared paper inside. Allow the cake to cool completely.

Unroll the cake and remove the paper. Spread over the apricot jam and roll up the cake again.

Dundee Cake

An imposing and handsome cake, Dundee Cake is packed with the goodness of dried fruits and nuts. Like other fruit cakes, it can be stored successfully for quite a long time in an airtight tin.

Preparation and cooking time: 2¾ hours
ONE 2-POUND CAKE

6 oz. [¾ cup] plus 2 teaspoons butter
  or margarine
1 tablespoon flour
6 oz. [1 cup] light brown sugar
4 eggs
8 oz. self-raising wholemeal flour
  [2 cups self-rising wholewheat flour]
⅛ teaspoon salt
12 oz. mixed dried fruit (currants,
  raisins, etc.)
2 oz. [⅓ cup] glacé cherries, quartered
  grated rind of 1 orange
3 tablespoons flaked almonds

Preheat the oven to moderate 350°F (Gas Mark 4, 180°C). Grease a deep 8-inch cake tin with the 2 teaspoons of butter or margarine. Sprinkle in the flour and tip and rotate the tin to distribute the flour evenly. Shake out any excess. Set the tin aside.

In a large mixing bowl, cream the remaining butter or margarine with a wooden spoon until it is soft. Beat in the sugar and continue beating until the mixture is light and fluffy. Add the eggs, one at a time, beating well between each addition.

Sift the self-raising flour and salt into the mixing bowl and blend it into the sugar and egg mixture. Fold in the dried fruit, glacé cherries and orange rind.

Spoon the mixture into the prepared tin and sprinkle over the flaked almonds. Place the tin in the oven and bake for 1 hour. Then reduce the oven temperature to warm 300°F (Gas Mark 2, 140°C) and continue baking for another hour, or until a knife inserted into the centre of the cake comes out clean.

Remove the cake from the oven and allow it to cool in the tin before turning it out on to a wire rack to cool completely.

Christmas Cake

This is a light, moist fruit cake, pale in colour, that takes a relatively short time to prepare, as most of the time is spent baking or cooling the cake.
Preparation and cooking time: 4 hours

ONE 9-INCH CAKE

8 oz. [1 cup] plus 1 teaspoon butter
  or margarine
6 oz. [1 cup] glacé cherries, chopped
1 lb. raisins
6 oz. [1 cup] currants
2 tablespoons finely chopped mixed
  candied peel
1 tablespoon finely chopped
  angelica
4 oz. [$\frac{4}{5}$ cup] walnuts, chopped
8 oz. [2 cups] plus 2 tablespoons
  self-raising flour
8 oz. [1$\frac{1}{3}$ cups] brown sugar
6 eggs
1$\frac{1}{2}$ teaspoons ground allspice
1 teaspoon salt
2 tablespoons sherry

Preheat the oven to cool 300°F (Gas Mark 2, 150°C).

Lightly grease a 9-inch cake tin with the teaspoon of butter or margarine. Line the bottom and sides of the tin with a double layer of greaseproof or waxed paper. Set aside.

Combine the cherries, raisins, currants, candied peel, angelica and walnuts in a medium-sized mixing bowl. Sprinkle the 2 tablespoons of flour on top and mix to coat the fruit and nuts well. Set aside.

In a large mixing bowl, cream the remaining butter or margarine and the sugar together with a wooden spoon until the mixture is light and fluffy. Add the eggs, one at a time, with a spoonful of flour, and beat well between each addition.

Fold in the remaining flour, allspice and salt. Stir in the fruit and nuts. Add the sherry and mix thoroughly.

Pour the batter into the prepared cake tin and place it in the centre of the oven. Bake for 2 hours, or until a skewer inserted into the centre of the cake comes out clean.

Remove the cake from the oven and let it stand in the tin for 1 hour. Turn the cake out on to a wire rack and peel off the paper. Leave the cake to cool for at least 12 hours before wrapping it in aluminium foil and storing it in an airtight tin.

Orange Currant Cake

Currants soaked in orange juice make this a moist and delicious cake. Serve it for tea and your family will be very pleased.
Preparation and cooking time: 4$\frac{1}{4}$ hours

ONE 8-INCH CAKE

8 oz. currants
8 fl. oz. [1 cup] orange juice
6 oz. [$\frac{3}{4}$ cup] plus 1 teaspoon butter
  or margarine
1 tablespoon flour
6 oz. [1 cup] light brown sugar
3 eggs
$\frac{1}{2}$ teaspoon vanilla essence
$\frac{1}{4}$ teaspoon salt
10 oz. self-raising wholemeal flour
  [2$\frac{1}{2}$ cups self-rising wholewheat flour]

Place the currants in a medium-sized mixing bowl and pour over the orange juice. The currants should be just covered, so add more orange juice if necessary. Leave the currants to soak for 3 hours.

Drain the currants and set them aside. Reserve the orange juice.

Preheat the oven to moderate 350°F (Gas Mark 4, 180°C). Lightly grease a 10- x 8-inch cake tin with the teaspoon of butter or margarine. Sprinkle in the tablespoon of flour and tip and rotate the tin to distribute the flour evenly. Shake out any excess flour and set the tin aside.

In a large mixing bowl, cream the remaining butter or margarine with a wooden spoon until it is soft and fluffy. Beat in the sugar. When the sugar is thoroughly incorporated, blend in one of the eggs with the vanilla essence and salt. Then beat in the other two eggs, one at a time, beating well between each addition.

Sift the flour into the bowl and throughly fold it into the egg mixture. Stir in the currants and 2 to 3 tablespoons of the reserved orange juice. The batter should have a dropping consistency, so add more of the orange juice if necessary.

Spoon the batter into the cake tin and place it in the oven. Bake for 1$\frac{3}{4}$ hours or until a skewer inserted into the centre of the cake comes out clean.

Cool the cake on a wire rack before serving.

Carrot Cake

This unusual American Jewish cake is made with eggs, carrots and ground almonds, but no flour. The finished cake has a moist consistency rather like cheesecake.
Preparation and cooking time: 1$\frac{1}{4}$ hours

ONE 9-INCH CAKE

1 teaspoon butter or margarine
6 eggs, separated
8 oz. [1 cup] sugar
12 oz. carrots, cooked and puréed
1 tablespoon grated orange rind
1 tablespoon brandy
12 oz. [2 cups] ground almonds

Preheat the oven to warm 325°F (Gas Mark 3, 170°C). With the butter or margarine, grease a deep 9-inch loose-bottomed cake tin. Set aside.

In a medium-sized mixing bowl, beat the egg yolks with a wire whisk until they are pale and frothy. Gradually add the sugar and continue beating until the mixture is thick and creamy and will make a ribbon trail on itself when the whisk is lifted. Add the carrot purée, orange rind, brandy and almonds and stir to mix.

In a large mixing bowl, beat the egg whites with a wire whisk or rotary beater until they form stiff peaks. With a metal spoon, carefully fold the egg whites into the carrot mixture.

Spoon the mixture into the cake tin and place it in the centre of the oven. Bake for about 50 minutes, or until a skewer inserted into the centre of the cake comes out clean.

Remove the cake from the oven and leave it to cool in the tin for 15 minutes. Turn the cake out carefully on to a wire rack to cool completely before serving.

Almond Soya Biscuits [Cookies]

These chewy biscuits [cookies] are made with semolina, soya flour and dark brown sugar. Serve them with a mousse or creamy dessert or as an after-school treat for the children.
Preparation and cooking time: 1 hour

20 BISCUITS [COOKIES]

4 oz. [$\frac{1}{2}$ cup] plus 1 teaspoon butter
  or margarine
4 oz. [$\frac{2}{3}$ cup] semolina
4 oz. [1 cup] soya flour
4 oz. [$\frac{2}{3}$ cup] dark brown sugar
$\frac{1}{2}$ teaspoon almond essence
2 to 3 tablespoons milk

Preheat the oven to fairly hot 375°F (Gas Mark 5, 190°C). Lightly grease a baking sheet with the teaspoon of butter or margarine. Set aside.

113

In a large mixing bowl, combine the semolina, soya flour and sugar. Add the remaining butter or margarine and cut it into small pieces with a table knife. With your fingertips, rub the fat into the flour until the mixture resembles coarse breadcrumbs.

Stir in the almond essence and enough of the milk to form a stiff dough. Form the dough into a ball and turn it out on to a lightly floured surface. Knead the dough until it is smooth.

Roll out the dough to a circle about ¼-inch thick. With a 2-inch pastry cutter, cut it into circles and place them on the baking sheet.

Place the sheet in the oven and bake the biscuits [cookies] for 20 minutes.

Remove the biscuits [cookies] from the oven and cool them on the baking sheet.

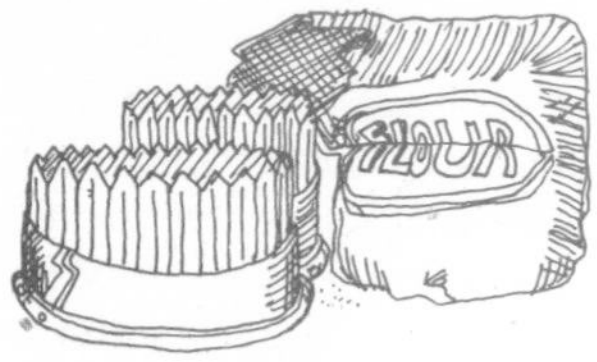

Black Pepper Cookies

This is an American recipe and these excitingly spiced chocolate cookies, with their sophisticated flavour and just a hint of pepper, are ideal to serve with afternoon tea or after-dinner coffee.

Preparation and cooking time: 1 hour

ABOUT 36 COOKIES

6 oz. [¾ cup] plus ½ teaspoon butter or margarine
¾ teaspoon freshly ground black pepper
¾ teaspoon ground cinnamon
¼ teaspoon ground cloves
1½ teaspoons vanilla essence
8 oz. [1 cup] sugar
1 egg, lightly beaten
6 oz. [1½ cups] self-raising flour
¼ teaspoon salt
3 oz. [¾ cup] cocoa

Preheat the oven to fairly hot 375°F (Gas Mark 5, 190°C). Lightly grease a baking sheet with ½ teaspoon of the butter or margarine. Set aside.

In a medium-sized mixing bowl, cream the remaining butter or margarine, pepper, cinnamon, cloves and vanilla essence together with a wooden spoon until the mixture is soft. Beat in the sugar and continue beating until the mixture is light and fluffy.

Beat in the egg.

Sift the flour, salt and cocoa into the bowl and blend the dry ingredients thoroughly with the butter or margarine and sugar mixture until a firm dough is formed.

Lightly flour your hands and roll spoonfuls of the dough into balls about 1-inch in diameter. Place the balls on the baking sheet, leaving a 1½-inch space between each one. With the heel of your hand, gently flatten the dough balls to ¼-inch thick.

Place the baking sheet in the centre of the oven and bake the cookies for 12 minutes.

Remove the baking sheet from the oven. Transfer the cookies to a wire rack and leave them to cool completely before serving.

Almond Petit Fours

These melt-in-the-mouth Almond Petits Fours are the perfect accompaniment for ice-cream or a fruit salad. They may be cut into a variety of shapes and decorated with halved glacé cherries, whole blanched almonds, chopped almonds or angelica.

Preparation and cooking time: 1½ hours

ABOUT 100 PETITS FOURS

12 oz. [3 cups] flour
5 oz. [⅝ cup] ground almonds
4 oz. [⅔ cup] light brown sugar
7 oz. [⅞ cup] butter
grated rind of 1 orange
1 tablespoon double [heavy] cream
2 tablespoons orange juice
1 egg, lightly beaten
1 teaspoon vegetable oil

Sift the flour into a large mixing bowl and stir in the almonds and sugar. Add the butter and cut it into small pieces with a table knife. With your fingertips, rub the butter into the flour until the mixture resembles coarse breadcrumbs.

Stir in the orange rind, cream, orange juice and egg. Knead the dough until it is smooth and pliable. Cover the bowl and place it in the refrigerator to chill for 30 minutes.

Preheat the oven to moderate 350°F (Gas Mark 4, 180°C). Lightly grease a baking sheet with the oil. Set aside.

Remove the bowl from the refrigerator and turn the dough out on to a lightly floured surface. Roll out the dough to a circle about ¼-inch thick. Using pastry cutters or a table knife, cut it into decorative shapes and place them on the baking sheet.

Place the sheet in the oven and bake the Petits Fours for 15 minutes or until they are lightly browned.

Cool the Petits Fours on a wire rack.

Blackberry Kiss Cakes

Succulent blackberry jelly is used to join these melting little cakes together. Blackberry Kiss Cakes make a very welcome addition to morning or afternoon coffee or a nibble any time.

Preparation and cooking time: 1 hour

25 BISCUITS [COOKIES]

1 teaspoon vegetable oil
4 oz. [½ cup] butter or margarine
4 oz. [½ cup] sugar
4 oz. [1 cup] self-raising flour
4 oz. cornflour [1 cup cornstarch]
⅛ teaspoon salt
2 eggs, lightly beaten
4 oz. blackberry jelly

Preheat the oven to moderate 350°F (Gas Mark 4, 180°C). Lightly grease a baking sheet with the oil. Set aside.

In a large mixing bowl, cream the butter or margarine with a wooden spoon until it is soft. Beat in the sugar and continue beating until the mixture is light and fluffy.

Sift the flour, cornflour [cornstarch] and salt into the bowl and blend the dry ingredients thoroughly into the butter and sugar mixture. Beat in the eggs.

Drop spoonfuls of the mixture on to the baking sheet. Place the sheet in the oven and bake for 15 minutes.

Remove the baking sheet from the oven and transfer the biscuits [cookies] to a wire rack to cool. When they are cool, sandwich pairs of biscuits [cookies] together with the blackberry jelly. Store the biscuits [cookies] in an airtight tin.

Cherry Biscuits [Cookies]

Children will enjoy making these Cherry Biscuits [Cookies]. *Just be sure they don't eat all the glacé cherries first!*

Preparation and cooking time: 1 hour

18-20 BISCUITS [COOKIES]

4 oz. [½ cup] plus 1 tablespoon butter or margarine
4 oz. [⅔ cup] soft brown sugar
½ teaspoon vanilla essence
4 oz. [⅘ cup] glacé cherries
4 oz. wholemeal flour [1 cup wholewheat flour]
1 teaspoon baking powder
4 oz. [1⅓ cups] rolled oats
2 to 3 tablespoons milk

Preheat the oven to fairly hot 375°F (Gas Mark 5, 190°C). Grease two large baking sheets with the tablespoon of butter or margarine. Set aside.

In a large mixing bowl, cream the remaining butter or margarine with a wooden spoon until it is soft and fluffy.

Gradually add the brown sugar, sifting it into the bowl if it is at all lumpy, and blend it into the butter or margarine. Stir in the vanilla essence.

With a sharp knife, coarsely chop half of the glacé cherries and stir them into the sugar mixture. Cut the remaining cherries in half and set them aside.

Sift the flour and baking powder into the mixing bowl. Add the rolled oats and stir to mix. Blend in enough of the milk to make a firm dough.

Turn the dough out on to a lightly floured surface and, with your hands, form it into a long roll about 1¼-inches in diameter. With a sharp knife, cut the roll into ½-inch thick slices. Place the slices on the baking sheets, leaving about a 1-inch space between each one.

With the blunt edge of a table knife, make three shallow indentations on the top of each slice. Place half a glacé cherry on the top of each slice.

Put the baking sheets in the oven and bake the biscuits [cookies] for 25 minutes, or until they are golden brown.

Cool the biscuits [cookies] on a wire rack.

Bergward Torte

A delicious flan, Bergward Torte is filled with the goodness of honey, ground nuts and plum jam. Serve it as a dessert after an omelet or cheese dish or cut it into 2-inch squares and serve with afternoon coffee.
Preparation and cooking time: 50 minutes
ONE 9-INCH TORTE

4 oz. [1 cup] Sweet Shortcrust
  Pastry dough
2 tablespoons clear honey
1 tablespoon golden [light corn] syrup
2 oz. [⅓ cup] walnuts, ground
6 oz. [1 cup] hazelnuts, ground
4 tablespoons plum jam

Preheat the oven to fairly hot 400°F (Gas Mark 6, 200°C).

On a lightly floured surface, roll out the dough to a circle about 12-inches in diameter. Lift the dough on your rolling pin and lay it over a 9-inch flan tin. Trim off any dough hanging over the sides of the tin and crimp the edges. Set the pastry case aside.

In a medium-sized saucepan, warm the honey and syrup over very low heat. With a wooden spoon, stir in the walnuts and hazelnuts, blending thoroughly. Remove the pan from the heat.

With a spatula or palette knife, spread the jam evenly over the bottom of the pastry case. Evenly spread the nut mixture over the jam. When the top of the nut mixture is smooth, mark it in a criss-cross pattern with a table knife.

Place the tin in the oven and bake for 25 minutes or until the pastry is golden brown. Check after 15 minutes—if the filling is browning too quickly, reduce the oven temperature to fairly hot 375°F (Gas Mark 5, 190°C) and continue baking.

Remove the torte from the oven and allow it to cool before serving.

Rough Puff Pastry

Rough Puff Pastry dough is quicker to make than shortcrust because the fat is not rubbed into the flour. The resulting pastry is light and melt-in-the-mouth. Remember that the yield is based on the amount of flour used.
Preparation and cooking time: 45 minutes
8 OUNCES [2 CUPS]

8 oz. [2 cups] flour
½ teaspoon salt
3 oz. [⅜ cup] butter or margarine
3 oz. [⅜ cup] vegetable fat
5 fl. oz. [⅝ cup] iced water

Sift the flour and salt into a large mixing bowl. Add the butter or margarine and vegetable fat and, with a table knife, cut them into small pieces. Add 4 fluid ounces [½ cup] of the water and, with the knife, mix to a dough which should be lumpy. Add more water if the dough is too dry.

Form the dough into a ball and wrap it in greaseproof or waxed paper. Place it in the refrigerator to chill for 30 minutes before using.

Cream Horns

You will feel great satisfaction when you present your family and friends with these magnificent pastry confections. They may be served as a light dessert, or with coffee.
Preparation and cooking time: 1½ hours
12 CREAM HORNS

8 oz. [2 cups] Rough Puff Pastry
  dough
1 egg, lightly beaten
2 tablespoons icing [confectioners']
  sugar
12 teaspoons jam
8 fl. oz. double cream [1 cup heavy
  cream], stiffly whipped

Dampen 12 cornet moulds. Set aside.

On a lightly floured surface, roll out the dough to a rectangle about 10-inches long and 12-inches wide. Cut out 12 strips of dough—each about 1-inch wide. Take one strip of dough and, starting at the pointed end, wrap it around a dampened cornet mould, slightly overlapping the dough at each turn. Trim off any dough hanging over the top, or open end, of the mould. Prepare the remaining cornet moulds in the same way.

Transfer the moulds to a baking sheet. With a pastry brush, coat each mould with a little beaten egg. Set the moulds aside for 10 minutes.

Preheat the oven to hot 425°F (Gas Mark 7, 210°C).

Brush the moulds with the beaten egg again. Place the baking sheet in the oven and bake the horns for 15 minutes. Remove the baking sheet from the oven and reduce the oven temperature to moderate 350°F (Gas Mark 4, 180°C). Sprinkle the cream horns with the icing [confectioners'] sugar and return them to the oven. Bake for a further 8 minutes or until the cream horns are golden brown.

Remove the baking sheet from the oven and allow the cream horns to cool. When they are cool enough to handle, carefully slip out the moulds. Transfer the cream horns to a wire rack and leave them to cool completely.

Spoon a teaspoon of jam into each cream horn. Pipe in the whipped cream and serve.

Welsh Tarts

Little rough puff pastry cases filled with jam and a mixture of ground rice, sugar and butter, Welsh Tarts are very tempting.
Preparation and cooking time: 1 hour
12 TARTS

8 oz. [2 cups] Rough Puff Pastry
  dough
12 heaped teaspoons jam
2 oz. [¼ cup] sugar
2 oz. [⅓ cup] ground rice
1 oz. [2 tablespoons] butter, melted
1 egg, lightly beaten

Preheat the oven to fairly hot 400°F (Gas Mark 6, 200°C).

On a lightly floured surface, roll out the dough to a circle about ¼-inch thick. Using a saucer as a guide, cut out 12 circles of dough and with them line 12 patty tins.

Place a heaped teaspoon of jam in each patty case. Set aside.

In a small mixing bowl, combine the sugar, ground rice and melted butter together. Add the egg and blend the ingredients well together.

Spoon the rice mixture into each of the patty cases on top of the jam.

Place the tins in the oven and bake for 15 to 20 minutes, or until the pastry and filling are lightly browned.

Remove the tins from the oven and turn out the tarts on to a wire rack. Cool the tarts completely before serving.

Desserts

Perfect ways to end perfect meals. That wonderful moment, just after the cheese and just before the coffee and liqueurs, when you present your guests with either a simple bowl of fresh fruit salad and cream or an impressive Bombe Coppelia!

You will find desserts for every season and occasion in this section.

Most desserts, in particular Zabaglione and Ricotta Cheese Pudding with Chocolate Sauce are rich with nutritious ingredients – eggs, butter, milk, cream, fruit or nuts. When you serve a bean casserole, vegetable stew or pasta dish, try to finish the meal with an egg-rich or sweet cheese dessert like these. Follow a heavy protein main dish with a lighter dessert such as a Jamaican Trifle or a fruit flan.

Some meals are, of course, sufficient without desserts. In such cases, cheese or fruit make ideal finishing touches.

Meringue Chantilly

This classic dessert is always a favourite. Meringues are really very easy to make— just follow the instructions carefully and remember that when folding in the sugar, you don't want to lose too much of the air that has been incorporated into the egg whites.

Preparation and cooking time: 2½ hours

6 SERVINGS

MERINGUES
  4 egg whites
  8 oz. [1 cup] plus 1 teaspoon castor [fine] sugar
CREME CHANTILLY
10 fl. oz. double cream [1¼ cups heavy cream]
  2 teaspoons castor sugar
  ½ teaspoon vanilla essence

Preheat the oven to cool 275°F (Gas Mark 1, 140°C). Line two baking sheets with non-stick silicone paper and set aside.

In a large mixing bowl, beat the egg whites with a wire whisk or rotary beater until they form stiff peaks. The egg whites should be so stiff that if you turned the bowl over they would not fall out. Add 4 teaspoons of the sugar and continue beating for 1 minute.

With a metal spoon, quickly and carefully fold all but 1 teaspoon of the remaining sugar into the egg whites.

Spoon or pipe the mixture in twelve mounds on the baking sheets. Sprinkle them with the reserved teaspoon of sugar. Place the baking sheets in the oven and bake the meringues for 1 hour, changing the sheets around halfway through baking, or until they are firm and lightly beige in colour.

Remove the baking sheets from the oven and turn the meringues over. Gently press the centres to make a shallow indentation in each meringue. Return the baking sheet to the oven and bake for a further 30 minutes.

Remove the baking sheets from the oven and allow the meringues to cool completely.

In a medium-sized mixing bowl, beat the cream with a wire whisk or rotary beater until it is very thick. Add the sugar and vanilla essence and continue beating until the cream is stiff.

Sandwich pairs of meringues with the flavoured cream and serve.

Jamaican Trifle

An exotic rum-flavoured trifle—layers and layers of biscuits [cookies], cream and pineapple, topped with pieces of pineapple or glacé cherries—Jamaican Trifle looks and tastes marvellous.

Preparation and cooking time: 50 minutes

4-6 SERVINGS

2 fl. oz. [¼ cup] water
2 fl. oz. [¼ cup] dark rum
  2 tablespoons dark brown sugar
10 fl. oz. double cream [1¼ cups heavy cream]
  3 tablespoons castor [fine] sugar
  1 teaspoon vanilla essence
12 sponge finger biscuits [cookies]
  1 small pineapple, skin and 'eyes' removed and flesh chopped
  2 tablespoons glacé cherries, halved (optional)

In a small saucepan, combine the water, rum and brown sugar over low heat. Cook, stirring constantly, until the sugar dissolves. Then increase the heat to moderately high and bring the syrup to the boil. Boil, stirring occasionally, for 4 minutes.

Remove the pan from the heat and set it aside to cool.

In a medium-sized mixing bowl, beat the cream with a wire whisk or rotary beater until it is thick. Add the castor sugar and vanilla and continue beating until the cream is very thick. Set the cream aside.

Pour the rum syrup into a shallow bowl. Dip half of the biscuits [cookies] into the syrup so that they become moistened but not completely saturated.

Arrange the biscuits [cookies] on the bottom of a medium-sized serving dish. Place half of the pineapple pieces on top and spoon over half of the whipped cream.

Moisten the remaining biscuits

[cookies] in the rest of the syrup and place them on top of the cream. Arrange a few more pineapple pieces on top, reserving some for decoration, and spoon over the rest of the cream.

Decorate with the remaining pineapple pieces or glacé cherries and serve.

Mocha Mousse

This superbly light and fluffy mousse, made with chocolate and coffee, must be chilled in the refrigerator for at least 6 hours before serving.

Preparation and cooking time: 6¾ hours

4 SERVINGS

4 oz. plain [semi-sweet] cooking chocolate
2½ fl. oz. [¼ cup plus 1 tablespoon] prepared coffee
4 eggs, separated
5 oz. [¾ cup] light brown sugar

In a small heavy-based saucepan or in a double saucepan, melt the chocolate in the coffee over low heat, stirring occasionally. As soon as the chocolate has melted, remove the pan from the heat and set it aside to cool for 10 minutes.

In a large mixing bowl, beat the egg yolks and sugar together with a wire whisk or rotary beater until the mixture is pale and thick. Beat in the cooled chocolate and coffee mixture. Set the bowl aside.

In a medium-sized mixing bowl, beat the egg whites with a wire whisk or rotary beater until they will hold stiff peaks.

With a metal spoon, carefully fold the egg whites into the chocolate and egg yolk mixture. Spoon the mousse into four individual glass serving dishes.

Place the dishes in the refrigerator and chill the mousse for at least 6 hours, or overnight if possible.

Crème Brulée
GLAZED BAKED CUSTARD

A rich, delicious dessert, with a topping of crisp caramelized brown sugar, Crème Brulée (krehm broo-lay) makes an impressive end to a dinner party.

Preparation and cooking time: 2¾ hours

4 SERVINGS

2 oz. [¼ cup] sugar
5 egg yolks
16 fl. oz. double cream [2 cups heavy cream], scalded
1 teaspoon vanilla essence
6 oz. [1 cup] light brown sugar

In a large mixing bowl, beat the sugar and egg yolks together with a wire whisk

until they are pale and smooth, and the mixture will form a ribbon trail on itself when the whisk is lifted. Gradually beat in the scalded cream.

Pour the mixture into a large, heavy saucepan. Place the pan over low heat and cook, stirring constantly with a wooden spoon, until the crème is thick enough to coat the spoon. Do not allow the crème to boil or it will curdle. Remove the pan from the heat and beat the crème for 1 to 2 minutes. Stir in the vanilla essence.

Strain the crème into a deep ovenproof serving dish. Allow it to cool and then place the crème in the refrigerator to chill for 2 hours.

Preheat the grill [broiler] to high.

Remove the dish from the refrigerator and sprinkle the surface of the crème with a ¼-inch thick layer of light brown sugar. Place the dish on a baking sheet and put it under the grill [broiler]. Cook for 3 to 4 minutes, or until the sugar melts and caramelizes, taking care to remove it before it burns.

Serve at once.

Coeur à la Crème

This is an attractive, light, classic French dessert. Coeur à la Crème (curr ah lah krehm) is often served with wild strawberries and sprinkled with sugar.

Preparation and cooking time: 13 hours

6 SERVINGS

1 lb. cream cheese
⅛ teaspoon salt
10 fl. oz. double cream [1¼ cups heavy cream]
2 egg whites
2 tablespoons soft brown sugar

Gently rub the cream cheese and salt through a strainer into a large mixing bowl. Using a wooden spoon, beat in the cream until it is thoroughly blended and the mixture is smooth.

In a medium-sized mixing bowl, beat the egg whites with a wire whisk or rotary beater until they form stiff peaks. With a metal spoon, carefully fold the egg whites into the cheese mixture.

With a layer of cheesecloth, line 6 *coeur à la crème* moulds if you have

them. If not, use 6 small moulds with perforated bottoms. Spoon the cheese mixture into the moulds.

Stand the moulds in a large soup dish or plate to catch the liquid that will drain out of the cheese mixture, and put the moulds and dish into the refrigerator. Leave for 12 hours or overnight.

Invert the moulds on to a serving platter and remove the cheesecloth lining. Scatter the tops of the coeurs with a little brown sugar and serve, accompanied by a jug of double [heavy] cream.

Ricotta Cheese Pudding with Chocolate Sauce

A very rich dessert that is so good for you, Ricotta Cheese Pudding with Chocolate Sauce best follows a light main course.

Preparation and cooking time: 1 hour and 10 minutes

4 SERVINGS

1 lb. ricotta cheese
2 tablespoons double [heavy] cream
2 oz. [¼ cup] sugar
2½ tablespoons orange-flavoured liqueur
2½ tablespoons coarsely chopped mixed candied fruit
2 oz. dark [semi-sweet] cooking chocolate, coarsely chopped
CHOCOLATE SAUCE
6 oz. dark [semi-sweet] cooking chocolate, cut into small pieces
3 fl. oz. [⅜ cup] strong black coffee
4 oz. [½ cup] unsalted butter, cut into ½-inch pieces and chilled

With the back of a wooden spoon, press the ricotta through a strainer into a medium-sized mixing bowl. With a wooden spoon, beat the ricotta until it is smooth. Add the cream, sugar and liqueur, beating until creamy. Fold in the chopped mixed candied fruit and chopped chocolate.

Loosely cover the bowl with plastic wrap or aluminium foil and place it in the refrigerator to chill for 1 hour.

Meanwhile, make the chocolate sauce. In a small, heavy saucepan, melt the chocolate with the coffee over low heat, stirring constantly. As soon as the chocolate has melted, remove the pan from the heat. Beat in the butter, one piece at a time. Continue beating until the sauce is smooth. Set the pan aside to allow the sauce to cool.

Remove the ricotta mixture from the refrigerator and pile it in an attractive serving dish. Spoon 2 tablespoons of the sauce over the pudding. Pour the remaining sauce into a sauceboat and serve it separately.

Sweet Orange and Black Grape Dessert

A delightfully different fresh fruit salad, Sweet Orange and Black Grape Dessert is a perfect light dessert to serve after a pilaff, risotto or pasta dish.
Preparation and cooking time: 1¼ hours
4 SERVINGS

8 oranges
4 oz. black grapes, halved and pitted
4 oz. [⅔ cup] light brown sugar
8 fl. oz. [1 cup] water
1 tablespoon light rum

Scrub one of the oranges and cut it in half. With a serrated-edge knife, cut each half into thin slices. Set aside.

Peel the remaining oranges, removing as much of the white pith as possible. Using the serrated-edge knife, slice the oranges.

Arrange the peeled orange slices and halved grapes decoratively in a glass serving dish. Set aside.

In a medium-sized saucepan, combine the sugar and water. Place the pan over low heat and cook, stirring constantly, until the sugar has dissolved. Increase the heat to moderately high and bring the syrup to the boil. Boil for 3 to 4 minutes, or until the syrup has reduced by about one-third of the original quantity.

Remove the pan from the heat and stir in the rum. Allow the syrup to cool for 15 minutes, then pour it over the orange and grape mixture. Garnish with the unpeeled orange slices.

Place the bowl in the refrigerator and chill for at least 30 minutes before serving.

Pears in Red Wine

A classic French dish, pears sweetened with honey and baked in red wine makes a simple but superb dinner party dessert.
Preparation and cooking time: 1½ hours
6 SERVINGS

6 ripe pears
1 tablespoon lemon juice
4 fl. oz. [½ cup] dry red wine
8 fl. oz. [1 cup] clear honey
1 cinnamon stick
   grated rind of ½ lemon

Preheat the oven to fairly hot 375°F (Gas Mark 5, 190°C).

Peel the pears and cut them in half lengthways. With a teaspoon, scoop out the cores. Place the pears, cut sides down, in a large shallow baking dish. Sprinkle over the lemon juice and set the baking dish aside.

In a medium-sized saucepan, combine

the wine, honey, cinnamon stick and lemon rind over moderate heat. Bring the syrup to the boil, stirring occasionally.

Pour the boiling syrup over the pears. Cover the dish with aluminium foil and place it in the oven. Bake the pears, basting occasionally, for about 20 minutes, or until they are tender when pierced with the point of a sharp knife.

Remove the dish from the oven and allow the pears to cool to room temperature. Then place the dish in the refrigerator and chill for 30 minutes. Remove the cinnamon stick before serving.

Fresh Peaches with Raspberry Sauce

Fresh peaches are not particularly high in vitamins (although they do contain a great deal of natural sugar), so it is best to serve this beautiful dessert after a heavy protein dish, such as an omelet or a quiche.
Preparation and cooking time: 1 hour
4 SERVINGS

10 fl. oz. [1¼ cups] water
 3 tablespoons clear honey
 4 fresh peaches, peeled, halved and
   stoned
 1 tablespoon kirsch
 8 oz. fresh raspberries

In a large saucepan, combine the water and honey over low heat. Place the peach halves in the pan and increase the heat to moderate. Simmer the peaches for 10 to 12 minutes, or until they are just tender but not mushy. Remove the pan from the heat.

With a slotted spoon, transfer the peach halves to a glass serving dish. Reserve the syrup in the saucepan. Sprinkle the kirsch over the peaches. Allow the peaches to cool to room temperature. Then place the dish in the refrigerator and chill for 30 minutes.

Rub most of the raspberries through a strainer into a small mixing bowl. Reserve a few whole raspberries for the garnish. Add 3 to 4 tablespoons of the reserved syrup to the raspberry purée to thin it slightly.

Remove the dish from the refrigerator. Spoon the raspberry sauce over the peaches. Garnish with the whole raspberries and serve.

Chilled Banana and Yogurt Dessert

Bananas, yogurt, honey, fruit and nuts— five particularly nutritious ingredients— make this a beautiful dessert.
Preparation and cooking time: 2¼ hours
4 SERVINGS

8 ripe bananas
4 tablespoons honey
1 pint [2½ cups] yogurt
4 tablespoons finely chopped
   walnuts
4 teaspoons raisins
4 maraschino cherries, with stems

Peel the bananas and slice them in half, lengthways. Place two bananas in each of four individual serving dishes. Sprinkle each with a tablespoon of honey and pour one-quarter of the yogurt over each dish.

Place the dishes in the refrigerator to chill for at least 2 hours.

Just before serving, sprinkle the tops with the walnuts and raisins and place a cherry in the centre.

Apricot Fool

This is a beautifully light, protein-rich summer dessert. Apricot Fool is a rich purée of nutritious dried apricots, orange juice and cream, decorated with fresh orange slices.
Preparation and cooking time: 10 hours
4 SERVINGS

8 oz. dried apricots
5 fl. oz. [⅝ cup] orange juice
3 oz. [½ cup] light brown sugar
1 teaspoon lemon juice
5 fl. oz. [⅝ cup] milk
5 fl. oz. double cream [⅝ cup heavy
   cream], stiffly whipped
4 slices fresh orange

Place the apricots in a medium-sized mixing bowl and pour over the orange juice. If the apricots are not completely covered, add a little water. Leave the apricots to soak overnight.

Transfer the apricots and soaking liquid to a medium-sized saucepan and stir in the sugar and lemon juice. Place the pan over low heat and cook, stirring constantly, until the sugar has dissolved.

Increase the heat to moderately high and bring the mixture to the boil. Reduce the heat to moderately low, cover the pan and simmer, stirring occasionally, for about 20 minutes, or until the apricots are very soft.

Strain the apricot mixture into a medium-sized mixing bowl, rubbing the apricots through the strainer with a wooden spoon. Alternatively, purée the mixture in a blender and transfer it to the mixing bowl.

Stir the milk into the purée and then fold in the cream. Spoon the fool into four individual glass serving dishes. Place the dishes in the refrigerator and chill for at least 1 hour.

Just before serving, decorate with the orange slices.

Yogurt and Orange Whip

A refreshing and tangy summer dessert, Yogurt and Orange Whip may be made with any fruit. You need a blender to make this dessert successfully.

Preparation and cooking time: 2¼ hours

4 SERVINGS

8 medium-sized oranges
2 tablespoons honey
1 pint [2½ cups] yogurt
4 tablespoons chopped walnuts, almonds or hazelnuts

Peel the oranges, removing as much of the white pith as possible. Reserve about 2 teaspoons of the orange rind and chop it finely. Set aside.

With a serrated-edge knife, chop the orange flesh into small pieces and place them in a blender. Add the honey and yogurt and blend at high speed for about 20 seconds, or until the ingredients are well combined.

Pour the orange mixture into four individual glass serving dishes. Place them in the refrigerator and chill for at least 2 hours.

Just before serving, sprinkle the tops with the nuts and reserved finely chopped orange rind.

Vanilla Ice-Cream

Made with a vanilla pod instead of vanilla essence, this is a rich, sumptuous ice-cream. The combination of cream and egg yolks makes it an excellent protein dessert to serve after a salad or vegetable casserole.

Preparation and cooking time: 4¼ hours

4-6 SERVINGS

1 vanilla pod, split
10 fl. oz. single cream [1¼ cups light cream]
3 oz. [⅜ cup] sugar
4 fl. oz. [½ cup] water
4 egg yolks

Set the freezer compartment of your refrigerator to its coldest setting.

In a small saucepan, warm the vanilla pod and cream together over very low heat for 5 minutes. Remove the pan from the heat and strain the cream into a small

mixing bowl. Set it aside. Discard the vanilla pod.

In another small saucepan, warm the sugar and water together over low heat, stirring constantly. When the sugar has dissolved, increase the heat to moderate and bring the syrup to the boil. Boil, without stirring, until the syrup reaches 215°F on a sugar thermometer (the short thread stage).

Remove the pan from the heat and allow the syrup to cool slightly.

In a medium-sized mixing bowl, beat the egg yolks with a wire whisk or rotary beater until they are pale and thick. Slowly pour in the sugar syrup, whisking constantly. When all the syrup has been incorporated, whisk in the cream.

Pour the mixture into two ice-cube trays, without divisions, and place the trays in the freezer compartment. Freeze for 30 minutes, or until the edges of the ice-cream begin to thicken.

Turn the ice-cream into a chilled large mixing bowl. With a wire whisk or rotary beater, beat the ice-cream for 4 minutes.

Return it to the ice-cube trays and replace the trays in the freezer compartment. Freeze for at least 3 hours before serving.

Bombe Coppelia

COFFEE ICE-CREAM MOULD WITH PRALINE AND RUM FILLING

A rich and unusual dessert, Bombe Coppelia (bawm koh-payl-yah) is a mouth-watering combination of coffee ice-cream and praline. To make this dessert, you will require either a large frozen food compartment in your refrigerator or a home freezer.

Preparation and cooking time: 12 hours

10-12 SERVINGS

3 pints [3¾ pints] coffee-flavoured ice-cream, slightly softened in the refrigerator
8 egg yolks
4 oz. [½ cup] sugar
3 tablespoons dark rum
1 tablespoon water
10 fl. oz. double cream [1¼ cups heavy cream]

PRALINE

1 tablespoon vegetable oil
3 oz. [⅜ cup] sugar
3 oz. [½ cup] blanched almonds

Prepare a chilled 3-pint [2-quart] bombe mould by spooning a little of the ice-cream into the base. Working quickly, so that the ice-cream does not thaw too much, spoon scoops of the ice-cream into the mould and, with the back of a metal spoon, pat the ice-cream firmly against

the sides of the mould. Press a chilled glass bowl, 1-inch smaller than the mould, inside the mould so that the ice-cream forms a solid wall between the bowl and the mould. With a knife, cut out more slices of the ice-cream to fill up any gaps in the walls.

Place the mould, with the bowl, in the freezer, and chill for 1 hour, or until all the ice-cream is completely firm. Chill the remaining ice-cream in a separate bowl for later use.

While the ice-cream is freezing, prepare the praline filling. Using a pastry brush, coat a baking sheet with the vegetable oil. Set aside.

In a small saucepan, melt the sugar over very low heat, stirring constantly. Add the almonds to the saucepan and cook, turning the nuts constantly with a metal spoon, until they are browned. Remove the pan from the heat. Pour the praline mixture on to the greased baking sheet. Leave the mixture to cool for about 10 minutes, or until it is firm.

Transfer the praline mixture to a sheet of greaseproof or waxed paper and cover with another sheet of paper. Pound the praline to a coarse powder with a wooden mallet or a rolling pin. Set the praline aside while you prepare the bombe mixture.

In a large mixing bowl, beat the egg yolks with a wire whisk or rotary beater until they are pale yellow and very thick.

Place the sugar, rum and water in a large saucepan and place it over low heat. Cook, stirring constantly, until the sugar has dissolved. Increase the heat to moderate and bring the syrup to the boil. Boil until the syrup reaches a temperature of 230°F on a sugar thermometer, or a few drops of the syrup spooned into cold water immediately form a soft ball. Remove the pan from the heat.

Slowly pour the hot syrup into the egg yolks, beating constantly. Continue to beat the mixture as it cools. Beat in the praline. Set aside.

In a medium-sized mixing bowl, beat the cream with a wire whisk until it is stiff. With a metal spoon, gently fold the cream into the praline mixture.

Remove the ice-cream mould from the freezer and take out the bowl. Pour the praline mixture into the centre of the ice-cream shell. Return the mould to the freezer and chill for 2 to 3 hours, or until the praline feels firm.

Remove the remaining ice-cream from the freezer. Allow it to thaw for a few minutes, or until it is soft enough to spread, but is not melting.

With a rubber spatula, smooth the softened ice-cream over the praline filling and ice-cream shell in the mould. Cover the mould with aluminium foil. Return the bombe to the freezer and freeze for 8 hours, or overnight.

When you are ready to serve the bombe, unmould it by dipping the mould quickly in hot water. Place a chilled plate, upside-down, on top of the mould. Holding the two firmly together, reverse them. The bombe should slip out smoothly. Serve at once.

Fruit Sorbets

A sorbet is a light, melt-in-the-mouth water ice. Filled with the goodness of vitamin-rich fruit, Fruit Sorbets are perfect summer desserts. Almost any ripe fruit, or combination of fruits, can be used in making Sorbets.
Preparation and cooking time: 3½ hours
4 SERVINGS

4 oz. ripe fruit
4 oz. [⅔ cup] light brown sugar
5 fl. oz. [⅝ cup] water
juice of 1 lemon

Set the freezer compartment of your refrigerator to its coldest setting.

Rub the fruit through a nylon strainer into a small mixing bowl. Set the resulting purée aside.

In a medium-sized saucepan, warm the sugar and water over low heat, stirring constantly. When the sugar has dissolved, increase the heat to moderate and bring the syrup to the boil. Boil for 5 minutes.

Remove the pan from the heat and allow the syrup to cool completely.

Stir the fruit purée and lemon juice into the cooled syrup. Pour the mixture into an ice-cube tray, without divisions, and place the tray in the freezer compartment. Freeze for 30 minutes, or until the edges of the sorbet begin to thicken.

Turn the sorbet into a chilled large mixing bowl. With a wire whisk or rotary beater, beat the sorbet for 4 minutes.

Return the sorbet to the ice-cube tray and replace the tray in the freezer compartment. Freeze for 2 hours.

One hour before serving, return the freezer compartment setting to normal.

Coupe Jacques
RASPBERRY AND LEMON SORBET WITH FRESH FRUIT

A classic French dessert, Coupe Jacques [coop jahk] is made of lemon and raspberry sorbet, served in individual shallow glass bowls, and moulded so that each half of the bowl is a different colour. The sorbet is topped with fresh fruit, steeped in kirsch, and decorated with blanched almonds. Any fruits suitable for fruit salad may be used.

120

Preparation and cooking time: 1½ hours
6 SERVINGS

1 pint assorted fresh fruit, cut into small pieces
2 tablespoons sugar
2 teaspoons lemon juice
7 tablespoons kirsch
1 pint raspberry sorbet [sherbet]
1 pint lemon sorbet [sherbet]
2 oz. [⅓ cup] blanched almonds, halved

In a medium-sized mixing bowl, combine the fruit, sugar, lemon juice and 6 tablespoons of the kirsch. Toss and mix the fruit well with a spoon. Cover the bowl and place it in the refrigerator to chill for 1 hour.

Rinse six shallow glass bowls in cold water.

Put a large tablespoonful of raspberry sorbet and another of lemon sorbet side by side in each bowl, leaving a small space between the two sorbets.

Remove the fruit from the refrigerator and put a large tablespoonful of fruit on top and in between the two sorbets.

Sprinkle the Coupe Jacques with the remaining kirsch and decorate with the blanched almonds. Serve immediately.

Cherries Jubilee

A colourful, flamboyant dessert that takes only a few minutes to prepare, Cherries Jubilee makes a splendid end to any dinner party. It is traditionally served with vanilla ice-cream.
Preparation and cooking time: 20 minutes
6 SERVINGS

14 oz. canned unsweetened, stoned black cherries
⅛ teaspoon ground cinnamon
1 tablespoon sugar
2 teaspoons arrowroot
2 fl. oz. [¼ cup] Cognac

Drain the cherries and set them aside, reserving 8 fluid ounces [1 cup] of the can juice.

In a medium-sized saucepan, heat the reserved can juice with the cinnamon, sugar and arrowroot over very low heat, stirring constantly with a wooden spoon. Cook for 3 to 4 minutes, or until all the ingredients have blended well and the juice is just warm. Add the cherries to the mixture and heat gently for another 1 to 2 minutes. Pour the cherries and juice into a serving bowl or chafing dish and set aside.

In a small saucepan, warm the Cognac over very low heat. Pour the Cognac over the cherries and ignite it. Serve as soon as the flames have died away.

Zabaglione
WHIPPED EGG YOLKS, MARSALA AND SUGAR

A favourite Italian dessert, Zabaglione [zah-bahg-lee-oh-nee] is a superbly light concoction that is the perfect ending for a meal based on pasta. It does require constant attention, but is well worth it.
Preparation and cooking time: 20 minutes
4 SERVINGS

3 egg yolks
4 oz. [½ cup] sugar
4 tablespoons Marsala

In a medium-sized, heatproof mixing bowl, beat together the egg yolks, sugar and Marsala. Place the bowl over a sauce-pan of simmering water over moderately low heat (the water should be just simmering, but not boiling).

With a wire whisk or rotary beater, whisk the mixture until it is thick and fluffy.

Remove the bowl from the heat and spoon the Zabaglione into four individual glass serving dishes. Serve immediately.

Bananas Beauharnais

A rich dessert, Bananas Beauharnais [bow-ahr-nay] is excellent for a lunch or dinner party. It is usually served hot, but is equally good cold.
Preparation and cooking time: 1 hour 10 minutes
4 SERVINGS

1 teaspoon butter or margarine
6 bananas
1 tablespoon light brown sugar
3 fl. oz. [⅜ cup] white rum
4 oz. macaroons, crushed
1 tablespoon melted butter or margarine
10 fl. oz. double cream [1¼ cups heavy cream]

Preheat the oven to moderate 350°F (Gas Mark 4, 180°C). Lightly grease a medium-sized baking dish with the teaspoon of butter or margarine.

Peel the bananas and place them in the baking dish. Sprinkle over the sugar and rum. Place the dish in the oven and bake for 15 minutes.

Remove the dish from the oven and set it aside to cool for 10 minutes.

In a small mixing bowl, mix together the crushed macaroons and melted butter or margarine. Pour the cream over the bananas and sprinkle the macaroon mixture on top.

Return the dish to the oven and bake for a further 20 minutes.

Remove the dish from the oven and serve, straight from the dish.

Grilled [Broiled] Grapefruit

This is a very quick-to-make dessert or first course. If you like, the grapefruit may be prepared in advance and then grilled [broiled] just before serving.

Preparation and cooking time: 30 minutes

4 SERVINGS

2 large grapefruit
4 teaspoons sherry
4 teaspoons dark brown sugar
1 tablespoon butter or margarine,
   cut into 4 small pieces

Preheat the grill [broiler] to high.

Cut the grapefruit in half. With a serrated-edge knife, loosen the segments and remove any seeds.

Place the grapefruit, cut sides down, on kitchen paper towels to drain for 2 minutes.

Arrange the grapefruit, cut sides up, on the grill [broiler] rack. Pour a teaspoon of sherry over each half and spread a teaspoon of sugar on each. Top with a piece of butter or margarine.

Place the grapefruit under the grill [broiler] and cook for 6 to 8 minutes, or until the butter or margarine has melted and the edges of the grapefruit are lightly browned.

Remove from the heat and transfer the grapefruit to four individual serving dishes. Serve immediately.

Fried Spiced Apples

Apples drenched in sugar, cinnamon and ginger, and then fried to a golden brown, make this a quick and easy dessert.

Preparation and cooking time: 35 minutes

4 SERVINGS

1 lb. cooking [greening] apples
2 tablespoons sugar
½ teaspoon ground ginger
½ teaspoon ground cinnamon
2 oz. [¼ cup] butter or margarine
6 fl. oz. single cream [¾ cup light
   cream]

Peel and core the apples. With a sharp knife, cut them into ½-inch thick slices.

In a shallow bowl or on a sheet of greaseproof or waxed paper, mix together the sugar, ginger and cinnamon. Dip the apple slices in the sugar and spice mixture, coating them on both sides.

In a large frying-pan, melt the butter or margarine over moderate heat. When the foam subsides, place the apple slices in the pan. Fry them for 3 to 5 minutes on each side, or until they are golden brown.

With a slotted spoon, remove the apple slices from the pan and arrange them on a warmed serving dish. Serve immediately with the cream.

Steamed Ginger Pudding

Serve this aromatic steamed pudding with Orange Custard Sauce for a warming winter dessert.

Preparation and cooking time: 3¼ hours

4-6 SERVINGS

1½ tablespoons butter or margarine
4 oz. self-raising wholemeal flour
   [1 cup self-rising wholewheat flour],
   bran sifted out
⅛ teaspoon salt
4 oz. [½ cup] vegetable fat
2 oz. [1 cup] fresh brown
   breadcrumbs
1 teaspoon ground ginger
2 oz. crystallized ginger [1 cup
   candied ginger], minced
4 oz. [⅔ cup] light brown sugar
2 eggs, lightly beaten
4 fl. oz. [½ cup] milk

Generously grease a 2-pint [5-cup] pudding basin with 1 tablespoon of the butter or margarine. Set aside.

Mix together the flour and salt in a large mixing bowl. Add the vegetable fat and cut it into small pieces with a table knife. With your fingertips, rub the fat into the flour until the mixture resembles coarse breadcrumbs.

Stir in the breadcrumbs, ground ginger, crystallized [candied] ginger and sugar. Make a well in the centre of the flour mixture and add the eggs and milk. Gradually draw the flour mixture into the liquid. Continue mixing until all the flour mixture is thoroughly incorporated and the mixture is smooth.

Spoon the mixture into the greased pudding basin. Cut out a circle of greaseproof or waxed paper 4 inches wider in diameter than the pudding basin. Grease the paper with the remaining butter or margarine. Cut out a circle of aluminium foil the same size as the paper circle. Place the two circles together, the greased side of the paper circle away from the foil, and holding them firmly together, make a 1-inch pleat across the centre. Place the paper and foil circles, foil upper-most, over the pudding basin and tie on securely with string.

Half fill a large saucepan with water and bring it to the boil over high heat. Place the pudding basin in the pan, adding more boiling water if necessary so that it comes up to the rim of the basin. Cover the pan, reduce the heat to moderately low and steam the pudding for 1½ hours, adding more boiling water when necessary.

Reduce the heat to low so that the water is just simmering, and continue steaming for a further hour.

Remove the basin from the pan and take off the paper and foil circles. Place a serving dish, inverted, over the top of the basin. Holding the two firmly together, reverse them. The pudding should slide out easily on to the dish.

Serve immediately.

Coriander Fruit Crumble

This unusual aromatic dessert is inexpensive, simple to make and has a very interesting flavour. Serve it either hot or cold, with cream.

Preparation and cooking time: 1¼ hours

4-6 SERVINGS

1 teaspoon butter or margarine
1½ lb. cooking [greening] apples,
   peeled, cored and thinly sliced
8 oz. fresh blackberries, washed and
   stalks removed
2 tablespoons brown sugar
1 teaspoon ground cinnamon
TOPPING
4 oz. [1 cup] flour
4 oz. [½ cup] sugar
2 oz. [¼ cup] butter or margarine
2 teaspoons ground coriander

Preheat the oven to moderate 350°F (Gas Mark 4, 180°C). Grease a 3-pint [7½-cup] baking dish with the teaspoon of butter or margarine.

Put the apples and blackberries in the baking dish and sprinkle them with the brown sugar and cinnamon. Set the baking dish aside.

To make the crumble topping, put the flour and sugar into a medium-sized mixing bowl. Add the butter or margarine and cut it into small pieces with a table knife. With your fingertips, rub the butter or margarine into the flour and sugar until the mixture resembles coarse breadcrumbs. Mix in the coriander.

Sprinkle the crumble topping over the fruit and place the dish in the oven. Bake for 45 minutes.

Remove the Crumble from the oven and serve immediately, straight from the dish.

Crème à la Vanille

CUSTARD SAUCE

Crème à la Vanille (krem ah lah vah-nee-yeh) *is a sweet vanilla-flavoured sauce that is usually served with fruit or puddings.*
Preparation and cooking time: 35 minutes
1 PINT [2½ CUPS]

16 fl. oz. [2 cups] milk
1 vanilla pod
4 egg yolks
2 oz. [¼ cup] sugar

Place the milk and vanilla pod in the top of a double saucepan or in a medium-sized heatproof bowl placed over a saucepan half full of simmering water. Scald the milk over moderate heat (bring to just below boiling point). Remove the pan or bowl from the heat, cover it and set it aside to cool for 10 minutes.

In a large mixing bowl, beat the egg yolks and sugar together with a wire whisk or rotary beater until the mixture is pale and creamy. Remove the vanilla pod from the milk and gradually add the milk to the egg yolk mixture, whisking constantly. Pour the custard back into the double saucepan or heatproof bowl and place it over the pan of simmering water.

Cook the custard, stirring constantly, for 3 to 5 minutes, or until it is thick enough to coat the back of the spoon. Do not let the custard boil or it will curdle.

Remove the custard from the heat and pour it into a serving jug. Serve warm or chilled.

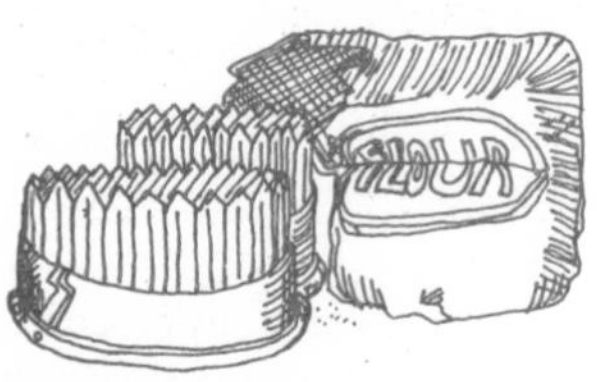

Orange Custard Sauce

A perfect accompaniment for a steamed pudding or a fresh citrus fruit salad, Orange Custard Sauce may be served hot or cold.
Preparation and cooking time: 45 minutes
16 FLUID OUNCES [2 CUPS]

2 sugar cubes
1 orange
16 fl. oz. [2 cups] unsweetened orange juice
4 egg yolks
2 oz. [¼ cup] sugar
1 teaspoon cornflour [cornstarch] **dissolved in 2 teaspoons water**

Rub the sugar cubes over the orange so that they absorb the zest from the rind. Place the sugar cubes in a medium-sized heatproof mixing bowl and mash them with the back of a wooden spoon. Set aside.

In a medium-sized saucepan, heat the orange juice over moderate heat until bubbles form around the edge. Remove the pan from the heat and set it aside to cool.

Add the egg yolks and sugar to the mashed sugar cubes. With a wire whisk or rotary beater, beat them together until the mixture is pale and creamy. Whisk in the cornflour [cornstarch].

Gradually add the cooled orange juice, whisking constantly. Place the heatproof bowl over a saucepan half full of simmering water. Cook the custard, stirring constantly with a wooden spoon, over moderate heat for 3 to 5 minutes, or until it is thick enough to coat the spoon. Do not let the custard boil or it will curdle.

Remove the custard from the heat and pour it into a serving jug. Serve warm or chilled.

Sweet Shortcrust Pastry

Ideal for fruit or sweet cheese flans and pies, Sweet Shortcrust Pastry is made with light brown sugar and an egg. As with the Shortcrust Pastry recipe, the yield indicates the amount of flour used to make the dough.
Preparation and cooking time: 45 minutes
4 OUNCES [1 CUP]

4 oz. wholemeal flour [1 cup wholewheat flour], bran sifted out
2 tablespoons light brown sugar
4 oz. [½ cup] butter or margarine
1 egg yolk
1 to 2 tablespoons water

In a medium-sized mixing bowl, combine the flour and sugar. Add the butter or margarine and cut it into small pieces with a table knife. With your fingertips, rub the fat into the flour until the mixture resembles coarse breadcrumbs.

Make a well in the centre of the flour mixture and add the egg yolk and 1 tablespoon of the water. With the knife, gradually mix the flour mixture into the egg yolk and water. Then with your fingers, knead the dough until it is smooth. Add more water if the dough is too dry.

Form the dough into a ball and wrap it in greaseproof or waxed paper. Place the dough in the refrigerator to chill for 30 minutes before using.

Lemon Meringue Pie

Golden meringue covering a rich lemon cream filling has made Lemon Meringue Pie a popular dessert for generations. Apart from their tangy refreshing flavour, lemons are an excellent source of Vitamin C.
Preparation and cooking time: 1¾ hours
4-6 SERVINGS

PASTRY

4 oz. wholemeal flour [1 cup wholewheat flour]
¼ teaspoon salt
2 oz. [¼ cup] vegetable fat
1 egg, lightly beaten

FILLING

6 oz. [¾ cup] sugar
⅛ teaspoon salt
1¼ tablespoons cornflour [cornstarch]
5 fl. oz. [⅝ cup] evaporated milk
5 fl. oz. [⅝ cup] boiling water
2 eggs, separated
juice and finely grated rind of 2 small lemons

Preheat the oven to hot 425°F (Gas Mark 7, 210°C).

Sift the flour and salt into a medium-sized mixing bowl, discarding the bran in the sifter. Add the vegetable fat and cut it into small pieces with a table knife. Using your fingertips, rub the fat into the flour until the mixture resembles coarse breadcrumbs.

Add the egg and mix and knead until a stiff dough is formed. If the dough is too dry, add a little water.

On a lightly floured surface, roll out the dough to a circle about 12 inches in diameter. Lift the dough on your rolling pin and lay it over an 8-inch pie dish. Gently ease the dough into the dish. Roll under any dough hanging over the edge of the dish and crimp the edge.

With a kitchen fork, prick the bottom of the pastry case several times. Line the pastry case with aluminium foil and add enough dried beans or rice to make a ½-inch layer on the bottom

Place the dish in the centre of the oven and bake for 10 minutes. Then remove the foil and beans or rice and continue baking for 5 minutes, or until the pastry case is golden brown.

Remove the dish from the oven and set the pastry case aside to cool. Reduce the oven temperature to fairly hot 375°F (Gas Mark 5, 190°C).

In a medium-sized saucepan, combine 2 ounces [¼ cup] of the sugar, the salt, cornflour [cornstarch], evaporated milk and boiling water over low heat. Cook, stirring constantly, until the sugar dissolves. Increase the heat to moderate and bring the mixture to the boil, still stirring. Simmer and stir for 5 minutes. Remove the pan from the heat.

In a small mixing bowl, lightly beat the egg yolks with a kitchen fork. Beat in about 4 tablespoons of the hot sugar and milk mixture. Stir the egg yolk mixture into the remaining sugar and milk mixture in the saucepan.

Return the pan to low heat and cook gently, stirring constantly, for 3 minutes. Remove the pan from the heat and stir in the lemon juice and rind. Set the pan aside.

In a medium-sized mixing bowl, beat the egg whites with a wire whisk or rotary beater until they are frothy. Gradually add the remaining sugar and continue beating until the egg whites will hold stiff peaks.

Turn the lemon mixture into the pastry case. Carefully spoon the egg white mixture on top.

Place the pie dish in the oven and bake for 7 minutes, or until the meringue topping is golden brown. Remove the pie from the oven and allow it to cool slightly before serving.

Apple Pie

This single-crust English Apple Pie is traditionally served with Crème à la Vanille, cream or, in Northern England, with cheese.
Preparation and cooking time: 1¼ hours
4 SERVINGS
1½ lb. cooking [greening] apples, peeled, cored and thinly sliced
¼ teaspoon grated nutmeg
¼ teaspoon ground cloves
6 oz. [1 cup] dark brown sugar
1 tablespoon butter or margarine, cut into small pieces
4 oz. [1 cup] Sweet Shortcrust Pastry dough
1 tablespoon castor [fine] sugar

Preheat the oven to fairly hot 400°F (Gas Mark 6, 200°C).

Arrange the apple slices in a medium-sized pie dish. Sprinkle over the nutmeg, cloves and brown sugar. Dot the top with the pieces of butter or margarine. Cover the dish with aluminium foil and place it in the oven.

Bake for 20 minutes, or until the apples are tender but still firm. Remove the dish from the oven and set aside.

On a lightly floured surface, roll out the dough to a circle about ¼-inch thick. Lift the dough on your rolling pin and lay it over the pie dish. Tuck under any dough hanging over the sides of the dish and crimp the edges.

With a pastry brush, lightly coat the dough with water. Sprinkle over the castor sugar. Place the dish in the oven and bake for 30 minutes, or until the pastry is golden brown.

Remove the pie from the oven and serve it at once.

Apricot Bourdaloue Tart

A pretty apricot tart with an orange-flavoured filling, Apricot Bourdaloue Tart is a super dessert. If you prefer to use fresh apricots, poach them in a sugar and water syrup until they are tender but still firm.
Preparation and cooking time: 2¼ hours
ONE 8-INCH TART
4 oz. [1 cup] Sweet Shortcrust Pastry dough
2 egg yolks
2 oz. [¼ cup] sugar
grated rind of 1 orange
1½ tablespoons each of cornflour [cornstarch] and flour, mixed
10 fl. oz. [1¼ cups] milk
1 egg white
14 oz. canned apricot halves
2 tablespoons toasted flaked almonds

Preheat the oven to fairly hot 400°F (Gas Mark 6, 200°C).

On a lightly floured surface, roll out the dough to a circle about 12 inches in diameter. Lift the dough on your rolling pin and lay it over an 8-inch flan tin. Gently ease the dough into the tin and trim off any pastry hanging over the sides. Crimp the edges.

With a kitchen fork, prick the bottom of the pastry case several times. Line the pastry case with aluminium foil and add enough dried beans or rice to make a ½-inch layer.

Place the pastry case in the centre of the oven and bake for 10 minutes. Then remove the beans or rice and foil and continue baking for 10 minutes, or until the pastry is golden brown.

Remove the pastry case from the oven and set it aside to cool.

In a medium-sized mixing bowl, beat the egg yolks and half of the sugar together with a wire whisk or rotary beater until the mixture is thick and will form a ribbon trail on itself when the whisk is lifted. Beat in the orange rind and cornflour [cornstarch] and flour mixture. Set aside.

In a medium-sized saucepan, scald the milk over moderate heat (bring to just under boiling point). Remove the pan from the heat and slowly pour the milk into the egg yolk mixture, beating constantly.

Pour the egg yolk and milk mixture into the saucepan and return it to the heat. Cook, stirring constantly, for 3 to 4 minutes or until the mixture is thick and smooth. Remove the pan from the heat and set it aside to cool.

In a medium-sized mixing bowl, beat the egg white with a wire whisk or rotary beater until it is frothy. Gradually beat in the remaining sugar and continue beating until the egg white will form stiff peaks.

With a metal spoon, carefully fold the egg white into the cooled egg yolk mixture. Set the crème bourdaloue aside.

Turn the pastry case out of the tin and place it on a decorative serving platter. Set aside.

Drain the apricots and put the can juice into a small saucepan. Place the pan over moderately high heat and bring the juice to the boil. Boil rapidly until the juice has reduced to about half the original quantity and is syrupy. Remove the pan from the heat and set it aside to cool.

Spoon the crème bourdaloue into the pastry case and spread it out evenly. Place the apricot halves on top of the crème so that it is completely covered. Sprinkle over the almonds and then pour over the reduced apricot juice. Allow this glaze to cool and set before serving.

Cream Cheese and Lemon Flan

Cream Cheese and Lemon Flan is a rich dessert that is high in protein. Serve it after a vegetable or rice main dish.
Preparation and cooking time: 1½ hours
6-8 SERVINGS
12 oz. cream cheese
6 oz. [1 cup] light brown sugar
4 eggs, lightly beaten
4 tablespoons lemon juice
2 tablespoons finely grated lemon rind
4 oz. [1 cup] Sweet Shortcrust Pastry dough

Preheat the oven to hot 425°F (Gas Mark 7, 210°C).

In a large mixing bowl, cream the cream cheese and sugar together with a wooden spoon until the mixture is light and fluffy. Beat in the eggs and lemon juice and rind. Set aside.

On a lightly floured surface, roll out the dough to a circle about 12 inches in diameter. Lift the dough on your rolling pin and lay it over an 8-inch flan tin. Gently ease the dough into the tin. Roll under the dough hanging over the sides of the tin and crimp the edges.

Spoon the cream cheese and lemon filling into the pastry case. Place the tin in the oven and bake for 15 minutes. Then reduce the heat to fairly hot 375°F (Gas Mark 5, 190°C) and continue baking for 35 minutes, or until a knife inserted into the centre comes out clean.

Remove the tin from the oven and allow the flan to cool to room temperature before serving.

Drinks, Dips and Spreads

There are lots of exciting new drinks and dips and spreads for you to try in this section.

Dips make very good appetizers. It is a nice idea to lay out some bowls of biscuits [crackers], pretzels and colourful raw vegetables alongside a spicy dip for your guests to eat with their pre-dinner drinks. Dips also make tasty additions to a buffet table and welcome snacks at cocktail parties.

For a cold winter's gathering, nothing could be more welcoming than hot mulled wine – nor, on a sunny afternoon, a refreshing fruit punch. Whatever the season or occasion – from a formal reception to a children's birthday party – you'll find a suitable drink in this section.

We have included a classic Swiss Fondue recipe, an irresistable combination of cheese and wine. A fondue party can be either a sophisticated candlelit affair or an informal cross-legged on-the-floor arrangement with everyone indiscriminately dunking pieces of bread in the pot!

Cheese and wine parties are great fun too – and so simple to prepare. All you need for a successful evening is a good supply of wines, lots of salads, dips, fresh crusty bread, as many different cheeses as you can find – and a group of cheerful people!

Grapefruit Punch

This non-alcoholic punch will be well received by both children and adults. Its citrus fruit flavour is very refreshing.
Preparation and cooking time: 30 minutes
8 SERVINGS

2 medium-sized oranges
1 tablespoon grated orange rind
2 fl. oz. [¼ cup] clear honey
2 pints [5 cups] unsweetened grapefruit juice
4 eggs
8 fl. oz. [1 cup] dry ginger ale
4 ice cubes
4 mint sprigs

Halve the oranges and squeeze their juice into a medium-sized saucepan. Add the orange rind and honey to the saucepan and place it over low heat. Cook the mixture, stirring constantly, for 3 minutes, or until the ingredients are well blended and warm. Remove the pan from the heat and strain the orange juice mixture into a medium-sized mixing bowl. Set aside to cool.

In a large punch bowl or mixing bowl, beat the grapefruit juice and eggs together with a wire whisk or rotary beater. Gradually add the cooled orange juice, beating constantly until all the ingredients are well blended.

Stir in the ginger ale, ice cubes and mint sprigs and serve.

Mulled Claret

There is nothing quite like a mulled, wine-based punch to brighten up a winter's party. This punch goes particularly well with a selection of good cheeses and crusty bread.
Preparation and cooking time: 30 minutes
3 PINTS [7½ CUPS]

2½ pints [6¼ cups], or 2 bottles, dry red Bordeaux wine
1 tablespoon finely grated orange rind
1 tablespoon finely grated lemon rind
8 oz. [1 cup] sugar
½ teaspoon ground cloves
½ teaspoon grated nutmeg
10 fl. oz. [1¼ cups] brandy

Put the wine, orange and lemon rinds, sugar, cloves and nutmeg into a medium-sized stainless steel or enamel saucepan. Place the pan over moderate heat and bring the mixture to the boil, stirring constantly to dissolve the sugar. Remove the pan from the heat and pour the wine mixture into a large punch bowl. Set aside.

In a small saucepan, warm the brandy over low heat until it is hot but not boiling. Remove the pan from the heat and pour the brandy into the punch bowl. Ignite the punch.

When the flames die down, serve the punch with a long-handled ladle.

Brandied Coffee Cream

A deliciously rich and warming drink, Brandied Coffee Cream is ideal to serve at the end of a very special meal.
Preparation and cooking time: 30 minutes
8 SERVINGS

4 oz. [½ cup] sugar
5 eggs
2 fl. oz. [¼ cup] brandy
10 fl. oz. [1¼ cups] milk
10 fl. oz. single cream [1¼ cups light cream]
1 pint [2½ cups] strong black coffee
2 fl. oz. double cream [¼ cup heavy cream], stiffly whipped
1 oz. plain or milk eating chocolate, grated

In a large mixing bowl, beat the sugar and eggs together with a fork or wire whisk until they are well blended. Set aside.

In a large saucepan, heat the brandy, milk, single [light] cream and coffee together over moderate heat until they are hot but not boiling. Remove the pan from the heat and gradually pour the brandy mixture into the egg-and-sugar mixture, whisking constantly until the ingredients are well blended.

Pour the brandied coffee into eight heatproof glasses. Top with a little whipped cream and grated chocolate and serve.

Golden Fruit Punch

A non-alcoholic and extremely refreshing summer drink, Golden Fruit Punch will be sure to delight the whole family.
Preparation and cooking time: 15 minutes
3½ PINTS [8¼ CUPS]

15 ice cubes
10 fl. oz. [1¼ cups] white grape juice
10 fl. oz. [1¼ cups] apple juice
 1 pint [2½ cups] pineapple juice
16 fl. oz. [2 cups] dry ginger ale
 1 small fresh pineapple, peeled,
   trimmed and finely chopped, or
   12 oz. canned pineapple pieces,
   drained
 4 borage sprigs

Put the ice cubes in a very large jug or punch bowl. Add all of the remaining ingredients and stir well with a long-handled spoon.
Serve immediately.

Hot Spiced Wine

A second mulled wine-based punch, Hot Spiced Wine will be a certain success at a winter party.
Preparation and cooking time: 30 minutes
4 PINTS [5 PINTS]

2½ pints [6¼ cups], or 2 bottles, dry
   red wine
 8 fl. oz. [1 cup] clear honey
 1 teaspoon grated nutmeg
 ½ teaspoon ground allspice
1¼ pints [3 cups] water

Combine all of the ingredients in a large stainless steel or enamel saucepan. Place the saucepan over moderate heat and bring the liquid to the boil, stirring constantly.
Pour the mixture into a punch bowl or very large jug and serve very hot.

Hot Spiced Ale

A marvellous and not-too-expensive drink, Hot Spiced Ale is perfect to serve your guests on cold winter nights. Serve with toasted marshmallows or toasted crumpets [English muffins] for a special treat.
Preparation and cooking time: 45 minutes
2½ PINTS [3¾ CUPS]

3 oz. [½ cup] light brown sugar
3 eggs
2 pints [5 cups] pale ale
1 teaspoon ground ginger
1 teaspoon grated nutmeg
5 fl. oz. [⅝ cup] brandy

In a medium-sized mixing bowl, beat the sugar and eggs together with a fork or wire whisk until they are well blended. Set aside.

In a large stainless steel or enamel saucepan, combine the ale, ginger and nutmeg over moderate heat. Bring to the boil, stirring frequently. Remove the pan from the heat and set aside.

In a small saucepan, warm the brandy over low heat until it is hot but not boiling. Remove the pan from the heat.

Combine all of the ingredients together in a very large jug or punch bowl, whisking until they are well blended. Serve hot.

Carnival Fruit Punch

The kind of fruit punch that will guarantee the success of a children's party, Carnival Fruit Punch is pretty to look at, marvellous to drink and full of goodness as well.
Preparation and cooking time: 25 minutes
4 PINTS [5 PINTS]

15 ice cubes
 2 pints [5 cups] unsweetened orange
   juice
 1 pint [2½ cups] unsweetened
   grapefruit juice
10 fl. oz. [1¼ cups] white grape juice
10 fl. oz. [1¼ cups] apple juice
 8 oz. black grapes, washed, halved
   and seeded
 8 oz. seedless white grapes, washed
   and halved
 4 spearmint sprigs
 4 borage sprigs (optional)

Put the ice cubes in a large punch or mixing bowl. Add all the remaining ingredients and, with a long-handled spoon, stir well to mix. Place the bowl in the refrigerator and chill the punch for at least 15 minutes before serving.

Strawberry Milk Shake

A popular drink with the whole family, Strawberry Milk Shake is very easy to make, especially if you have a blender. However, it is possible to make a perfectly adequate shake without a blender, as you can see in the following recipe.
Preparation and cooking time: 30 minutes
1¼ PINTS [3 CUPS]

4 oz. fresh strawberries, washed and
   hulled
2 tablespoons clear honey
1 pint [2½ cups] milk

In a large mixing bowl, mash the strawberries and honey together with a fork until they are well blended. With a wire whisk, gradually beat in the milk and continue beating until the mixture is smooth and slightly thick. Alternatively, put all of the ingredients in an electric blender and blend them together for 30 seconds.

Pour the milk shake into a large screw-top jar and place it in the refrigerator to chill for 15 minutes. Just before serving, shake once or twice.

Strawberry Rum Punch

A delightful—and potent—drink, Strawberry Rum Punch is especially good for summer evening parties in the garden. It is expensive—but it's worth it!
Preparation and cooking time: 3½ hours
4½ PINTS [5½ PINTS]

2 lb. fresh strawberries, washed,
   hulled and sliced
8 oz. [1 cup] sugar
12 fl. oz. [1½ cups] light rum
15 ice cubes
2½ pints [6¼ cups], or 2 bottles, white
   Rhine wine
 4 borage sprigs (optional)

In a large mixing bowl, combine the strawberries, sugar and rum together, stirring until the strawberries are well coated with both the sugar and the rum. Place the bowl in the refrigerator to chill for 3 hours, stirring occasionally.

Remove the strawberry mixture from the refrigerator and set it aside. Put the ice cubes in a large punch bowl. Add all the remaining ingredients, including the strawberry mixture, and mix well with a long-handled spoon. Serve cold.

Party Fizz

An excellent non-alcoholic punch for a cocktail party, Party Fizz will delight your tee-total guests.
Preparation and cooking time: 1¼ hours
3¾ PINTS [9½ CUPS]

 4 lemons, thinly sliced
 3 medium-sized oranges, thinly
   sliced
 2 tablespoons castor [fine] sugar
 2 pints [5 cups] ginger ale
1½ pints [3¾ cups] soda water
 4 oz. crystallized ginger [⅔ cup
   candied ginger], very finely chopped
15 ice cubes

Place the lemon and orange slices in a large punch bowl and sprinkle over the sugar. Place the bowl in the refrigerator and chill for 1 hour.

Add all of the other ingredients to the bowl, stirring with a long-handled spoon until they are all well blended. Serve immediately.

Citrus Ponets

A light, white-wine-based punch, perfect for summer garden parties, Citrus Ponets tastes as fresh as it sounds. Serve with lots of fruit and cheese. Wines such as Rüdesheimer and Niersteiner are particularly good in this punch.

Preparation and cooking time: 15 minutes

3½ PINTS [8¾ CUPS]

15 ice cubes
2½ pints [6¼ cups], or 2 bottles, white Rhine wine
5 fl. oz. [⅝ cup] vodka
5 fl. oz. [⅝ cup] soda water
juice of 6 medium-sized oranges
juice of 2 large grapefruit
juice of 1 lemon
1 small fresh pineapple, peeled, trimmed and finely chopped
4 oz. bottled cocktail cherries, drained

Place the ice cubes in a large punch bowl. Add all of the remaining ingredients and, with a long-handled spoon, mix well to blend. Serve immediately.

Egg Fondue

Fondues make marvellous party dishes—it's hard to be stand-offish, after all, when you're sharing the same cooking pot. Serve accompanied by lots of green salad and a delicious well-chilled white wine—try the Swiss wines Fendant or Neuchâtel, the traditional accompaniments to a Swiss fondue.

Preparation and cooking time: 20 minutes

8 SERVINGS

1 garlic clove, halved
1 pint [2½ cups] dry white wine
8 oz. Emmenthal cheese, grated
8 oz. Gruyère cheese, grated
2 teaspoons cornflour [cornstarch] dissolved in 1 tablespoon water
½ teaspoon salt
¼ teaspoon black pepper
½ teaspoon ground mace
12 hard-boiled eggs, halved
2 long loaves crusty bread, cut into 2-inch pieces

Rub the garlic halves around the insides of a medium-sized saucepan and discard. Put the wine, cheeses and cornflour [cornstarch] mixture into the pan and place it over moderate heat. Cook, stirring constantly, until the cheese melts and the mixture becomes thick and creamy. Stir in the salt, pepper and mace.

Pour the fondue mixture into a fondue pot and place it over a spirit burner on the table. The fondue is now ready to serve.

Place the eggs on one plate and the bread pieces on another. Put an egg half on the end of a fondue fork or skewer and dip into the fondue mixture. Eat. Then place a piece of bread on the fondue fork or skewer and dip into the fondue. Continue alternating the two.

Egg and Onion Scramble

Serve this flavourful mixture of eggs, onions, garlic, parsley and lemon rind hot or cold on toast or savoury biscuits [crackers].

Preparation and cooking time: 20 minutes

8 SERVINGS

2 oz. [¼ cup] butter or margarine
2 medium-sized onions, finely chopped
1 small garlic clove, crushed
8 eggs
2 tablespoons chopped fresh parsley
2 teaspoons grated lemon rind
½ teaspoon salt
¼ teaspoon black pepper
⅛ teaspoon cayenne pepper
2 tablespoons single [light] cream

In a large frying-pan, melt the butter or margarine over moderate heat. When the foam subsides, add the onions and garlic. Fry them, stirring occasionally, for 5 to 7 minutes, or until the onions are soft and translucent but not brown.

Meanwhile, in a medium-sized mixing bowl, beat the eggs, parsley, lemon rind, salt, pepper and cayenne together, mixing until they are well blended. Add the egg mixture to the frying-pan and cook, stirring frequently with a fork, for 4 minutes, or until the eggs are just beginning to scramble. Pour in the cream and cook, stirring constantly, for 1 minute, or until the cream is absorbed and the eggs are scrambled.

Remove the pan from the heat and serve.

Paté d'Aubergine

AUBERGINE [EGGPLANT] PATE

Serve this smooth, creamy Paté d'Aubergine (pah-tay doh-bair-jeen) *with triangles of toast at a wine and cheese party or as a special appetizer with drinks. A well-chilled white wine, such as Frascati or Côtes de Provence, would be a good complement.*

Preparation and cooking time: 1¾ hours

6-8 SERVINGS

2 medium-sized aubergines [eggplants]
1 large garlic clove, crushed
1 tablespoon lemon juice
1 teaspoon salt
½ teaspoon black pepper
⅛ teaspoon cayenne pepper

Preheat the oven to moderate 350°F (Gas Mark 4, 180°C).

Place the whole, unpeeled aubergines [eggplants] on a baking sheet and place the baking sheet in the oven. Bake for about 40 minutes, or until the aubergines [eggplants] are soft. Remove the aubergines [eggplants] from the oven and set them aside to cool.

When the aubergines [eggplants] are cool, slice them in half, lengthways. With a teaspoon, scoop out the flesh and transfer it to a medium-sized mixing bowl. Discard the shells.

Stir the garlic, lemon juice, salt, pepper and cayenne into the aubergine [eggplant] flesh and, with a fork, mash the mixture to a pulp. Place the bowl in the refrigerator to chill for 30 minutes before serving.

Crudités avec Aïoli

RAW VEGETABLES WITH GARLIC MAYONNAISE

Crudités are raw, trimmed vegetables served as appetizers or party fare, which are dipped into various sauces and eaten. Aïoli sauce is a perfect complement to the vegetables—as are the other dips in this section. You may feel that this recipe will produce a sauce with too strong a garlic flavour for your tastes. If so, use only 2 garlic cloves.

Preparation and cooking time: 1 hour

8-10 SERVINGS

AIOLI SAUCE

4 garlic cloves, peeled
½ teaspoon salt
2 tablespoons lemon juice
2 egg yolks, at room temperature
10 fl. oz. [1¼ cups] olive oil
4 parsley sprigs

VEGETABLES

4 celery stalks, thinly sliced and chilled
1 head of fennel, peeled, thinly sliced and chilled
4 carrots, scraped, thinly sliced and chilled
1 small cauliflower, washed, broken into flowerets and chilled
1 green pepper, white pith removed, seeded, cut into thin strips and chilled
1 red pepper, white pith removed, seeded, cut into thin strips and chilled
1 cucumber, chopped into bite-sized pieces and chilled
8 oz. small [cherry] tomatoes, chilled

First make the sauce. Crush the garlic cloves in a garlic press, with a pestle in a mortar, or with the flat side of a table knife. Transfer the crushed garlic to a medium-sized mixing bowl and add the salt, lemon juice and egg yolks. With a wire whisk or rotary beater, whisk the ingredients together thoroughly.

Gradually add the oil, a few drops at a time, whisking constantly. When about one-third of the oil has been added, the remainder may be whisked in more quickly. When all the oil has been incorporated, the mayonnaise should have the consistency of thick cream. If the Aïoli is too thick, whisk in a little more lemon juice.

Place the bowl in the refrigerator and chill the Aïoli for 30 minutes.

Arrange the vegetables on a large serving platter, leaving room for the sauce in the centre. Spoon the Aïoli into a serving dish and place it in the middle of the vegetables. Garnish the sauce with the parsley and serve.

Dips and Spreads

Try serving a selection of the following dips and spreads at your next party. You can prepare canapés ahead of time, by spreading savoury biscuits [crackers] or small triangles of toast or bread with the dips and spreads. Or let your guests help themselves to the dips, spreads, savoury biscuits [crackers], bread or toast and crudités (raw vegetables).

All the dips and spreads take a very short time to prepare.

Blue Cheese Dip

5 OUNCES [⅝ CUP]

4 oz. Danish Blue cheese, softened
2 tablespoons single [light] cream
6 large pecans, finely crushed
1½ tablespoons finely snipped fresh chives

Combine all the ingredients in a large mixing bowl, beating with a wooden spoon until they are well blended. Serve at room temperature.

Spicy Cheese and Brandy Dip

1 POUND

10 oz. [2½ cups] Cheddar cheese, grated
3 oz. [⅜ cup] butter
6 fl. oz. single cream [¾ cup light cream]
½ teaspoon Tabasco sauce
3 fl. oz. [⅜ cup] brandy

Cream the cheese and butter together in a medium-sized mixing bowl with a wooden spoon. Gradually beat in the cream, then the Tabasco sauce and brandy, beating until the mixture is smooth and thick. Serve at room temperature.

Mint and Chive Spread

2 OUNCES [¼ CUP]

2 oz. [¼ cup] unsalted butter
1 tablespoon very finely chopped fresh mint
1 tablespoon finely chopped fresh chives
½ teaspoon freshly squeezed lemon juice

Combine all the ingredients in a medium-sized mixing bowl, beating with a wooden spoon until they are well blended. Place the bowl in the refrigerator and chill for 30 minutes before serving.

Speckled Tomato Spread

5 OUNCES [⅝ CUP]

2 medium-sized tomatoes, blanched, peeled, seeded and chopped
4 oz. [1 cup] Cheddar cheese, finely grated
1½ tablespoons finely chopped fresh parsley
1½ tablespoons finely snipped fresh chives

Combine all the ingredients in a large mixing bowl, beating with a wooden spoon until they are well blended. Place the bowl in the refrigerator and chill for 30 minutes before serving.

Herb Spread

5 OUNCES [⅝ CUP]

4 oz. cream cheese
1 tablespoon mayonnaise
1 teaspoon finely chopped fresh parsley
1 teaspoon finely snipped fresh chives
1 teaspoon finely chopped fresh sorrel leaves
¼ teaspoon salt
⅛ teaspoon white pepper

Combine all of the ingredients together in a medium-sized mixing bowl, beating with a wooden spoon until they are well blended. Place the bowl in the refrigerator and chill for 30 minutes before serving.

Gherkin Spread

6 OUNCES [¾ CUP]

4 oz. [½ cup] butter or margarine, softened
2 oz. [½ cup] Lancashire or any hard white cheese, finely grated
4 small pickled gherkins, finely chopped
½ teaspoon capers

Combine all the ingredients in a medium-sized mixing bowl, beating with a wooden spoon until they are well blended. Serve at room temperature.

Hot and Cold Spread

5 OUNCES [⅝ CUP]

4 oz. mild cream cheese
1 tablespoon mayonnaise
1 tablespoon finely chopped radishes
1 tablespoon finely chopped fresh watercress

Combine all of the ingredients in a medium-sized mixing bowl, beating with a wooden spoon until they are well blended. Place the bowl in the refrigerator and chill for 30 minutes before serving.

Cheese Spread

8 OUNCES [1 CUP]

1 oz. [2 tablespoons] butter or margarine
3 tablespoons cornflour [cornstarch]
5 fl. oz. [⅝ cup] milk
1 garlic clove, crushed
4 oz. [1 cup] Lancashire or any hard white cheese, finely grated
½ teaspoon dry English mustard
1 teaspoon paprika

In a medium-sized saucepan, melt the butter or margarine over moderate heat. When the foam subsides, remove the pan from the heat and, with a wooden spoon, stir in the cornflour [cornstarch] to make a smooth paste. Gradually add the milk, stirring constantly.

Stir in the garlic.

Return the pan to low heat and cook the sauce, stirring constantly, for 2 to 3 minutes, or until it is thick and smooth. Remove the pan from the heat and set it aside to cool slightly.

When the mixture is cool, stir in the cheese, a little at a time, beating until the mixture is smooth. Then add the mustard and paprika, mixing well to blend.

Spoon the spread into a small serving dish and place it in the refrigerator. Chill for 30 minutes before serving.

Index